THE BOOK OF VISUAL STUDIO .NET

THE
BOOK OF VISUAL STUDIO .NET

A GUIDE FOR DEVELOPERS

Robert B. Dunaway

NO STARCH PRESS

San Francisco

Publisher: William Pollock
Editorial Director: Karol Jurado
Cover and Interior Design: Octopod Studios
Composition: 1106 Design, LLC
Developmental Editor: William Pollock
Copyeditor: Kenyon Brown
Proofreader: Mei Levenson
Indexer: Broccoli Information Management

Distributed to the book trade in the United States by Publishers Group West, 1700 Fourth Street, Berkeley, CA 94710; phone: 800-788-3123; fax: 510-658-1834.

Distributed to the book trade in Canada by Jacqueline Gross & Associates, Inc., One Atlantic Avenue, Suite 105, Toronto, Ontario M6K 3E7 Canada; phone: 416-531-6737; fax 416-531-4259.

For information on translations or book distributors outside the United States and Canada, please contact No Starch Press, Inc. directly:

No Starch Press, Inc.
555 De Haro Street, Suite 250, San Francisco, CA 94107
phone: 415-863-9900; fax: 415-863-9950; info@nostarch.com; http://www.nostarch.com

The information in this book is distributed on an "As Is" basis, without warranty. While every precaution has been taken in the preparation of this work, neither the author nor No Starch Press, Inc. shall have any liability to any person or entity with respect to any loss or damage caused or alleged to be caused directly or indirectly by the information contained in it.

Library of Congress Cataloguing-in-Publication Data

Dunaway, Robert B.
  The book of Visual Studio .NET / Robert B. Dunaway.
    p. cm.
Includes index.
  ISBN 1-886411-69-7 (pbk.)
 1. Microsoft Visual Studio. 2. Microsoft.net framework. 3. Web
 site development--Computer programs. I. Title.
  TK5105.8885.M57 D86 2002
  005.2'76--dc21   2001030346

DEDICATION

To Tamarah:

Your steadfast love has inspired me to become a better man.

I love you.

To my Grandfather:

The principles and love you have shown me remain.

I miss you.

ACKNOWLEDGMENTS

This book is the product of a combined effort. My thanks to all involved at No Starch Press.

I would like to thank Bill Pollock for believing in me as a first time writer and for his patience throughout the writing of this book. Thank you for the countless hours you spent guiding and editing my work so that it would be more enjoyable and understandable to read.

Special thanks to Karol Jurado, the Editorial Director, for coordinating the entire effort and fielding my many questions. You've help make this an experience I would like to repeat.

I would also like to thank Ken Brown, the copyeditor, and Mei Levenson, our proofreader. I know that catching my grammatical errors is no trivial task.

Special thanks to William H. Bennethum, whose friendship, criticism, and encouragement means the world to me. Your comments and insight concerning this book have been invaluable.

Thanks to Cheryl and Jeffery Dunaway, for your love and for teaching me that nothing was out of my reach.

Thanks to Michael and Cathy Browning, for your guidance in my career and your continued support.

Special thanks to my Grandmother, Maude Jump, for your continued love and support.

Robert B. Dunaway
Cincinnati, Ohio

BRIEF CONTENTS

CONTENTS IN DETAIL

Introduction
INTRODUCING .NET

1
WHY .NET

2
EVOLUTION OF TIER DEVELOPMENT

3

VISUAL STUDIO .NET WALKTHROUGH

4

THE .NET FRAMEWORK

5

VISUAL STUDIO .NET TOOLS

6

DESIGNERS, DATABASE AND MONITORING TOOLS

7

A VISUAL BASIC.NET CRASH COURSE

8

ASP.NET

9

PROMOTING APPLICATION SCALABILITY

10
WEB SERVICES

11
COM INTEROP

12

ENTERPRISE SERVICES

Index
351

INTRODUCING .NET

When designing the contents, format, and general layout of this book, the challenges that developers face when implementing Microsoft .NET technologies were considered. The .NET initiative offers both a new set of technologies and a new paradigm for development, because it is not only a development environment but also an entire suite of servers and services that work together to deliver solutions to solve today's business problems. The book could have perhaps more easily addressed a single vertical portion of the .NET suite of technologies, but then how would you know how or where that portion fits into .NET model, and how could you take advantage of other services that are provided by the vast set of .NET technologies? The truth is that you probably could not.

One book simply cannot adequately cover all of the technologies that are required to deliver a complete .NET solution. .NET encompasses several new technologies, including new versions and enhancements of nearly every current technology. These products include SQL Server, Windows XP, .NET Enterprise Server, and industry-standard technologies such as XML and SOAP.

This book provides you with a solid understanding of Visual Studio .NET and of how to use it to implement a variety of .NET solutions (a considerable challenge, given the number of technologies that make up the .NET framework). You'll focus mainly on Visual Studio 7 .NET, while still getting an overview of several .NET-related technologies. In fact, you'll get quite a bit more than a simple overview of Visual Studio .NET and related technologies; you'll learn exactly where each technology fits into the big picture of .NET, and you'll run sample code that demonstrates your ability to take advantage of that technology today! Good luck and enjoy.

Level of Expertise

The Book of Visual Studio .NET assumes that you are familiar with Windows-based programming, object-oriented programming, Windows 2000 Advanced Server, Windows XP, or .NET Enterprise Server. It will also be helpful for you to understand SQL Server, COM, and COM+ because they are required to build a scalable and reliable Windows DNA application. Knowing these technologies will make the transition to the .NET Framework easier for you to handle. While the book assumes this knowledge, it will discuss much of this technology throughout because of the way .NET integrates it to build business solutions. If you are lacking in any one of these areas, do not fear; you won't be by the time you finish this book.

NOTE *While many of the examples are written in Visual Basic (VB), and the book has included a chapter on Visual Basic .NET, don't expect to learn Visual Basic .NET here. If you already know Visual Basic, you will be better able to take advantage of these code examples. If not, you will get an introduction to areas of Visual Basic .NET that you will need to explore in a book that is geared more toward learning the Visual Basic .NET language.*

Who Should Read This Book?

This book is only a starting point for understanding the .NET suite of technologies, which is essential for any successful .NET delivery. Once you are finished with this book, you will be able to relate whatever you are doing to some portion of the .NET framework.

The Book of Visual Studio .NET is for intermediate and advanced developers who want to build scalable, reliable, flexible, and manageable systems using Visual Studio .NET. If you are a developer, an architect, or a manager of a software development team, this book is for you.

You will also find this book helpful if you aspire to become a software architect with an understanding of how the pieces of .NET technology fit together to form a business solution.

Finally, while every development manager does not need to understand the details of COM+/Enterprise Services, ASP.NET, ADO.NET, or SOAP/Web Services, an understanding of the issues that are involved in integrating multiple .NET technologies will enable you to better lead your team. You will be better prepared to deal with the complexities of the next wave of software development for both the Internet and the desktop.

Goals of This Book

This book does not take an exhaustive look at any one language or technology. While you will gain new insights into these technologies, you will not learn the technologies themselves.

You will, however, learn to use Visual Studio .NET to implement a variety of .NET technologies as we take an exhaustive look at the .NET Framework. The book covers many new and updated .NET tools (with tutorial-like examples of how to use them). As you learn, you will see, in great detail, the process of building compiled components has significantly changed compared to how classic COM has been implemented. The book also discusses how languages have been enhanced and DLLs changed. Finally, the book examines a variety of nuances introduced by .NET and Visual Studio .NET.

By the end of this book, you should have a firm grasp on what this new world of .NET development technology is all about. You will be able to answer the question, "What is .NET?" with confidence, and communicate the benefits of .NET. But more importantly, you will be able to use all of the .NET tools and implement other .NET technologies by using Visual Studio .NET.

1

WHY .NET

.NET, like any other technology, must be carefully evaluated
before an educated decision can be made concerning its use.
Before we continue discussing the values of .NET we will briefly look at
how problems can be solved using .NET.

Business Problems Addressed by .NET

Many Internet solutions have been patterned after the mainframe's centralized
model. New technologies in the PC world, such as transaction support and messaging, are mature technologies in the mainframe world, and in many ways, the
mainframe has paved the way for the Internet. However, it is important to
understand that the mainframe, while incorporating many technologies, leans
toward centralization. In this chapter we will cover key architectural designs
leading to today's application designs as they are implemented using .NET.

In many ways, the PC world itself has made a few paradigm shifts as it has
moved from computing on separate, unconnected workstations to the PC network and a client/server relationship. Network file and print servers provided a
way to share information and a single point of administration. The addition of
file services turned the PC into an application server.

The birth of client/server computing helped to reduce the workload on the client PC and to increase performance and reliability. Rather than relying on the client application to manipulate and manage its own e-mail files, services ensures that the client's responsibilities are limited to requests and replies while the server does the work, thus improving reliability because the PC could no longer damage its own data in the event of a crash.

The first PC networks involved file and print servers with a centralized means of sharing information and a single point of administration, as shown in Figure 1-1. The server simply serves the files required to run an application. This is a client/server model only in the context of file and print services; the application itself isn't really a true client/server application, and it only takes advantage of certain client/server services that are needed to run the application from a central location.

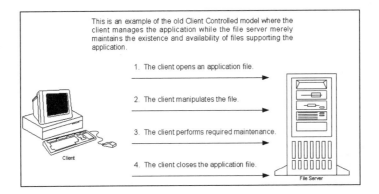

Figure 1-1: This diagram represents the old client-controlled model.

The problems with this centralized computing model range from loss of performance to data corruption. Performance is slow because the client application must do all the work necessary to make the application functional, with the network as intermediary. Due to the ever-present risk of client instability, the potential for data corruption is also high. If the client fails while handling files on the file server, it can easily corrupt application or data files.

The true client/server model, shown in Figure 1-2, never allows the client to actually touch the application or data. The client has no impact on the application or data files, performance is improved, and the risk of data corruption by the client is significantly reduced. The server maintains the application data.

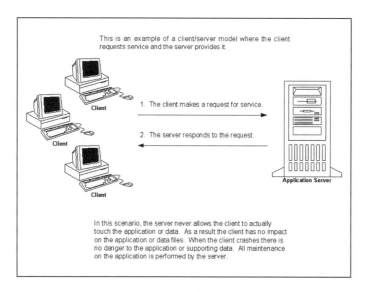

Figure 1-2: This diagram represents a client/server model.

Today, a single server performs all Internet-related application services, from authentication to data access. This may not present many challenges on a small scale, but when the frequency of data access exceeds the database server's capabilities and the application server receives more requests than it can respond to, we have problems.

And what about reliability? If any portion of this solution, which in many cases resides on a single server, is overwhelmed or crashes, the business solution fails, and the business depending on this solution may be damaged.

Likewise, the client browser can have difficulty manipulating or intelligently handling data. The web browser is basically dumb and, for the most part, does what it's told, thus greatly reducing the browser's ability to meet an individual's specific needs.

The .NET suite of technologies includes everything from development tools to Web Services in an effort to increase scalability, reliability, flexibility, and manageability, thus addressing these business issues. As such, .NET frees the web server from its limited communication with the client web browser, and allows it to communicate with other web servers on the client's behalf (see Figure 1-3). For instance, if you schedule a service to be provided by a business, like canceling or rescheduling a flight, and if that business is unable to fulfill your request, your provider's Web Services will work with other Web Services to find another provider to satisfy your needs.

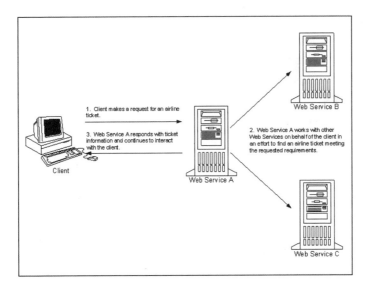

Figure 1-3: A server working with other Web Services on behalf of the client.

Performance and Scalability

If a system is not scalable, there's not much point in building systems to support large numbers of concurrent users. In fact, when considering large systems, performance is important, but scalability is still more important.

Performance refers to the number of processor cycles that are necessary to complete any given task, or the time that is required to complete a single task. *Scalability* is the number of concurrent users that are able to perform a task at the same time. For example, say you run a component that returns information at an incredible rate. The cost of this transaction is 100 percent CPU utilization. While the *performance* of this task is good, its *scalability* is poor because the CPU can support only one or two concurrent users who are requesting this transaction.

Scalability is almost entirely determined by your application's architecture and adherence to good coding practice. Even one poorly written routine or transaction can reduce an application's performance. You'll learn about these topics and more in Chapter 2 in which tiered development is covered.

The Benefits of .NET

For the developer, the answer to the question "Why .NET?" revolves around the benefits of Visual Studio .NET and the meaning of ".NET."

.NET is a set of cross-platform technologies, including time-tested and accepted protocols, such as HTTP, and platform-independent standards like XML. These two technologies allow COM and CORBA to interoperate, through Web Services, like never before. Issues concerning the platform are now removed, so developers can concentrate on business requirements.

As we witnessed with the rise and fall of Windows DNA, Microsoft often changes the names of its new technology suites. .NET (pronounced "dot net") was first called NGWS, Next Generation Windows Services.

.NET is a moving target and is clearly in a state of flux. While much of what we know about .NET is not likely to change, new methodologies and paradigms are sure to arise that will add to what we already know and understand. And, as these new and innovative technologies emerge, some will fail to achieve industry acceptance and will be discarded or will simply disappear.

Before the Internet, most application development was limited to Windows-based forms. As the Internet's popularity rose, the development of web applications increased and the world began to change.

Early web technologies were limited to creating static pages with click-and-link functionality. This satisfied users initial web requirements because people were simply happy to be able to surf the Web and even more pleased to contribute to its growth. For the most part, this also satisfied the requirement of providing information to a growing Internet population. However, as businesses began building static websites, they realized quickly that consumers wanted more dynamic pages that would reflect new and changing products.

Acceptance of Open Standards

One of the most important aspects of .NET is Microsoft's acceptance of open industry standards. The full acceptance and implementation of XML is significant. While XML is not the "end all" technology that some people think it is, it's one of the few available ways to integrate disparate systems. Without an open standard like XML, developers would need to rely on proprietary third-party applications for data integration.

Nearly every one of Microsoft's current servers (see Table 1-1) will be a .NET server that supports XML and the .NET Framework. (Previous versions of SQL Server had very limited XML support.) The implementation of industry standard protocols in .NET and throughout Microsoft servers marks Microsoft's effort to create cross platform applications, as services—nothing less than a paradigm shift for traditional Microsoft application developers.

Table 1-1: Current and future .NET servers

Server	Description
Microsoft Application Center Server 2000	Manages clusters and deploys web applications.
Microsoft BizTalk Server 2000	Implements business processes and provides data through an agreed-upon interface.
Microsoft Commerce Server 2000	Helps in building e-Commerce applications.
Microsoft Exchange 2000	Enables messaging and collaboration (e-mail).
Microsoft Host Integration 2000	Allows communication with the mainframe.
Microsoft Internet Security and Acceleration Server 2000	Operates as a firewall and web cache.
Microsoft SQL Server 2000	Offers database storage and analysis services.

Web Services

One concept that may be entirely new to you is that of Web Services; a principle that underlies much of the .NET strategy. Web Services are services exposed by an Internet application for consumption by another service or client application. Web Services are built using industry-standard tools (such as XML and HTTP), and are platform and development-environment independent, which means that you don't need to use .NET to deliver them. Developing Web services requires a paradigm shift: we need to move away from the single-server, single-application model to a more distributed-services model.

This ability to create loosely coupled applications increases the flexibility of applications requiring disconnected data services, like sales applications that require a sales representative to complete a deal out of the office or on the road without Internet connectivity. Loosely connected data-access relieves the data-base server from having to maintain a database connection for everyone using it; instead, database connectivity is established when convenient or when necessary to transmit new records. Loosely connected data also enables disconnected devices that require read access to a specific subset of data for the user to analyze offline. (Chapter 9, "Retrieving Data," discusses Microsoft's ADO.NET, implemented by Visual Studio .NET, the relevant piece here.)

The use of industry standard protocols is key to the wide adoption of the .NET initiative. While loosely connected applications promote flexibility, .NET's support of industry-standard protocols brings reliability. By combining HTTP with XML to produce SOAP (Simple Object Access Protocol), .NET offers a reliable web-enabled development solution. SOAP, which is XML traveling over an HTTP transport layer, is the foundation of Web Services. Not only can SOAP take advantage of COM, but it can also take advantage of other standards, such as CORBA (Common Object Request Broker Architecture). These technologies make up a majority of middle-tier solutions, making SOAP a significant addition to the Microsoft set of tools. (See Chapter 10, "Implementing Web Services," for more detail.)

Visual Studio .NET Development Features and Enhancements

While the look and feel of Visual Studio .NET has changed from its predecessors, the real enhancements of Visual Studio .NET are the underling technologies the development environment is based on. It is these technologies that allow for rapid development with the stability and reliability of classic development environments such as C++.

Visual Studio .NET Designers

Visual Studio .NET provides easy access to underlying server functionality by giving developers access to server functions like message queuing and event logging, as well as a variety of designers from the VS .NET environment. Designers are the key component of Visual Studio .NET; allowing developers to be guided through complex development of specific components. These designers, including XML Data Designer, Web Services Designer, Windows Forms Designer, and Web Forms Designer, provide easy access to generated code based on class frameworks. The generated code is accessible to the developer, allowing the developer to modify or add code.

Visual Studio .NET's Visual Web Page Editor's WYSIWYG interface eliminates the need to master HTML. Developers can still modify their HTML but need not spend time reinventing the wheel. The most significant enhancement of the Visual Studio .NET Web Designers is the separation of presentation and business logic code.

Common Language Runtime

One significant enhancement to Visual Studio is the addition of a language-independent runtime called the *Common Language Runtime* or CLR. CLR offers the ability to develop in any language in a managed environment that is less susceptible to memory leaks and that provides metadata for components to allow for type checking and debugging.

CLR's security and version-control features, which we'll discuss throughout this book, make it easier to deploy applications and to sell them as a service rather than simply as an application. CLR makes it easier, faster, and safer to create web applications than with Microsoft's previous Package and Deployment Manager. (We discuss this further in Chapter 4, "The Framework.")

.NET Languages

Microsoft created the C# language (pronounced "C sharp") to give you the power of Visual C++ and the ease of use of Visual Basic. That's Microsoft's story and they're sticking to it. The truth is that the two main .NET languages, C# and Visual Basic .NET, have very similar capability.

All .NET languages support a minimum subset of CLR functionality, and their level of support will vary. For many applications, language choice will have little impact; however, of the 20-plus .NET languages coming available, some will be better suited for scientific calculations while others are ideal for financials or most efficient for processing IO. The issues of languages should not cause heart pain for organizations. However, companies that limit their development by over simplifying standards will miss out on the full functionality of the CLR.

NOTE *While C# and Visual Basic .NET are high performing object-oriented languages, you may encounter situations in which Visual C++ offers performance advantages. (In most cases, though, performance is enhanced more through good design and best practices than by the language used to build any individual component.) While you'll find other comments about C# throughout this book, you won't find C# tutorials. You can find plenty in the .NET Framework SDK.*

Intermediate Language

.NET's new Intermediate Language (IL) supports multiple languages and is CPU independent. All .NET code is first compiled into this IL and, because the IL is CPU independent, the component can be platform independent. IL has its costs, too: For the component to be platform independent, it must be compiled for the specific platform to which it is deployed in its native format just before it is used. This just-in-time (JIT) compilation uses resources and takes time and we'll address these issues in Chapter 4, "The Framework."

Server-to-Server Communication

Server-to-server communication is another .NET initiative. Before .NET, Internet developers were happy to simply redirect the browser to the server maintaining the data the client required. Consequently, before .NET, if a client needed access to several Internet services, it would first need to be redirected to the appropriate sites and then be connected to each web server. Technologies such as SOAP/Web Services enable clients to connect to services that are provided by other web servers on a different platform. This server-to-server communication allows a company to create a high-demand service (anything from an identification site to your future e-wallet) and expose it, because that service is maintained by the organization that specializes in a given service.

Summary

In this chapter, you learned:

- .NET will take a few years to be completely realized. In the meantime, we will learn how to use the pieces of .NET that are released to design our applications in a way that will allow an easier transition to .NET.
- One of .NET's goals, to make all web applications available on any device, requires decoupling data and business rules from the client and supporting them in the business and data service tiers.
- Microsoft's implementation of Web Services with SOAP is an industry-standard implementation with a focus on cross-platform integration. Web Services provide a mechanism for server-to-server communication on behalf of the user rather than redirecting the user to another site.
- Deployment is made easier with CLR, the Common Language Runtime.
- .NET includes a set of servers that have been upgraded to support XML.
- .NET's goals are manageability, scalability, flexibility, and reliability.
- Visual Studio .NET Intermediate Language (IL) makes it possible for us to use several programming languages, all hosted in one environment.
- The adoption of industry-standard protocols and related technologies is the largest initiative of .NET, making use of time-tested technologies such as HTTP, HTML, and XML. XML and HTTP have been rolled into SOAP.

2

EVOLUTION OF TIER
DEVELOPMENT

Component-based programming is valuable because it lets you divide general program functionality into more generic, manageable components. This encourages code reuse, flexibility, and horizontal tiers that break the application into logical sections based on its services. This chapter gives you a complete understanding of tier development, its advantages, and some of its disadvantages. By the end of this chapter, you should have a good idea of how to place functionality within your components.

You'll learn how tiered development has evolved from a centralized environment to today's distributed multiple-tier server farms. The chapter examines centralized management, distributed computing, performance, scalability, business rules, and the user experience. You'll also learn about a couple of proven n-tier models and their specific implementation issues.

Once you've learned about tier modeling, the chapter discusses the implementation of business rules, including the advantages and disadvantages implementing them in different tiers of the application. You'll learn the differences between business rules, data-specific business rules, and business processes, and how and where to implement each type. Next, the chapter covers the challenges that are presented by application state. You will learn why application state presents performance and scalability problems and some proven solutions to this problem.

Finally, you'll learn about Web Services and its role in the tier model.

Evolution of Tier Development

An application tier is a functional layer of an application. Each functional layer performs a specific application task, effectively creating a logical division of functionality within an application. The implementation of application tiers can more easily be physically divided to deliver a distributed application among multiple machines.

The tier development model was designed to solve many application challenges. Some of the issues that are addressed by tier development are centralized management, distributed computing, performance, scalability, and the user experience.

Centralized Management

In a *centralized-management* environment, configuration changes made to the central location are distributed and applied to the surrounding system. A system with centralized management can be managed from a limited number of locations.

Microsoft's Application Center 2000, a deployment and management tool, is one example of a system that uses centralized management. With its ability to manage server clusters, Application Center increases an application's scalability and reliability. More importantly, it centrally manages the application supported by the cluster, configuration of the application, and server configurations properties.

Centralized management makes managing a group of servers almost as easy as managing a single server. When application components are updated, or a server configuration is changed, the changes are automatically distributed to all servers participating in the Application Center cluster.

Distributed Computing

In a *distributed-computing* environment, processing is spread across multiple systems and, if necessary, across multiple locations. The goals are to increase scalability, fault-tolerance, and network efficiency.

Performance

As stated in Chapter 1, "Why .NET," *performance* is a measure of the number of processor cycles that are necessary to complete any given task. While a task may be completed quickly, indicating good performance, this good performance does not necessarily mean that the task is scalable. Users generally perceive performance in terms of an application's response time. When an application does not scale well, the user thinks that the application is performing poorly. It is therefore important for a developer to understand the difference between performance and scalability.

Scalability

As mentioned in Chapter 1, *scalability* is a measure of the number of users who can perform a task concurrently. While performance is considered good when a task is performed quickly, the key to building scalable applications is to create a component that performs quickly using the fewest possible resources. The desired result is an application that allows for concurrent use with a reasonable response time. ("Concurrent use" and "reasonable response time" are subjective terms and will need to be replaced with real numbers that will depend on your application's requirements.)

Business Rules

Business rules describe the business's constraints on an application. The application of business rules, while subjective at times, affects the data integrity of an application, and the failure to adequately enforce these rules can negatively affect the business. While there may not be a single right way to implement business rules, there are usually several acceptable implementations. In contrast, there are many wrong ways to implement them. These issues are discussed throughout this chapter.

User Experience

In a world where perception is reality, it is fruitless to spend time, money, and critical thought on an application's architecture and design if the basic application is difficult to use, unreliable, or inflexible. That is to say, even if an application performs like a top and is scalable to 100,000 concurrent users, what good is it if your users hate to use it? While this chapter doesn't show you how to improve your users' experience, it demonstrates a few .NET tools that are designed to make this task easier.

Two-Tier Development

The two-tier development model is commonly referred to as the client/server model; the terms are used interchangeably throughout this book. In a two-tiered model, a client application requests information or a service, such as e-mail, from a single server or service.

Client/server environments distribute application processing between the client and the server. The client application displays the user interface and receives input from the user. The server application provides a service, usually data or communication services.

Figure 2-1 shows a simple client/server model with clients accessing one server. While this is an accurate, logical diagram, keep in mind that most applications require many concurrent users, so while the logical diagram is correct, a physical diagram would show many clients talking to one server at the same time.

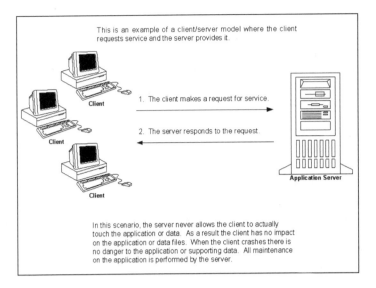

In this scenario, the server never allows the client to actually touch the application or data. As a result the client has no impact on the application or data files. When the client crashes there is no danger to the application or supporting data. All maintenance on the application is performed by the server.

Figure 2-1: The two-tier (client/server) model.

The following sections cover a few critical two-tier topics.

Two-Tier Code Management

There are two aspects to managing code in a client/server environment, namely the management of both client and server. (*Client* refers to an application executable that runs on a client computer.)

The challenges in managing a server are relatively straightforward. Unless the server is part of a cluster, server code must be managed and deployed in a single location. If the server is part of a cluster, the code must be sent to each server (manually or automatically) using cluster-management software, such as Microsoft's Application Center 2000.

On the other hand, the client application is much trickier to manage than the server. Changes made to components of the client application must be distributed to every client, in many cases simultaneously. Such simultaneous deployment requires a high level of coordination and, depending on the number of clients who receive new components, a reliable deployment package.

Client deployment presents other potential issues, including coordination with the server. Changes to the server application may dictate that the client application needs updating, which can render the entire application useless until all clients are updated.

Performance

The use of the client/server model also affects network performance. Because all data and service requests must be transferred across the network in the client/server model, the network can become overwhelmed easily, creating a bottleneck. This problem is magnified when you consider the traffic that is created by many users using the same application at the same time. Performance bottlenecks typically appear during times of peak usage, such as during month-end processing or during peak hours of the day.

As network performance degrades, service requests begin to queue and a cascading effect begins. Often the only fix is a quick one: Disconnecting all clients, rolling back all transactions, and sometimes rebooting the server.

Depending on the network protocol that is used, it may be nearly impossible to distribute a client/server application globally because the client application may need to reside on the same local area network (LAN) as the server.

Data Access

Data access must also be considered when evaluating performance. Not only must clients know how to connect to the database server, they often require their own dedicated database connection (as shown in Figure 2-2). This arrangement is costly both in terms of licensing fees and in the use of database resources that are required to maintain each connection. Also, these database connections cannot be shared between applications, thus limiting the application's scalability.

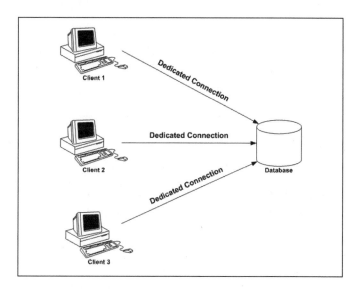

Figure 2-2: Three clients requiring their own dedicated database connection.

Business Rules

The client/server model offers only two locations for maintaining and enforcing business rules: The client application and the server application that provides the database services. The server is the preferred location for implementing business rules because it avoids the possibility that a client might not receive a modified or new business rule during an update.

Implementing business rules on the server's database also avoids another possibly sticky situation. In many cases, multiple applications will need to access the same data, and it would be very easy for a developer to implement a business rule in one application and forget to add it to another application. If the business rule is implemented in the server's database, there is no way around it.

Three-Tier Development

The three-tier model (shown in Figure 2-3) improves on the two-tier model by dividing applications into service tiers: User Services, Business Services, and Data Services. These divisions allow for greater scalability and reliability.

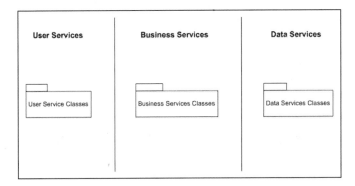

Figure 2-3: The logical three-tier model.

User Services

The User Services tier, also referred to as the presentation layer, is made up of windows executables and/or web pages, such as dynamic HTML or Active Server Pages. User Services tier is the interface that is used to display data to the user and to receive input. In a three-tier model, it is unnecessary for the client or the User Services tier to know anything about the database or any other service that is provided by the Data Services tier.

Business Services

The second tier is the Business Services tier, which is responsible for knowing exactly how to access data. These responsibilities include requesting data on behalf of the User Services tier and returning query results. The Business Services tier can, and in many cases should, maintain business rules.

The Business Services tier, as shown in Figure 2-4, exposes all the functionality that the User Services tier requires. While its main purpose is to decouple the User Services from the Data Services, the Business Services tier does much more. Any function, including calculations and other application-specific tasks, are available through the Business Services tier. All User Services have access to the Business Services tier, which physically resides on a server accessible via the network. Any new or modified business rule needs only be deployed to the Business Services tier, thus eliminating the need to redistribute anything to the client application.

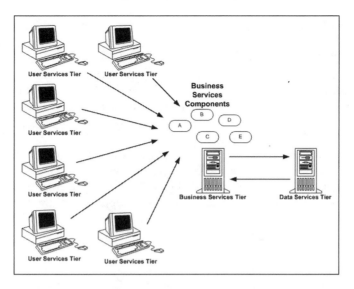

Figure 2-4: Business Services tier components being used by all User Services.

Data Services

In a further effort to decouple application services so that they can be more easily managed and supported, the Data Services tier provides data access to the Business Services tier, which in turn passes this data on to the client application in the User Services tier. ADO.NET and the Database Management System (DBMS) are both maintained in the Data Services tier. ADO.NET is Microsoft's solution for universal data access, and SQL Server is Microsoft's solution for the DBMS. Both provide data access: ADO.NET provides a method for getting at data and SQL Server provides the database engine that is required for maintaining the data itself.

Code Management

Code management in a three-tier application is much easier to support and less problematic than with a two-tier application. Since the application is logically and physically divided, there is no need for a single development team. Presentation developers can build the user interface without having access to data, business tier developers no longer need to understand user interface requirements, and database programmers can focus on relational data and the implementation of known business rules. Because each service tier is physically separated, they can each be compiled and/or reconfigured without involving the other services, thus freeing up the developers and reducing coordination requirements.

Scalability

Scalability is greatly improved in three-tier applications because database connections can be disconnected or maintained for use by other clients, reducing the number of concurrent database connections that are needed to support an application. Processing is transferred from the client to the Business Services server, and network performance can increase because the Business Services server can communicate with the database server on the same network, reducing the amount of network traffic.

Scalability is also enhanced through the clustering of the Business Services and database servers. Business components loaded into memory can remain loaded through services provided by COM+ and Enterprise Services—this increases the number of users that can be supported by the Business Services server because the time required to load a component from the hard drive into memory is significantly reduced.

Business Rules

With one exception, there is no real right way to implement business rules. That exception is that you should never place business rules in the client application or User Services tier where the client applications can easily bypass them. As a result, if a rule is placed in one client application, it must be placed in every application accessing the database.

You can reliably enforce business rules in either the Business Services or Data Services tier. When placing business rules in the Business Services tier, make sure that all applications accessing your data are also using your Business Services tier's components. If an application can bypass the Business Services component that enforces the business rule, the rule itself is not enforced. When enforcing business rules in the Data Services tier, no application can bypass the business rules, hence the advantage of placing business rules here.

Programming languages such as Visual Basic .NET, Visual C++, and C# are well suited to implementing business rules. However, the objects and languages that are available in SQL Server for enforcing business rules are column-level constraints, table-level triggers, and Transact SQL (Microsoft's SQL Server programming language). Although SQL Server's Transact SQL is not a particularly flexible language, with a little effort and a lot of practice you can implement almost any business rule.

NOTE *When Transact SQL is not sufficient, Microsoft provides stored procedures for calling COM components. These stored procedures are sp_oacreate, sp_oagetproperty, sp_oasetproperty, sp_oamethod, and sp_oadestroy. For more information on these stored procedures, refer to Microsoft's online SQL Server documentation.*

N-Tier Development

Strategically dividing an application into tiers can greatly improve an application's scalability, performance, flexibility, and manageability. Giving each tier a specific task allows the development and system configuration to focus on the needs of the tasks that are performed by that tier. Further dividing these tiers can let you further separate out the tasks of the tier.

Any application with three or more tiers is considered an N-tier application. "N" represents any number greater than two. For the purposes of this section, N-tier refers to a five-tier model, which is the same as the three-tier model with the Business Services tier divided into three tiers or tier classes (as shown in Figure 2-5): Facades, Main Business, and Data Access.

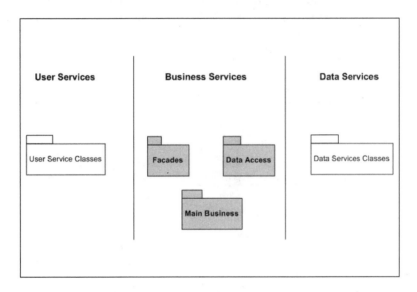

Figure 2-5: The divided Business Services classes.

Dividing Business Services

Once you have divided the Business Services tier into three tier classes, the three new tiers reside in the Business Services logical model while supporting a more defined set of functionality. Even though these more defined tier classes are part of the Business Services tier, they can be packaged separately and deployed on separate servers to increase scalability.

NOTE *This book doesn't discuss in detail how to implement these services. To learn more about how to implement the N-tier model, read* Designing for Scalability with Windows DNA *(Microsoft Press). Keep in mind that this book was written at the beginning of 2000, meaning that the code examples are provided for Visual Studio 6 and require modification to work under Visual Studio .NET. This is not a problem. In fact, consider it good practice.*

Facades Class

The Facades classes, shown in Figure 2-6, act as a buffer between the User Services tier (or presentation layer) and the functionality provided by the Business Services tier, which offers several advantages. One less obvious advantage of the Facades classes is that you can create sub-classes; thus, you can create a Facades class to return statically embedded data, allowing the User Services developer to more quickly begin development and prototyping.

Another more significant advantage is that the Facades classes remove the complexity of accessing business functionality. Business Services components are, or should be, built so that their functionality is generic and can be used by a number of applications. As such, any User Services form or web page will need to *instantiate*, or load, several components to perform any task. With the Facades classes, the User Services developer needs only to instantiate the Facades class, and the Facades class deals with the complexity of business-functionality instantiation.

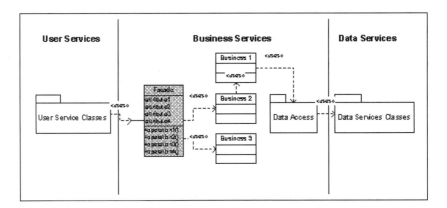

Figure 2-6: The Facades classes as a buffer component.

Main Business Class

The Main Business classes or Business Level Layer (BLL) provide actual business functionality, including enforcing business rules, maintaining collection classes, ensuring business functionality, and providing access to data components. The Main Business classes provide the actual intelligence of the application. The Facades classes call the appropriate main business components (Figure 2-7), and the Data Access components only access data they are told to access. You'll learn about Data Access components in the next section.

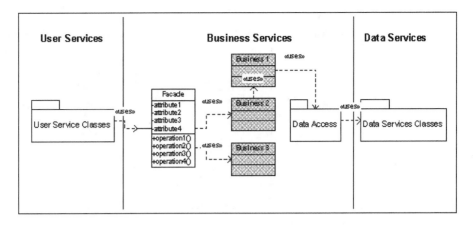

User Services · Business Services · Data Services

Facade

-attribute1
-attribute2
-attribute3
-attribute4

+operation1()
+operation2()
+operation3()
+operation4()

User Service Classes

«uses»

Business 1
Business 2
Business 3

Data Access

Data Services Classes

Figure 2-7: The relationship of the Main Business classes to Facades and Data Access classes.

Data Access Class

Data Access components (Figure 2-8), or Data Access Layer (DAL), perform data access on behalf of the Main Business classes. These components know about the Database Services tier, and as long as this is the only tier that is required to know how to access data, the transition from one type of database server to another is as simple as modifying this tier alone. The rest of the application is shielded from the burden of knowing how to access data.

ADO.NET is Microsoft's preferred method for accessing data, no matter what the database provider is. ADO.NET provides access to a multitude of data sources and methods, including SQL Server, Oracle, Sybase, MS Access, MS Word, MS Excel, and so on. In tier development, the data source is typically a DBMS (Database Management System) that provides a variety of data access methods. When using ADO.NET, application developers tend to use the query components of ADO.NET, although other database-specific methods are available. For example, in the case of SQL Server, stored procedures provide a way to collect and return data that is up to 40 percent faster and less demanding on database resources. Whenever possible, try to use platform-specific features. Of course, the downside of using platform-specific features is reduced portability across platforms, but this is a judgment call. Try to use platform-specific features when it makes sense, even at the expense of platform independence.

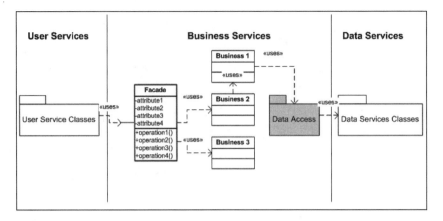

Figure 2-8: The Data Access component ready to access and pass data to the Business Services tier.

Data-Specific Business Rules

As mentioned earlier, dividing an application into tiers improves both its flexibility and manageability, such as in the implementation of business rules. In a tiered model, you can implement business rules strategically for maximum enforcement.

You should implement business rules in the Data Services tier whenever possible because the database is the lowest common denominator. However, this is only valid if you can implement the rule simply (examples might be setting the default values of a field, enforcing data relationships, or ensuring data uniqueness). Also, the rules that you implement in the database should be data-specific rules and not business processes because all applications that wish to fetch, modify, or insert data must access the database.

More complex rules, or rules more closely related to business processes, such as invoice processing, should be implemented at the Business Services tier. Avoid the Business Services tier for data-specific rules because business rules that you implement at the Business Services tier can be bypassed.

NOTE *The following sections relate to the implementation of business rules through the Data Services tier. The information is very basic and can hardly be considered more than a primer on how to take advantage of database constraints. If you want a glimpse into how the database can help you, these brief explanations should suffice. If you are an experienced database developer, you may wish to skip down to the "Application State" section.*

Business Processes

A business process is a rule-based, predefined set of tasks that is designed to complete a transaction. While the database can easily handle many business processes using triggers and stored procedures, you should always implement business processes in the Business Services tier and limit access to the database. If you don't, you'll likely reduce an application's scalability and cripple data services.

For example, a credit card transaction only needs access to modify the database when recording the purchase and other information. Building this process into the Business Services tier makes the application more scalable by allowing for the use of additional distributed servers.

Constraints

Use data-specific business rules to protect data, not to implement business processes, and remember that simply ensuring that data inserted into a database that meets the data type requirement does not mean your data is necessarily protected. For example, consider what happens when you modify an employee's ID when the ID is used in other tables. If this kind of modification is permitted and no other actions are taken, the data related to this employee will become orphaned (meaning that the data will no longer relate to anything) and will become useless or corrupt.

It is important that you don't accidentally modify key information when data in other tables depends on it. For instance, in a parent-child relationship in which the child is dependent on the parent table's data, the child can be orphaned if data is incorrectly modified or deleted from the parent table. (Foreign keys address this problem by enforcing referential integrity: If a parent record is modified or deleted, those changes are cascaded, or replicated, to all the child tables.)

Another business rule might be that you cannot duplicate a certain type of data in the database. The business rule might state that while a customer can have many records relating to him or her, the customer itself cannot be duplicated in the database. This data can be implemented at the database level by using a UNIQUE constraint. Often, if the column that requires uniqueness is also the subject of the table, adding a primary key is a good practice. This procedure allows you to take advantage of the FOREIGN KEY constraint. Or, a business rule might require additional information before you can insert a record into a table. Within the database, you can configure the columns that require data not to accept null values. On the other hand, you can apply a default value where data is not available.

GUIDs

One way to take advantage of default values is to use globally unique identifiers (GUIDs). GUIDs are an excellent way to guarantee uniqueness for records that will be replicated across databases. Obviously, the person entering customer information could care less about whether the customer is globally unique. Nor does the Business Services tier care. However, when you use the NewId() function (that is provided by SQL Server) as the default value, all customers will always have a globally unique identifier that is used for database replication or simply for uniqueness within a table. Use GUIDs for table uniqueness if you've had to add GUID columns to tables that you have not created with the foresight to include replication. You'll learn more about this in Chapter 9, "Retrieving Data."

Using a CHECK Constraint

Rather than focusing on database referential integrity, many business rules concern the specific values that are allowed. These are values that make business sense and are specific to a column. For example, if a customer is entered into a system with a customer category, chances are that there are sets of valid category numbers. A CHECK constraint can be placed on a column to ensure that only a specified range of values is entered.

Triggers

Triggers are an excellent means of rule enforcement. I recommend that you make sure there is no other way to implement the rule, and if there is not, use a trigger. The reasoning for this is based on the amount of processing that occurs before the rule is enforced. In the case of a CHECK constraint, the data is validated before it reaches the table. A trigger doesn't validate data until the data has already been entered into the table. If data checked by a trigger violates some rule, a rollback is required, meaning that not only is the record rejected but now it must be removed from the database. In defense of triggers, they are sometimes the only means for comparing data in a way that meets the business requirements. For example, if the data must be compared to data in another table, a trigger is your best bet.

The Downside

After examining all the reasons for placing data-specific business rules in the database, you need to understand the downside. You have to consider the possibility that the database platform might one day change—perhaps from SQL Server to Oracle, or vice versa. The point is that all business rules implemented at the database level may one day need to be reimplemented in another database system. This can be a considerable challenge when you consider that functionality can vary between systems. Regrettably, this is a good argument for implementing all business rules, except for the very basic data-integrity rules, in the Business Services tier.

What to Do?

Your choice of approach depends on the situation and inevitably involves trade-offs. For example, suppose that by using SQL Server stored procedures (which is an SQL Server-specific feature), performance can be increased an average of 40 percent with a stored query plan. The use of these stored procedures may cause additional development in the event that a database platform change is required. Even so, a performance gain of 40 percent probably will justify the use of this platform-specific feature. In any case, there are many ways to implement the same solution correctly. Make the best decisions concerning your application architecture and be flexible enough to change if you've made a mistake.

NOTE *For more information on SQL Server and how to take full advantage of rule implementation and performance, I recommend Kalen Delaney's* Inside Microsoft SQL Server 2000 *(Microsoft Press). There are many books available, but this is a definitive guide covering many aspects of SQL Server 2000 not found anywhere else.*

Application State

The concept of state applies to several contexts of an application. One such context is system state. The system that supports an application must know information about itself (for instance, computer name, date and time, networking protocols, and installed applications). This is not the kind of state that is discussed here. The state you are learning about is application-specific state, and more specifically, a single user's session state.

The application state represents the values that are necessary to support the user's session-specific environment. Take a user password for example. It's unreasonable to expect a user to enter his or her password every time the person navigates to another page. On the other hand, you cannot expect an application to accept a user blindly without a password. The solution is to make the password part of the user's session state and to maintain it as long as necessary. (In the Microsoft world, the password is not part of the user's session state. Instead, once authenticated, the user is given an access token.)

Consider another example: The information necessary to complete a purchase online. As you navigate from page to page, giving the application your name, mailing address, and payment information, the application must preserve this information to complete the ordering process. Without the persistence of application state, the application would forget your name and what you wanted to buy as soon as you loaded the next page.

Application state is quickly becoming one of the hottest issues in Internet application development because Internet applications need a way to track users, their application preferences, and sometimes orders that are processed on the behalf of the user. For example, think of a web farm, typically a group of server clusters. When a browser connects to a web farm, it can connect to a different server every time a new page is loaded. Any user information that is maintained by the application server is lost if the user's web browser connects to another server in the server farm. A simple fix to this complex problem is to tie a user into the first server to which the person connects for the duration of their session.

To build a scalable application, you need to aim for stateless components with the state being maintained elsewhere. The database and/or client are two great places to maintain application state because both of them typically place more permanent stateful information in the database and less stateful information in the client.

Maintaining Application State in the Database

There are many different ways to maintain session state in a database—you can create either a session-state database or a couple of tables in your current database. If you're relying on the client, you will need to use cookies, as shown in Figure 2-9. The GUID value that the cookie maintains is related to data that is stored in the session-state database, and this relationship is the key to maintaining information about any user's session.

The best way to maintain application state within the database is to create a series of related stored procedures specifically designed to maintain state. Whenever the user refreshes a page or moves to another page, your stored procedure would first check whether session state is stored in the database and, if not, the stored procedure would begin a process to initiate session state. If it finds a session state for this user, the information is collected and used when necessary.

While this is a fairly simple solution to implement, it may come with a performance cost because every time you access the database, you take time that would normally be used to process user requests. On the other hand, this solution will almost always perform and scale better than solutions that use stateful components.

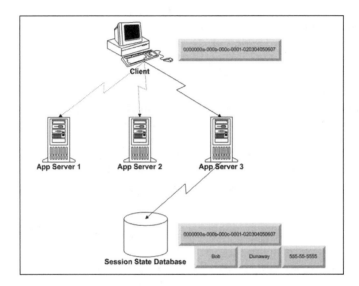

Figure 2-9: Application state in the database.

Maintaining Application State in the Client

One preferred method for maintaining application state in the client is to use ADO in the client application (See Figure 2-10). This method is fast and easier to implement than using stored procedures because it doesn't require you to invent new technologies or to build new database tables or stored procedures; all you need to do is store session information in an ADO object on the client.

The ADO method requires that the client supports ActiveX. While DHTML supports ADO, HTML pages do not; consequently, in the interest of allowing the largest number of browsers to access your application, the session state database is probably your best bet. If, however, your client is a DHTML client, you're in business; DHTML allows all session states to be maintained on the client as ADO.

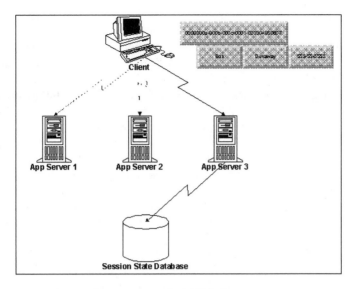

Figure 2-10: Application state in the DHTML client.

The ASP.NET Solution

ASP.NET, the next generation of Microsoft's Active Server Pages, introduces a new way to maintain application state. The old ASP method of maintaining state is undesirable for large scalable applications because it maintains application state in the session object on the application server, thus severely limiting the application's scalability, lowering performance, and making a server farm almost impossible to implement.

ASP.NET supports out-of-process session state, meaning that user sessions can come and go while leaving the session-state process open and available to anyone within a server farm. A few configuration changes to the config.web file are all that is required to make ASP.NET point to a common server. Of course, there is a performance trade-off; accessing a remote server for session-state information is always slower than accessing an in-process application running on the same server. If you want scalability, use the out-of-process model.

NOTE *The book will not cover the implementation of session state using ASP.NET.*

Final Thoughts on Session State

Session state is an issue that many applications will have to face. One of the most challenging aspects of application state is implementing it in a legacy application. Many web applications were built with session state maintained on the application server. Microsoft is partly to blame, because they did not anticipate application state to be a scalability problem. For years, you had to invent your own method of state management. Microsoft has finally identified application state as a scalability problem when it is implemented on the application server, and now provides methods to address it as previously described concerning ADO.NET.

Web Services

A Web Service is a method or set of methods that is made accessible through the Internet using a combination of XML to represent the data and HTTP for transport. Web Service methods are similar to COM or .NET Components, which expose methods and properties in a black box. The *consumer* is a client application that calls the Web Service method. As a result, Web Services fits very well into the N-tier model as an extension tier.

Web Services introduces a new way of thinking. Historically, applications were built and distributed as stand-alone products. If you wanted to make a data repository available as an application service, you not only had to make the data available, but you also needed to create all the functionality that applications typically provide, including the user interface, data-access methods, navigation, and application-state management. As a result, duplicate development effort was required.

Web Services allows you to provide access to functionality without having to build a complete application. A developer building the consuming client application can use one or more Web Services to create a new application or complement an existing one.

Web Services Tier Model

Like the Facades tier, Web Services wrap up functionality and reduce complexity for the consuming application. In fact, if you are building a Web Service for an application that was previously built using Facades, Main Business, and Data Access tiers, all you really need to do is wrap up the Facades tier with the Web Service while the Facades tier wraps up the remaining functionality.

Figure 2-11 shows the Web Services Wrapper logical model, while another Web service is providing new functionality not provided by the Facades tier. (You'll learn about all this and more in Chapter 10, "Implementing Web Services.")

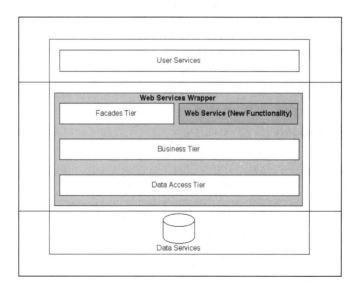

Figure 2-11: A Web Service can wrap current functionality and provide new functionality.

Why Web Services?

Why bother with Web Services when we can use DCOM (Distributed Component Object Model), Microsoft's solution for accessing remote methods, to provide remote functionality? The reason is platform independence. While DCOM solves many application-distribution and scalability problems, it is platform dependent. While once reasonable, this limitation is no longer necessary, and industry standard technologies like HTTP, XML, SOAP, and ASP.NET make it possible to bridge the platform gap.

RPC (Remote Procedure Call), DCOM, and MSMQ (Microsoft Message Queue Server) all attempted to bridge the Internet gap and, while successful within the Microsoft platform, they fail to bridge the platform gap as shown in Figure 2-12. Web Services succeed in bridging the platform gap, paving the way for rapid data availability, reduced development effort, and an enhanced user experience.

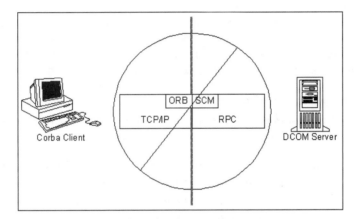

Figure 2-12: The incompatibilities of remote functionality without standard protocols.

Making Data Available

The need for information has been the driving force behind the Internet, and Web Services can make any data repository available. Information is a major commodity with regard to complimentary services.

For example, consider a subscription-based data service like Chrome data. Chrome data maintains information about every vehicle ever built and sells a subscription to this data on a CD-ROM, which must be periodically updated because the data changes frequently. Chrome data allows dealers to trade used cars because they can readily identify the vehicle even if they don't normally sell it. If Chrome made their data available through Web Services, subscribers would not need to maintain the data locally; they could simply call it up over the Web.

Reducing Development

Web Services reduces development because using it requires no intimate knowledge of its inner workings. This leaves the developer with more time to focus on meeting business requirements. When accessing other vendor's Web Services, there is no need to coordinate efforts with the Web service author. Web Services are self-describing, and methods for discovering how to interact with Web Services are available. You will learn about this in more detail in Chapter 10, "Implementing Web Services."

Enhancing the User Experience

Web Services greatly enhance the user experience. Customers no longer need to be redirected to another URL because Web Services can access other Web Services on behalf of the user, much like the Facades class of our N-tier solution. A single Web Service can provide a number of services, thus reducing or eliminating the need to send users away.

Web Services also save money. Rather than buying and installing an application locally, with many features that users don't need or want, Web Services provide flexibility in the cost of an application. Customers are charged for only the features they use and the frequency with which they use them.

Candidates for Web Services

Any data repository or function is a good candidate for a Web Service. The following is a short list of applications or data that might benefit from Web Services:

- Volatile data, such as the one example that was mentioned earlier, is data that is provided by Chrome for vehicle make and model.

- Applications that require data and process integration between two or more applications. Historically, data integration requires messaging while process integration is loosely enforced through some type of request-reply solution. Web Services provides ways to integrate both data and business processes without the overhead that is required by messaging technologies.

- Application APIs can be wrapped and exposed as Web Services.

- Web Services can also provide Facades-like interfaces to a set of other Web Services (which are provided by partnering businesses). One example might be a financial organization that partners with lenders and credit bureaus in an effort to provide its customers with a full range of services.

- Proprietary algorithms and other services that might be too difficult or impractical for other businesses to implement can be exposed through Web Services.

Summary

In this chapter you learned that programmers have been forced to choose models that support a variety of solutions throughout the evolution of tiered development. When you choose a model, the distinction between performance and scalability must be clearly defined. Performance is a measure of the number of processor cycles that are necessary to complete any given task while scalability is a measure of the number of users able to perform a task concurrently.

The implementation and enforcement of business rules is another critical aspect to building stable and reliable applications. Placing business rule enforcement as close to the data source is preferable. As there is a trade-off between enforcing business rules at the Data Services Layer and in compiled code at the Business Services Layer, the decision should be to enforce data specific rules in the Data Services Layer while enforcing all other business logic in the Business Services Layer. Implementing business logic in the presentation layer should be avoided at almost all costs.

3

VISUAL STUDIO .NET
WALKTHROUGH

Visual Studio .NET is Microsoft's most recent and successful attempt to integrate all Microsoft development environments into a unified Integrated Development Environment (IDE). Visual Studio .NET provides an IDE that can be shared by all .NET languages. Furthermore, Visual Interdev features have been rolled up into Visual Studio .NET so that all .NET languages have access to Internet functionality.

One advantage of using a single IDE for all .NET languages is that it reduces the learning curve needed to learn new languages and to build, debug, and deploy applications. This makes the decision as to what language to use more of a personal or company preference (with the exception of languages that expose special CLR functionality such as financial and scientific calculations).

In this chapter you'll learn about the Visual Studio .NET installation, customizing the IDE, the development environment, and Visual Studio .NET options. You'll also take a quick walkthrough of common applications that are built with Visual Studio .NET.

Installing Visual Studio .NET

To install Visual Studio .NET, you'll need not only the installation media (of course) but also certain minimum hardware. Visual Studio .NET cannot be installed on a network drive. Another point is that Visual Studio .NET can be installed along side of MS Office 2000 and Visual Studio 6 development tools.

The Visual Studio .NET hardware requirements and Microsoft's recommendations are:

Processor: Pentium II 450 MHz (required); Pentium III 733 MHz (recommended)

Memory: 128 MB (required); 256 MB (recommended)

Disk Space: 3 GB required for the full installation

Monitor Settings: 800x600 with 256 colors (required); High Color 16-bit resolution (recommended)

Operating Systems: Supported operating systems are Windows 2000, Windows ME, Windows NT4, Windows XP, .NET Enterprise Server, and Windows 98.

CD ROM drive: required

Installation Walkthrough

To install Visual Studio .NET, follow these steps:

1. Insert CD 1. The Visual Studio .NET Setup page is displayed (as shown in Figure 3-1).

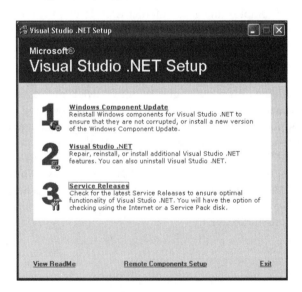

Figure 3-1: The Visual Studio .NET setup screen.

The three choices here should be obvious. If you have not already installed Visual Studio .NET, choose Windows Component Update. If you've already installed Visual Studio .NET and want to reinstall, add new components, or repair broken components choose Update Visual Studio .NET.

NOTE *From time to time you will need to check the Internet for updated Visual Studio .NET components. In Visual Studio 6 you had to search Microsoft's download pages for updated components such as MDAC (Microsoft Data Access Components) or Visual Studio service packs. With Visual Studio .NET, all you need to do is pop in CD 1 of the Visual Studio .NET installation and select Service Releases.*

2. Select Windows Component Update. The Visual Studio installation will ask for the Windows Component Update CD.

3. Place the Windows Component Update CD into the CD-ROM drive and press OK. You should see the dialog box that is shown in Figure 3-2.

Figure 3-2: The Automatic Log On dialog box.

This dialog box is designed to collect your credential information so the rest of the installation will be able to reboot and log back in without your assistance.

4. Select the Automatically Log On check box, type your password into the Password text box, and press the Continue hyperlink.

5. Press Install Now. A red arrow will indicate the current windows components being installed or updated as indicated in Figure 3-3. The Visual Studio .NET installation program will reboot your computer a few times throughout the installation of these components.

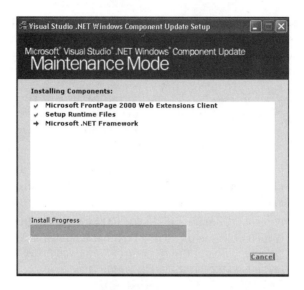

Figure 3-3: You can update, install, or repair Windows components.

6. Once the Windows Component Update is complete you'll get the first installation dialog box. Select Update Visual Studio .NET.

7. The next dialog box (Figure 3-4) provides three more options. Choose Add/Remove Features.

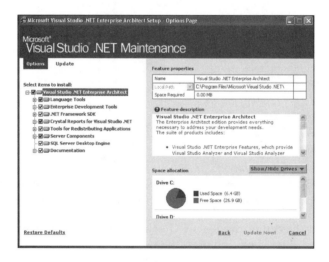

Figure 3-4: You can customize the Visual Studio .NET installation.

Before you continue, observe the features of this dialog box. You can expand the options on the left and select any option and view the installation path and space required on the right. You may also change the path but remember to use only local hard drives in your path. You cannot select a network drive letter.

8. Press Update Now! to continue. When the installation is complete, you will have the opportunity to view the error and installation logs.

9. When you are finished, press Done.

Customizing the Visual Studio .NET IDE

One of the new advances in Visual Studio .NET is its customizability. You can customize Visual Studio .NET with a familiar environment to make tasks easier to perform and duplicate. Customizing the environment enables you to automate common and repetitive tasks.

The Start Page

To open Visual Studio .NET, select Programs from the Start bar, then select Microsoft Visual Studio .NET 7.0 from the Microsoft Visual Studio .NET 7.0 program group.

The first time you run Visual Studio .NET, My Profile (Figure 3-5) provides customization options. You will always have the opportunity to customize Visual Studio .NET, although this particular Start Page is displayed the first time you start Visual Studio. (To access this page in the future, click the My Profile hyperlink.)

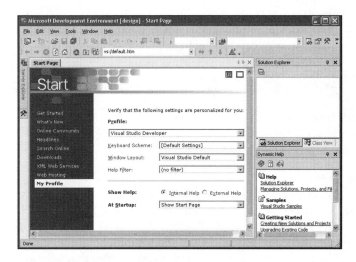

Figure 3-5: The My Profile Start Page used for customizing Visual Studio .NET.

The Visual Studio .NET Start Page provides links to related development information. On the left hand side of the Start Page, hyperlinks point to Get Started, What's New, Online Community, Headlines, Search Online, Downloads, XML Web Services, Web Hosting, and My Profile. These links help to provide quick and easy access to related .NET development information.

Get Started

The Get Started Start Page offers all of your recently opened solutions in a hyperlink list. Click a link to begin working with an existing solution.

What's New

The What's New page provides links to the latest information for each language and Visual Studio .NET Extensibility components, and allows you to look at Visual Studio .NET updates.

Online Community

The Online Community page provides a host of news group links.

Headlines

The Headlines page provides a list of hyperlinks that point to Visual Studio .NET news links. One of these, http://msdn.microsoft.com/default.asp, is packed with information including the MSDN Magazine, featured articles, news, columns, technical articles, and training and event information. This is an excellent place to begin researching any Microsoft related subject as well as to help keep up with the latest information.

Search Online

The Search Online page provides portal access to the MSDN library.

Downloads

The Downloads page provides easy access to the latest product updates, sample code, and software development kits.

XML Web Services

The XML Web Services page allows you to search for and register web services.

Web Hosting

The Web Hosting page provides access to companies that host .NET applications.

My Profile

The My Profile page is the first Start Page that is displayed after installation, and provides a means for customizing the Visual Studio .NET IDE. This page includes your profile. Other developers can work on the same machine and maintain their own sets of customized settings.

The profile drop box lists predefined profiles that help to leverage your personal preference and reduce the learning curve when first using Visual Studio .NET. The Keyboard Scheme and Windows Layout provides Visual Studio .NET with a set of predefined keyboard schemes.

Microsoft Solution Developer Network (MSDN) is an online technical reference for developers. Previous versions of Visual Studio integrated MSDN by loading MSDN with a related topic (in its own stand-alone application) when help was requested. Visual Studio .NET fully integrates MSDN so that all searches and search results are managed within the Visual Studio .NET IDE.

The Help Filter option of the My Profile Start Page allows you to search a subset of help topics specific to their needs. This helps to reduce unnecessary search time. For example, when you are searching for how to implement ADO.NET using Visual Basic .NET, you don't have to also search and return the equivalent information for each of the other .NET languages.

Auto Hide

The Auto Hide feature is an attempt to reduce screen clutter and complexity. Auto Hide displays tool windows as tabs; placing the mouse over one of these tabs expands the hidden window. By default, Visual Studio .NET provides a hidden Toolbox and Server Explorer.

Dockable Windows

Not only can you hide the tool windows, but if you turn Auto Hide off, you can view the contents of a tool window without it floating around the IDE. (They are made dockable to the side of the IDE.)

Navigation Buttons

Browser-like navigation buttons (like those shown in Figure 3-6) provide a familiar and efficient way to navigate through opened windows.

Figure 3-6: The navigation buttons.

Favorites

The Favorites menu item of both Internet Explorer and the Windows environment are integrated into both Visual Studio .NET and MSDN. You don't have to worry about loosing all your favorite links when you upgrade to new versions of MSDN!

Multi-Monitor Support

A lack of screen real estate is a constant constraint for developers; this is now addressed with such features as Auto Hide and dockable windows. Furthermore, Visual Studio .NET supports the use of multiple monitors to increase available screen real estate. This feature can help to display more tool windows to aid you without cluttering the development environment.

Visual Studio .NET Macros

Macros provide easy access to the Visual Studio .NET IDE. They are another method for customizing the Visual Studio IDE from a task-oriented perspective. Macros are used to not only customize how the Visual Studio .NET IDE behaves but also for automating repetitive tasks and extending the IDE to do more than it does out of the box.

Macros save time and effort when a task needs to be repeated or automated. One advantage of macros over other automation methods such as Add-ins, which are discussed in the next section, is that they are easier to create than Add-ins. Macros can be created easily with an editor, or recorded.

To access the Visual Studio .NET Macro development environment (shown in Figure 3-7), press ALT+F11 or select Macros from the Tools menu option. This development environment is feature rich and provides a single location for creating, modifying, and running macros.

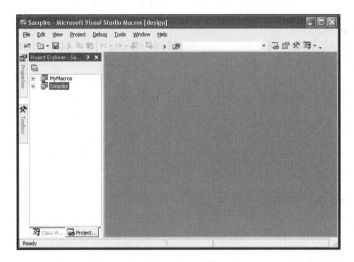

Figure 3-7: The Microsoft Visual Studio .NET Macro development environment.

The Macro Recorder

The Macro Recorder allows you to create macros with record and playback functionality without coding (though it does provide access to the code that is used by the macros). With this code accessible, it's easier to modify macros and to manage versions. In addition, you can learn a lot from code generated by the Macro Recorder.

The following steps walk you through creating a simple macro with the Macro Recorder. This will be a temporary macro that displays your Task Window:

1. Select Macros from the Tools menu option, then press Record Temporary Macro. At this point the Macro Recorder is recording every click and action taken within the Visual Studio .NET IDE.

2. Select Other Windows from the View menu option and press Task List. The Macro Recorder recorded the click events just made.

3. Close the Task List window.

4. To run this temporary macro, select Macros from the Tools menu and press Run Temporary Macro.

    You'll notice that the Task List window is added to the Visual Studio .NET IDE.

Macro Explorer

The Macro Explorer (Figure 3-8) displays all available Macros in a hierarchical or tree view. The various macros can be expanded by left-clicking the plus "+" sign to view their supporting modules and then further expanded to display each modules supporting functions. To run, edit, or view a macro, double-click on it. (The development environment is loaded, providing access to all available macro components such as supporting code.)

The Macro Explorer provides quick and easy access to all available macros, making the management of macros simpler.

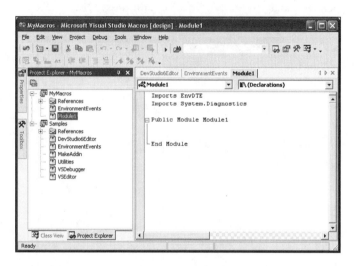

Figure 3-8: The Macro Explorer.

Add-ins

Macros provide a simple way to manipulate and access Visual Studio .NET's extensible features. For additional extensibility and distribution, use an Add-in. Much like macros, Add-ins allow you to automate repetitive tasks, reducing the time and effort that are required to perform a variety of tasks.

One significant difference between macros and Add-ins is their programmability. Add-ins are .NET assemblies that implement the IDTExtensibility2 interface, Microsoft's dual-interface that provides five methods that are required for Add-ins. These methods support events that respond to startup and shutdown conditions.

The programmability of Add-ins offers several benefits. For one, compiled Add-ins are easy to deploy and implement and are language independent. You can run Add-ins from a variety of locations within the interface, including the Add-in Manager, toolbars, the Command Window, and during the Visual Studio .NET startup.

Add-in Wizard

The Add-in Wizard makes it easier to develop add-ins by providing the basic framework. Once the framework is created, all you need to do is to add code. Very little knowledge of the Add-in framework is required.

To create a simple Add-in, follow these steps:

1. Select New from the File menu, then press Projects. The New Project dialog box appears as shown in Figure 3-9.

2. Expand the Other Projects folder and select Extensibility Projects.

3. Select Visual Studio .NET Add-in and press OK.

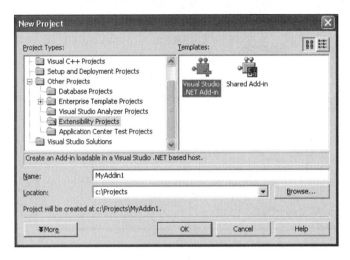

Figure 3-9: The New Project dialog box displaying the Visual Studio .NET Add-in option.

Now the Add-in Wizard (Figure 3-10) walks you through the necessary steps to create the Add-in framework.

Figure 3-10: The Extensibility Wizard Start Page for creating an Add-in.

4. The next Wizard page (Figure 3-11) allows you to select the language used to build the Add-in. Select your language and press Next.

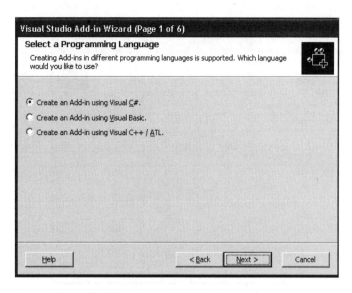

Figure 3-11: Add-in Wizard page displaying language options.

5. This Wizard page (Figure 3-12) allows you to select the host or application where the Add-in is to be executed. Select the host environment and press Next.

Figure 3-12: Add-in Wizard page displaying available Application Hosts.

6. This Wizard page (Figure 3-13) allows you to provide information about the Add-in, such as the name and description of the Add-in. Enter these values and press Next.

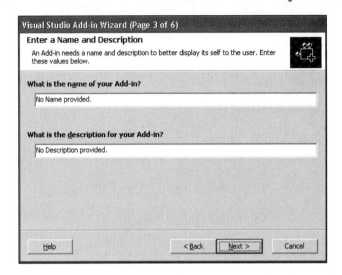

Figure 3-13: Wizard page for entering the name and description of the Add-in.

7. The next Wizard page (Figure 3-14) provides a variety of Add-in options. The first option allows you to specify whether the Add-in supports a user interface or not. The next two options provide a means for optimizing the Add-in, and the final option manages the security of the Add-in, determining who has permission to run the add-in.

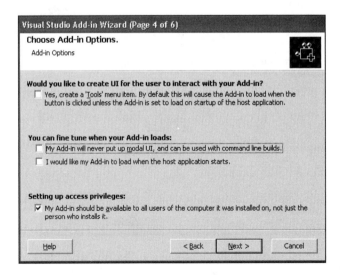

Figure 3-14: Wizard page displaying additional interface and startup options.

8. This Wizard page also provides a means for adding "about" information. Press Next.

9. The final page provides summary information. If you chose the wrong setting or want to change a setting that you chose previously, use the Back button to make the appropriate modification. If the summary information is correct, press Finish.

The end result is an Add-in project with the Add-in framework ready for code, as shown in Figure 3-15.

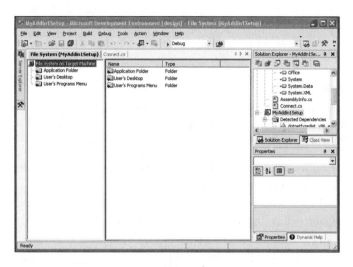

Figure 3-15: The project created by the Add-in Wizard.

The Visual Studio .NET Development Environment

Before taking the time to develop macros and Add-ins, it is helpful for you to understand the tools that are available out of the box. Now that you know how to customize your personal development environment with My Profile, let's look at the tools provided by Visual Studio .NET.

Preferred Access Connection

This option determines the means of access your projects will use when creating and modifying your web projects. To use the option, follow these steps:

1. From the Tools menu select Options. The Visual Studio .NET Options dialog box appears.

2. Select Projects, then choose Web Settings. The Preferred Access Method option allows you to build web applications using a file share or FrontPage extensions.

3. Select the File Share option and press OK.

Solution Explorer

In Visual Studio .NET "speak," a solution is a combination of projects that uses programs to solve business problems. The Solution Explorer displays a list of all projects, files, and directories of the current solution in a hierarchical or tree view. In addition, all files and directories beneath the project are displayed and accessible.

Dynamic Help

Finding documentation on specific key words and Visual Studio .NET components can be difficult and time-consuming. Dynamic Help provides list of help topics that are constantly changing based on what is selected and where the cursor is placed. Links that are provided by Dynamic Help point to articles and help topics in MSDN.

Searching Help

To search the MSDN knowledge base, select Search from the Help menu. As with the stand-alone MSDN application, you have a variety of search options from which to choose:

- *Filter by*: Allows you to limit your search results to a specific language. This reduces unnecessary search time.
- *Titles only*: Searches for words in the title of MSDN articles.
- *Related words*: Searches not only for the words placed in the search criteria but for different tenses of the word as well as plural forms of each word.
- *Highlight search hits:* Make it easy to find the information you are looking for within an article.
- *Search Results Window:* Displays the results of your search with the article's title, location, and rank. Each of these columns can sort the results by clicking the column heading.

Task List

The Task List, formerly part of Visual Interdev and Visual J++, is a central location where you can track a variety of tasks. The Task List provides a place for keeping notes about the code and indicating the status of a task or a section of code. You also can filter the different types of tasks; for example, you can decide to view only those tasks that are generated by compile errors.

To display the Task List window, select Other Windows from the View menu and then click Task List. Double-click a task to display code related to it. Follow these steps:

1. Open any project and place the following comment within any portion of code:

You should see the task automatically created in the Task Window.

---

2. Close the code window and double-click the task in the Task List that you just created. The code that is related to the task is displayed.
3. Right-click anywhere within the Task List to sort and filter tasks.
4. Left-click the task under the "!" column of the Task List window to select a task's priority.
5. Left-click the check box in the status column for your task to remove the task and the tasks comment in code.

The Task List is an important tool for documenting and tracking work you want to perform, and for managing general notes for a section of code. Certain tasks are automatically generated, such as when errors occur during compilation.

Command Window

The Command Window, which was introduced with Visual J++, provides more direct access to the Visual Studio IDE through the keyboard. The Command Window allows you to search and navigate through the application as well as to execute commands and run programs.

Commands that search and navigate as well as run commands and programs can also be made into aliases. You can create aliases for commonly-used commands, reducing the number of keyboard strokes that are required to complete routine tasks.

Command Window commands also provide flexibility through the use of switches and arguments. Many of the rules for Command Window commands support rules that are similar to legacy DOS commands using switches and parameters. All arguments must be given in the correct order while switches don't have to adhere to any specific order. Like DOS, arguments with spaces must have quotation marks around them. (For a full list of Command Window commands with arguments and switches, see the Visual Studio Command with Arguments article from the Visual Studio .NET SDK.)

To open the Command Window, select Other Windows from the View menu and press Command Window. The following are a couple Command Window tasks to help familiarize you with the Command Window.

Creating a New Project
In the Command Window, type File.NewProject or type NewProj.

Creating a New Project with a Predefined Alias
The alias for a new project is np. Type np in the Command Window to create a new project.

Creating an Alias for Creating a New Project

To create an alias name for a command, enter the `alias` keyword, the alias name, and the command the alias represents. An example of an alias name is

```
Alias NewP File.NewProject
```

The alias is available for use immediately. To test the new alias, enter `NewP` in the Command Window. A new project is created.

Creating a New Project Using Switches and Parameters

Enter the following command statement in the Command Window:

```
File.NewProject "Visual Basic Projects\Windows Application" "Project1" "C:\Temp"
/sln:cmdSolution
```

You can also adapt this command statement when you create C# applications or any other .NET application; use the the parameters to determine exactly the type of project you want to create. You'll notice in the first parameter, `Visual Basic Projects\Windows Application`, that the first part of the parameter is the same as the Visual Basic Projects folder and the second part of the parameter is the type of Visual Basic project to be created. In this case, a Windows Application is created although this project could just as easily be a Class Library or Web Service.

The second parameter is the project's name. In this case, the project that you create is named Project1. You add the Project1 project to the `cmdSolution` solution as indicated by the `/sln:` switch, which, in turn, is passed the name of the solution. The third parameter determines where the project will be created. These values effectively represent what would normally be entered when you create a project manually as shown in Figure 3-16.

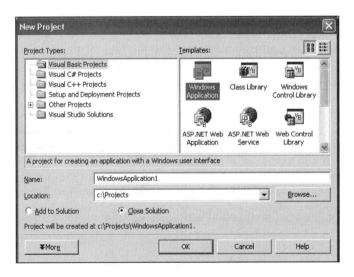

Figure 3-16: These values can be used at the command line.

Closing the IDE

When closing the Visual Studio .NET IDE, you would normally either left-click the X box in the upper-right corner of the IDE or select Exit from the File menu. From the command line, you can simply type File.Exit.

I've described only some of the tasks that are available to the Command Window. To effectively cover all the features of the Command Window and its associated commands goes beyond the scope of this book. Take some time to experiment and try commands to see the benefits the Command Window commands might provide to you.

Tool Box Window

The Tool Box Window, shown in Figure 3-17, is a container for controls that are used by the .NET forms designers, including both Windows Forms and Web Forms. Tools that are contained in the Tool Box Window change depending on the designer being used.

Figure 3-17: The Tool Box Window.

Some of the controls that are available include Form controls for Windows Forms and Web Forms, ActiveX Controls, Web Services, HTML Elements, objects, and the Windows clipboard. In addition to components, the Tool Box Window can hold code snippets, which helps to save time and improve productivity.

To add a code snippet to the Tool Box Window, simply highlight the code that you want to add to the Tool Box and copy it.

You can access code snippets that are stored in the Tool Box Window from the Clipboard Ring tab. From this point, you can rename the new item in the Clipboard by right-clicking and then selecting Rename, or you can drag the code snippet into the code window.

Server Explorer

The Server Explorer development console provides access to computer resources on the network including message queues, performance counters, services, processes, event logs, and database objects. The Server Explorer also aids development by providing information about Web Services such as the methods and schema that are used by the Web Service. You can use drag- and-drop functionality to create references to Web Services in order to reduce the time that is necessary to prepare for programming remote methods.

Accessing Remote Network Resources

To add a remote computer to the Server Explorer double-click Add Server (Figure 3-18).

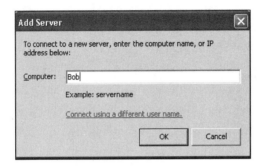

Figure 3-18: Connecting to a remote server resource.

After entering the name of the server that you want to add to the Server Explorer, you can select the different user name hyperlink to connect with a different user ID. Once you've connected, a variety of resources are available for drag-and-drop programming (Figure 3-19).

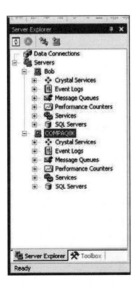

Figure 3-19: Remote server resources.

Adding a new server to the Server Explorer makes including server components such as error handling and performance counters easier to add to your project.

Document Window

The Document Window allows you to write and edit code, and include all windows that display actual content such as the Visual Studio .NET home page and MSDN articles. The Document Window is loaded when a component in the Solution Explorer is selected.

The Document Window is a simple component, but it does have some interesting features. One feature is IntelliSense, which helps to reduce the potential for writing error-prone applications. Another feature is the tabular feature, which enables you to load and access multiple Document Windows easily. The tabs for each Document Window are located at the top of the Document Window screen.

Properties Window

The Properties Window describes the properties or information about a component or Visual Studio .NET object, such as those found in the Server Explorer window. The Properties Window is opened by default with Visual Studio .NET; if it appears closed, select Properties Window from the View menu to reopen it.

The Properties Window is a simple tool that provides you with several benefits. You can save time when you program by using new components because information about each component is readily available and graphically configurable. You can change the properties of the component at design-time as well as properties for the project and project solution.

Object Browser

The Object Browser provides you with access to a variety of information about a particular component that you specify (such as properties, methods, and events) or components that are already referenced by your project. Information about the component's namespace, classes, structures, variable, constraints, and so on, are available. You can access the Object Browser by selecting Other Windows from the View menu and then selecting Object Browser (or by pressing CTRL+ALT+J or F2 alternatively) as shown in Figure 3-20.

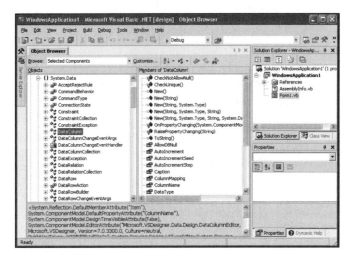

Figure 3-20: The Object Browser.

Customization Options

The Visual Studio .NET IDE wouldn't be complete without providing you with a set of options to completely customize the development environment to meet your specific needs. The Options dialog box, which is accessible when selecting Options from the Tools menu, enables you to change default settings that provide more flexibility and control of the IDE. It's not necessarily important for you to memorize all the options that are available, but it can be helpful.

Environment

You can use the Environment tab to change default settings of the IDE. The General page shows the most commonly-used options for configuring the IDE, one of which is to set Visual Studio .NET's start-up behavior. For example, you can customize the IDE so that the Open Project dialog box appears or the last-used project can be automatically loaded.

Source Control

Visual Source Safe is version-control software where you can store code, as well as check out code for modification and check the code back in. The Source Control tab allows you to change default settings for source control software. Some of these settings include the role of a developer, who may be an individual, or a developer role that is required in order to work with a team of developers.

Text Editor

The Text Editor tab allows you to change settings that related to text editors.

Database Tools

The Database Tools tab manages options for database projects, such as how to deal with error conditions and default field lengths for creating database tables.

Debugging

The Debugging tab provides a number of options for debugging applications.

Projects

The Projects tab provides options for projects. The most significant option to configure under the Projects tab is the Preferred Access Method on the Web Settings tab. As you learned earlier in this chapter, the Preferred Access Method determines how web projects are accessed.

Visual Basic .NET

Visual Basic .NET is Microsoft's latest release of Visual Basic and has been redesigned from the ground up to build .NET applications, including .NET assemblies, class inheritance, web applications, and web services. Visual Basic .NET also includes CLR support for protocols such as XML, HTTP, and SOAP for promoting of loosely coupled applications.

Creating a Visual Basic .NET Application

The following section enables you to cut your teeth on Visual Basic .NET. The purpose of this section is not to teach you Visual Basic .NET, but to introduce you to it. With Visual Studio .NET and application templates, you can create applications easily. The following steps guide you through creating a Visual Basic .NET application:

1. Start Visual Studio .NET.
2. From the File menu, select New and then select Project.
3. In the New Project window, select the Visual Basic Projects folder. You can select from a series of template applications or create an empty one.

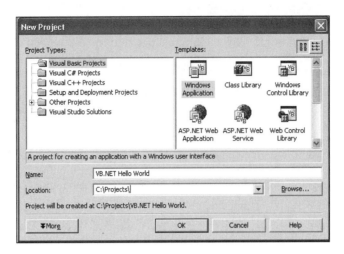

Figure 3-21: Creating the VB.NET "Hello World" sample.

4. Select the Windows Application project icon.

5. Before pressing OK, select the project name and location. Type the following values in the Name and Location text boxes (Figure 3-21):

   In the Name text box, enter `VB.NET Hello World`..
   In the Location text box, enter `C:\Projects\`..

6. Press OK. The Visual Basic .NET project, supporting files, and references are created.

NOTE *The directory you create for this project is the location plus the project name. This means that if you create a new project and use a directory with the project name after defining the location, you will end up with a directory structure that seems to duplicate the project name within it. Just remember that the project name also becomes part of the new directory structure and you'll be okay.*

Adding "Hello World" Code

Now you'll add "Hello World" to the text area of the control bar:

1. Right-click on the Form1.vb object in the Solution Explorer window and select View Code.

2. You will first need to expand the "Windows Form Designer generated code" region. Under the comment, "'Add any initialization after the InitializeComponent() call" add the following code:

```
Form1.text = "Hello World"
```

Your screen should look like Figure 3-22.

Figure 3-22: The results of adding the "Hello World" code.

Building the Project

To check for errors, build the Visual Basic project by selecting Build from the menu bar and then select Build again (or CTRL+SHIFT+B). When you run the build, an output screen appears at the bottom of Visual Studio. If there are no problems, you should see the following output:

```
Build: 1 succeeded, 0 failed, 0 skipped
```

Running the "Hello World" Application

To run your new windows application, select Debug from the menu bar and then select Run. You have now created a .NET Windows Application.

C#

C# is the first programming language that is written for component-based oriented languages. Microsoft has taken the best of C and C++, the ease of use of Visual Basic, and the .NET Framework features such as garbage collection, exception handling, and type safety, to create the new C# language. Like Visual Basic .NET and the .NET Framework, C# supports loosely coupled applications through the use of XML, HTTP, and SOAP.

Creating a C# "Hello World" Application

To create the "Hello World" application in C#, follow the same steps that are provided for Visual Basic .NET with the following exceptions (Figure 3-23):

- When selecting a project template choose from the C# Projects folder.

- Name your project CSharp Hello World.

- Place the following code after "// TODO: Add any constructor code after InitializeComponent call":

```
this.Text = "Hello World";
```

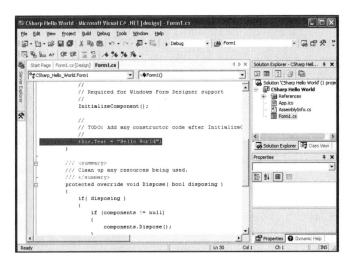

Figure 3-23: The C# sample application.

Building, Running, and Debugging C# Code

Building, running, and debugging C# code is exactly the same as Visual Basic .NET, which we covered in the previous section. The Visual Studio .NET IDE integrates and shares these functions with all .NET languages.

ASP.NET

ASP.NET is used for creating web forms with scripting in either Visual Basic or Visual C#. It can take advantage of all the Visual Studio .NET controls as well as debugging and error handling. One of the biggest differences between ASP.NET and its predecessor ASP is that the Visual Basic or Visual C# code is compiled, which allows for better performance and strong typing of variables. Before ASP.NET became available, all variables in classic ASP were declared as variant, which is the lowest performing data type. ASP.NET also includes two new methods for managing application state.

Creating the "Hello World" ASP.NET project

The following series of steps result in creating an ASP.NET application. Before you begin, you need to have IIS5 or greater installed. For IIS5 to have the extensions that are required to support ASP.NET, you need to install Visual Studio .NET after installing IIS5. Follow these steps to create the ASP.NET application:

1. Start Visual Studio .NET and select the Web Application project under the Visual Basic Projects folder.

2. Before pressing OK, you must set up the project directories with the following parameters (Figure 3-24):

Name   HelloWorld

Location   http://localhost/

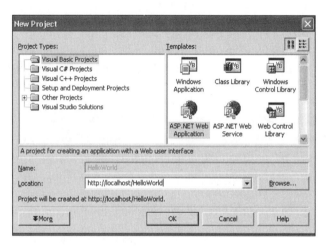

Figure 3-24: The New Project dialog box.

NOTE *After adding the new HelloWorld web project, you may see the dialog box that's shown in Figure 3-25. If you do, simply press OK. The Virtual Directory in IIS5 should be automatically created. If not, consider uninstalling and then re-installing IIS5 and reapplying the Windows Component Update.*

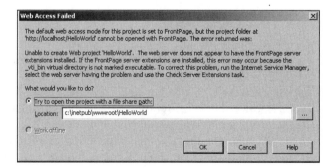

Figure 3-25: The Web Access Failed dialog box.

Once you've created the web project you can begin developing it.

Creating the "Hello World" ASP.NET Page

To create the HelloWorld ASP.NET page, follow these steps:

1. Rename the file WebForm1.aspx to HelloWorld in the Solution Explorer window or simply delete the WebForm1.aspx file and add a new one with the desired name.

NOTE *Be sure to close the WebForm1.aspx file from the editor window before you rename it (Figure 3-26).*

If you were to rename this file a few more times you would get a dialog with several options, as shown in Figure 3-26. You have the option to save this file as a different file altogether, leaving the contents of the original file unchanged. The Overwrite options overwrite the old WebForm1aspx file with the new HelloWorld.aspx file, which is what you want to do. If you navigate to C:\Inetpub\wwwroot\HelloWorld, you will find that the actual file names have also been renamed. The Conflicting Modifications Detected dialog box is extremely helpful and informs you when your intentions are not clear.

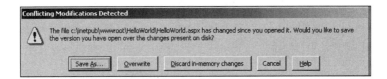

Figure 3-26: The Conflicting Modifications Detected dialog box.

2. Select the HelloWorld.aspx file and press the View Designer button in the Solution Explorer window.

3. Drag a Label control from the Toolbox on the far right. Right-click on the label and select Properties.

4. In the Properties Window, type "This is my first ASP.NET application." in the Text property box. You could do more, but more detail will be covered in Chapter 8, "Building Forms."

Viewing the "Hello World" Page

Before you view your page, be sure to save your project in Visual Studio .NET.

To view the page, select View in browser from the File menu. The page appears in preview mode as the new ASP.NET page within the Visual Studio .NET IDE. Right-click the URL text box and select the Copy option. Start Internet Explorer, paste the URL into the text box, and press ENTER. Your page runs independently of the Visual Studio .NET IDE. (The URL of the ASP page appears in the URL text box near the top of the Visual Studio .NET IDE. This is an easy place to copy the URLs for the ASP pages and paste them into Internet Explorer for testing.)

NOTE *Because an ASP.NET page is compiled the first time you view the page after you create or modify it, the page takes a little longer to display. After the first compile, the page displays more quickly.*

XML

The eXtensible Markup Language (XML), is a predefined set of elements that are used for describing data contained in a document. This standard, created by the XML Working Group of the W3C, is extendable when new elements are needed to better describe data. One of the more important aspects of XML is its openness to all platforms, including but not limited to Windows 2000, UNIX, Linux, OS2, and Mac. XML's extensibility allows for new elements to describe business or industry specific data types, some of which might include data specific to the banking industry, automobile industry, musical scores, or biological sciences, such as DNA research data.

XML is used in nearly all of Microsoft's new .NET Servers. SQL Server 2000 can return data in the form of XML and receive XML data updates from data grams. BizTalk has also been retrofitted to support XML for Enterprise Application Integration (EAI) solutions and workflow processing. The loose coupling of data is made possible by XML and its platform independent nature.

XML can be used to describe structured documents, everything from the data descriptions to how the data is presented. XML is also an excellent way to store database schemas. There are many other uses of XML, but these are currently the most widely implemented.

Examining a Simple XML Document

To give you an idea of what XML looks like, here's a very simple example. This example does not include data type definition (DTDs), but it does describe name-value pairs for data about the *The Book of Visual Studio .NET:*

```
<?xml version="1.0"?>
<!-- File Name: Book.xml -->
<BOOK>
    <TITLE>The Book of Visual Studio .NET</TITLE>
    <AUTHOR>Robert B. Dunaway</AUTHOR>
    <PUBLISHER>No Starch</PUBLISHER>
    <PAGES>687</PAGES>
    <PRICE>$45.49</PRICE>
    <Rating>5</Rating>
</BOOK>
```

Web Services

Web services, as discussed in Chapter 2, "Evolution of the Tier Development," provide a way of exposing remote methods. These methods provide programming logic with access to other assemblies and data. Web services also fit nicely into the .NET architecture by introducing loosely connected components.

Web services offer a variety of advantages over classic COM development. For one, they take advantage of XML and HTTP to provide a method for creating distributed applications that can pass through firewalls, thus increasing an applications potential customer base. Another advantage is the services' self-describing nature. Visual Studio .NET automatically generates XML data structures that are used to describe your web service so other developers know what public functions are available, the input parameters and data types, and the return data types. This information is available by accessing the URL of a service's disco file which stores discovery information describing the service.

Creating a Simple Web Service

Here's a simple example of a web service that accepts two numbers and returns their sum:

1. Start Visual Studio .NET
2. From the File menu, select New and then select Project.
3. In the New Project window, select the Visual Basic Projects folder.
4. Select the Web Service project icon.
5. Before clicking OK, you must select the project name and location. Use the following information to populate the Name and Location text boxes:

Name   Sum_WebService

Location   http://localhost/

NOTE *This value should be in the text box by default unless you've already created a web service with a different location. Visual Studio .NET tracks the last used location to make programming multiple web services a little easier.*

6. Press OK. The web service project and supporting files and references are created. The dialog box should look like Figure 3-27. If you receive another dialog box entitled Web Access Failed (Figure 3-28) and you're given the option to "Try to open the project with a file shared path," press OK to create your project.

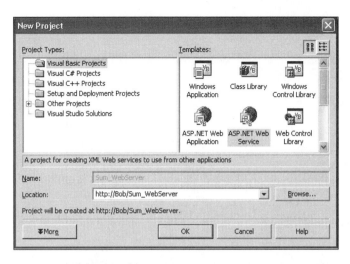

Figure 3-27: The Name and Location of the web service.

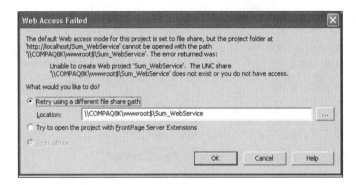

Figure 3-28: The Web Access Failed dialog box.

NOTE *Now you have a project with references and supporting files, which include the Sum_WebService.disco file that is used to provide discovery information for developers of your web service.*

7. Rename the Service1.asmx file to Sum_WebService.asmx.

8. Right-click on the Sum_WebService.asmx object in the Solution Explorer window and select View Code.

9. Type the following code after the remark **WEB SERVICE EXAMPLE:**

```
Public Function <WebService()> Sum_WebService(ByVal a As Integer, _
                            ByVal b As Integer) As Integer
        Sum_WebService = a + b
End Function
```

Your screen should look like Figure 3-29.

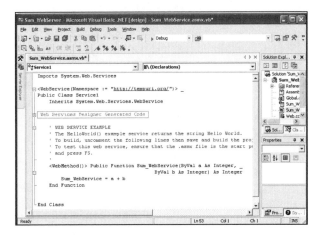

Figure 3-29: The results of adding the web service code.

To check for errors, you can build the VB project by selecting Build from the menu bar and then Build again (or CTRL+SHIFT+B). When you run the build, an output screen appears at the bottom of Visual Studio .NET. If there are no problems, you should see the following output:

```
Build: 1 succeeded, 0 failed, 0 skipped
```

Running the Sum_WebService Application

Visual Studio .NET has already generated all the information that is needed to use the Sum_WebService and a page for testing it. To view this page, right-click the Sum_WebService.asmx file and select Build and Browse, or browse to the file using Internet Explorer. You should see the screen that is shown in Figure 3-30.

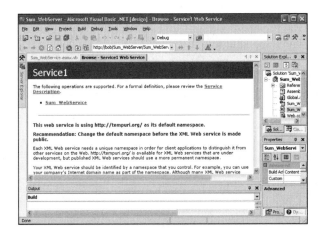

Figure 3-30: The Service1 disco web page.

Testing the Web Service

To test the web service, follow these steps:

1. Type 2 in the parameter a text box and 3 in the parameter b text box.
2. Click the Invoke button. The results should look like Figure 3-31.

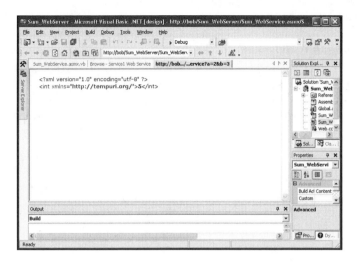

Figure 3-31: The XML results of the Service1 web service.

A new Internet Explorer page launches with the answer embedded in an XML document. An application will know how to parse the XML document to retrieve the results. Because this is a simple web service, you should be able to parse the document easily in a visual manner.

ADO.NET

ADO.NET can deliver a variety of features for creating scalable web applications. ADO developers are able to take advantage of ADO.NET objects, although while some behaviors may be different, many of the older ADO programming techniques still apply.

Scalability

Scalability is one of ADO.NET's primary goals. ADO.NET supports disconnected DataSets to address problems of database resource usage. Many applications are tightly coupled to their databases because record sets are not easily passed between layers, requiring that a data connection be maintained while data is manipulated. This overuse of database connection resources restricts those same resources from use by other instances of the application. ADO.NET DataSets can be disconnected from the data source and passed between application layers, and when the DataSet data is modified, it only requires database resources when applying the newly modified data. This allows for the use of database resources when absolutely necessary, which helps the application scale better.

XML Persistence

Portability of data is another ADO.NET goal. ADO.NET supports persistence of data in XML. XML steams are used for passing data between components and allow for portability because many platforms already understand XML formats. XML can also be persisted to a file for use at a later time. Most importantly, XML can be passed through firewalls where anything not on port 80 might be blocked.

Creating a Simple ADO.NET Project

You'll learn about the differences between ADO and ADO.NET in more detail in Chapter 9, "Retreiving Data." For now, here's a simple ADO.NET example that writes a DataSet to the window console.

To create the "ADO to XML File" project, follow these steps:

1. Create a new project with name ADOSample.

2. Drag a button from the toolbox to Form1.vb and change the text property to ADO Start.

3. Double-click on the button and type the following code:

```
        Dim oDS As DataSet
        Dim oCMD As SQLDataSetCommand
        Dim strConn As String
        strConn = "Initial Catalog = pubs;Data Source = localhost;" & _
            "User ID = sa;password="

        oDS = New DataSet()
  oCMD = New SQLDataSetCommand("Select title, price from titles"_
, strConn)

        oCMD.FillDataSet(oDS, "TitleList")

        Dim oRow As DataRow
        For Each oRow In oDS.Tables(0).Rows
            Console.WriteLine(oRow(0).ToString() & " " & _
            oRow(1).ToString())
        Next
        Console.In.Read()
```

4. Notice that the project doesn't understand what SQLDataSetCommand is and indicates this by underlining the code. By placing the mouse over the underlined code, the message, User-Defined type not defined: SQLDataSetCommand, is displayed.

5. Scroll to the top of the code window and type the following code under the previous Imports statements:

```
Imports System.Data.SQL
```

> **NOTE** *The last line of code* Console.In.Read() *is only to pause the Console long enough for you to see the results and press ENTER to exit the application.*

.NET Assemblies

At their most basic level, assemblies offer a programmatic method for exposing reusable code through properties, methods, and events. Assemblies allow you to reuse code, which enable other programs that are written in any .NET language to use them. Properties provide a means of maintaining data as each property holds a value. Methods are the actions the components perform. Events are invoked programmatically when certain conditions are met.

Compatibility

Microsoft has moved away from the binary compatibility standard because it does not encourage support for all languages. A binary component written in Visual C++ can be used by a Visual Basic application as long as all types used are available in Visual Basic. While multiple languages can take advantage of a binary COM component, the component is "vanilla." COM components are often built to take advantage of a specific language, restricting the richness of the solution. Type-safe compatibility guarantees that any .NET language can use all data types of any component written in any other .NET language by requiring the enforcement of the CTS (Common Type System).

The important distinction to remember is that COM is not a part of .NET's components. While components may act and feel the same as classic COM, the plumbing has been changed. There is no more COM. COM+ and Enterprise Services are a different matter and are addressed in Chapter 12, "COM+."

Building Blocks

.NET assemblies are the building blocks of the middle tier. These components include the Facades assemblies for simplifying or buffering the User Services tier from the complexity of Business Services assemblies. The Business Services assemblies provide business functionality, collections classes, business rules, and access to Data Access assemblies. The Data Access components perform data access on behalf of all business components. All these services and anything outside Data Services and User Services are considered .NET assemblies.

This section gives you a glimpse of components as well as a little hands-on experience with building components and creating a test application. Very little of this should be new to seasoned developers except for compatibility changes between classic COM and .NET assemblies. You'll walk through the creation of a very basic .NET assembly and test application. More detailed information is covered in Chapter 11, "Other .NET Topics" and Chapter 12, "COM+", respectively.

Full Name Example Component

The full name example component demonstrates how to build a simple assembly and a test application. The assembly takes the first and last name as entered by the user, and returns the full name in a label control.

To create the CompFullName assembly, follow these steps:

1. Create a new Visual Basic Class Library project with a project name of CompFullName.
2. View the default class, Class1, in the code window. Change the public class to Public Class CFullName and rename the Class1.vb file to CFullName.vb.
3. Type the following code before the End Class statement of the CFullName class:

```
Public Function FullName(ByVal FName As String, _
ByVal LName As String) As String
      FullName = FName & " " & LName
   End Function
```

To create the test application, follow these steps:

1. Add a new Visual Basic Windows project and name it CompFullNameTest.
2. Make CompFullNameTest the startup project.
3. Drag 2 text boxes, one label and one button, onto the form.
4. Clear the text property of the boxes and label text.
5. Type Submit Names in the button text property.
6. Right-click on the CompFullNameTest project references folder and select Add Reference.
7. Select the Projects tab and double-click the CompFullName then press OK (Figure 3-32).

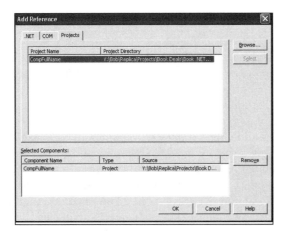

Figure 3-32: The Add Reference dialog box.

8. Add Imports CompFullName to the beginning of the CompFullNameTest code window.

NOTE *This will allow you to use the properties, events, and methods of the CompFullName component. In this case, you will only use a single method.*

9. Double-click the button entitled Submit Names.

10. Type the following code:

```
Public Function FullName(ByVal FName As String, _
ByVal LName As String) As String
        FullName = FName & " " & LName
    End Function
```

11. Run the program.

NOTE *At this point your application should look similar to the one that is shown in Figure 3-33, providing access to the CompFullName component's business logic.*

Figure 3-33: The CFullName test application.

Summary

In this chapter you learned about a host of subjects that were centered on how to take advantage of Visual Studio .NET. Visual Studio .NET is highly customizable and flexible, and integrates several tools that provide information and easy access to common tasks and utilities. The chapter examined these tools and discussed:

- The *Preferred Access Connection* option allows you to develop web applications through file share access.

- The *Solution Explorer* displays a list of all projects, files, and directories of the current solution in a hierarchical or tree view.

- *Dynamic Help* provides a hyperlink list of help topics that are constantly changing, based on what you select and where you place the cursor.

- The *Task List* is a central location where you can track a variety of tasks.

- The *Command Windows* provides you with direct access to the Visual Studio IDE through the use of the keyboard.

- The *Tool Box Window* is a container for controls that are used by the .NET forms designers, including both Win Forms and Web Forms.

- The *Server Explorer Window* is a new server development console that provides you with access to remote computer resources.

- The *Document Windows* are windows in which you can write and edit code.

- The *Properties Window* is a window that describes the properties or information about a component or Visual Studio object, such as those that you find in the Server Explorer window.

- The *Object Browser* provides access to a variety of information about a particular component that you specify or components that are referenced by your project.

4

THE .NET FRAMEWORK

Cross language integration, cross platform communication, easy access to common classes and interfaces, installation, and versioning are all developmental issues that commonly plague programmers. We'll discuss all of these issues and more in this chapter since they are addressed by the .NET Framework.

The .NET Framework provides a platform for building highly scalable and distributable applications. The .NET Framework also allows for cross-language interoperability as well as other features that are discussed throughout this chapter (Figure 4-1).

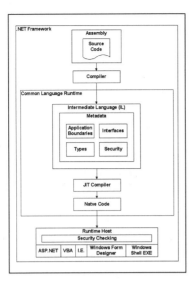

Figure 4-1: The .NET Framework.

The Common Language Runtime

The *Common Language Runtime* (CLR) is an execution engine that provides the .NET Framework services. This is the core of the .NET Framework, providing both the execution environment for .NET assemblies during run time, as well as services to aid developers during the creation of .NET components.

Among the services provided by the CLR are those that aid in assembly execution. These services include the Microsoft Intermediate Language, just-in-time compilers, metadata, application domains, memory management, and runtime hosts. CLR also provides services for developers such as the Common Type System, the namespace, and the .NET Class Framework. We'll discuss all of these throughout this chapter.

Managed Code

The .NET Framework consists of managed code that is designed to target the .NET Framework using the CLR. Managed code provides developers with services such as cross-language integration between all .NET languages, component security, version control, and deployment features.

Microsoft Intermediate Language

Visual Studio .NET compiles code into the *Microsoft Intermediate Language* (MSIL) which is processor independent and portable to a number of platforms. All .NET languages are compiled to the same MSIL, making performance between languages relatively the same.

When MSIL code is generated from the source code, all the necessary metadata describing the methods, properties, events, and data types are created.

(We'll discuss metadata later in this chapter.) One drawback to MSIL code is that it closely resembles the original source code, which makes it more difficult to protect intellectual copyright.

Just-In-Time Compilers

Microsoft provides a set of *Just-in-Time* (JIT) compilers for each supported platform. These compilers compile MSIL code into native machine code, so the JIT compiler is no longer needed to run the component. The compilation results in slower method calls the first time the code is run. However, it is compiled to native machine code, the code performs faster. The JIT compiles the code to machine code that is specific to the processor running the code. This offers a considerable performance advantage.

NOTE *Unlike previous Microsoft compilers, the JIT compilers only compile methods that are being used. The code can be executed more quickly because this reduces the time that is needed to compile the MSIL code.*

Assembly

The *assembly* is a collection of one or more files that maintain a developer's code and all the information that is required by the CLR execution environment. The assembly is the unit of deployment that is used to install a .NET application, including all resource files required by the application. These files can be bitmaps, JPEGs, and any other file type that is required by the application.

Note that applications may have more than one assembly. Every unit or application building block will have at least one assembly, but many applications require several building blocks. This is perfectly acceptable as assemblies can be configured to communicate with each other and take advantage of code in the other assemblies.

Assemblies can also be designated as "private" or "shared." A private assembly can be used by only one application and must be stored in the same directory or in a subdirectory of the calling application. Other assemblies can use a shared assembly that can only be updated by the author, making version control safer and malicious hacking more difficult. Usually a shared assembly is installed in the global assembly cache (discussed later in this chapter), which is a local cache of assemblies.

The Manifest

Part of the assembly includes a *manifest* which holds information about the assembly. This self-describing method of the assembly allows for easy deployment through the use of the XCOPY command from the command line prompt. Historically, this type of metadata was stored in the Windows Registry and required the registration of every *COM* (Common Object Model) component. This is no longer necessary because the information is stored exclusively in the assembly manifest.

The manifest can be stored in a separate file or as part of a module, such as an .EXE (executable) file or DLL (dynamic link library).

Among the information that is stored in the manifest is the name and version of the assembly. This is essential when an application is dependant on a specific version of an assembly. All other assemblies that depend on the assembly are stored in the manifest and help to determine if all required code for the application is available. To allow other components to communicate with the assembly, all of the assembly's data types are described in the manifest.

Additional security information for the assembly is also described by the manifest and includes three possible security settings and the assembly public key, which guarantees uniqueness of the assembly and identifies the source of the assembly. The possible security settings are

- Required security.
- Optional security.
- Denied security settings.

Providing the ability to store all metadata within the assembly has an additional benefit. Because .NET assemblies no longer require a special installation to record metadata about the assembly in the Windows Registry, you can simply copy all .NET assemblies to a given location and run them. As a result, .NET assemblies can be run directly from a CD-ROM that, by its very nature, is read-only. This also means that complex installation programs are no longer needed. You can simply write a program that installs your .NET application and run it when the CD-ROM is inserted into the CD-ROM tray.

The metadata that is stored in the manifest is fully accessible through the use of the Reflection API. By using this API, the metadata can be extracted into XML format.

Assembly Versioning

Assemblies simplify versioning and interface development, allowing developers to determine the versioning rules by specifying the version the assembly is allowed to use.

Interface development in COM required that all assemblies maintain backward compatibility when upgrading an assembly to support new features; COM allowed only a single version of an assembly to be registered with the operating system at any given time. .NET assemblies, however, are not specific to a machine but specific to an assembly, allowing the installation of multiple versions of the same assembly on the same physical computer. When a .NET assembly is upgraded, the older assembly can remain installed to maintain backwards compatibility for applications that are still using it.

Global Assembly Cache

Assemblies that are designated as "shared" are stored in the Global Assembly Cache. These assemblies are accessible by multiple applications on the computer. (Installing assemblies in the Global Assembly Cache requires administrative privileges to the machine where the assemblies are installed.)

Assemblies that are installed in the Global Assembly Cache are similar to COM components; the components cannot be accessed except through a single controlling force. In the case of assemblies, this is the Global Assembly Cache, whereas in COM it was the Windows registry.

Application Domains

Applications have historically separated or isolated memory access and application variables through process boundaries, which could not communicate directly with each other. Application assemblies, however, can access each other and run within the same process. To provide boundaries for assemblies, the CLR enforces boundaries through *Application Domains* that improve both performance and scalability; they eliminate the high overhead that is required to communicate across processes.

Common Type System

With classic COM, the standard by which a binary component could be classified as a COM component, which allowed other types of components to understand interfaces even other components that were written in a different language. The problem with binary compatibility, however, is that each language supports different data types that are not necessarily understood by other languages. As a result, components intended for use by multiple languages were forced to cater to one language or the other. Also, type conversions needed to be performed every time data was exchanged.

With the Common Type System, all data types are provided as objects in the System.Object class. This class is accessible by all .NET programming languages and enforced by the CLR. With the Common Type System, it is no longer necessary to cast data types between assemblies that are written in different languages. The Common Type System provides for a new standard for .NET Assemblies, which is called *Type Safe Compatibility*. Binary compatibility is a thing of the past except for backwards compatibility.

To accommodate this Type Safe Compatibility, some languages will have to adjust their data types. For example, the Visual Basic .NET integer is no long a 16-bit data type but a 32-bit one.

Table 4.1 identifies .NET data types and their corresponding sizes. Each .NET language must adhere to the specifications of these data types. Some languages, such as Visual Basic .NET, may support their own name for these data types, but the language compilers must convert the specific data types to the data types that are shown in the following table. For example, to declare a System.Int32 data type, Visual Basic permits the use of the Integer keyword. The variable that is declared as an Integer is actually of type System.Int32. It is safer and a better practice to use the Qualified Names of data types because these are common among all .NET languages.

Table 4.1: .NET Data Types and their Corresponding Sizes

Qualified Name	Data Type	Size	Description
System.Boolean	Boolean	32-bit or 4-byte	Holds values 1 (true) or 0 (false).
System.Byte	Byte	8-bit or 1-byte	Holds unsigned integer values 0 to 255.
System.Char	Char	16-bit or 2-byte	Holds unicode characters.
System.Decimal	Decimal	96-bit or 12-byte	Holds values up to 28 digits on either side of the decimal.
System.Double	Double	64-bit or 8-byte	Holds negative values from -1.79769313486231E308 to -4.94065645841247E-324 and positive values from 4.94065645841247E-324 to 1.79769313486232E308.
System.Int16	Short	16-bit or 2-byte	Holds signed integer values -32,678 to 32,767.
System.Int32	Integer	32-bit or 4-byte	Holds signed integer values -2,147,483,648 to 2,147,483,647.
System.Int64	Long	64-bit or 8-byte	Holds signed integer values -9,223,372,036,854,775,808 to 9,223,372,036,854,775,807.
System.Object	Object	32-bit or 4-byte	A reference to an instance of a class.
System.Sbyte	sbyte	8-bit or 1-byte	Holds signed integer values 0 to 255.
System.Single	Single	32-bit or 4-byte	Holds negative values from -3.402823E38 to -1.401298E-45 and positive values from 1.401298E-45 to 3.402823E38.
System.String	String	Up to 2 Billion Characters	Unicode characters.
System.UInt16	ushort	16-bit or 2-byte	Holds unsigned integer values -32,678 to 32,767.
System.UInt32	uint	32-bit or 4-byte	Holds unsigned integer values -2,147,483,648 to 2,147,483,647.
System.UInt64	ulong	64-bit or 8-byte	Holds unsigned integer values -9,223,372,036,854,775,808 to 9,223,372,036,854,775,807.

Runtime Host

The Runtime Host that is provided by the CLR creates and maintains the environment for .NET applications. Visual Studio .NET currently ships with the ASP.NET, Internet Explorer, and Shell Executable runtimes. Third-party developers are able to develop more runtime hosts with APIs that Microsoft provides.

Namespace

The concept of a namespace is important to .NET. The .NET Framework object library has been organized hierarchically, and access to an object within the object hierarchy can be through a fully qualified name. This fully qualified name includes the root and every level leading to the object; for example, in `System.Diagnostics.Debug`, `System` is the root.

Before developers can access an object, the root of the object must be imported. The `Imports` statement makes the namespace available so you don't have to use a fully qualified name of the namespace. After the desired object has been imported, it can be accessed through the qualified name; however, it is easier to access the object when you import part of the hierarchy with the root. This means that you can use only the unique object name; the same object can exist in multiple areas of the hierarchy because it is the path to the object that makes the object reference unique. If the same class name is used in more than one imported namespace, the fully qualified namespace or at least enough of the namespace to distinguish the class must be used.

All projects have a namespace property that is accessible through the Solution Explorer. When a project is created, a default namespace is created; however, this default namespace can be changed so that your objects can be accessed through the same namespace.

.NET Class Framework

The .NET Class Framework, also referred to as the .NET Base Classes, is a set of object models that provides easy access to base functionality thought a common namespace. All objects in this framework are accessible to all .NET languages. The .NET Class Framework provides a variety of base services divided among a variety of second-level namespaces under the `System` namespace. These second-level namespaces include base services such as data access, security, collections, XML, error handling, and threading.

Before the .NET Class Framework, each programming language required its own class libraries. All .NET languages share the .NET Class Framework, requiring no special-language specific libraries. Developers no longer need to learn the Visual Basic or Visual C++ class libraries for accessing data or debugging because all languages use the same Class Framework. Even the syntax that is used to perform the same task between .NET languages looks the same because you must use the same namespace and parameters. All language-specific features have been moved into the .NET Class Framework to enable all .NET languages to take advantage of the functionality.

Base functionality that is provided by the .NET Class Framework aids in a number of regular programming tasks. For instance, all data access is accessible through the System.Data namespace. Access to debugging information and security are accessed through System.Diagnostic and System.Security, respectively.

Table 4.2 includes second-level services that are provided by the .NET Class Framework. All .NET Framework development relies heavily on the classes that are available in these namespaces. You will benefit by becoming familiar with each namespace and its related classes.

Table 4.2: Namespaces and Their Related Classes

Category	Namespace	Description
Data Access	System.Data	Contains a set of classes supporting ADO.NET data access.
	System.XML	Contains XML classes that provide standards-based support for processing XML.
Component Model	System.CodeDOM	Contains classes that represent the elements and structure of a source code document.
	System.ComponentModel	Contains classes used for building .NET components.
Configuration	System.Configuration	Contains classes for configuring assemblies and writing installation programs.
Framework Services	System.Diagnostic	Contains classes for debugging applications.
	System.DirectoryServices	Contains classes necessary for accessing the active directory.
	System.ServiceProcess	Contains classes for installing and running services.
	System.Messaging	Contains classes for sending and receiving messages on the network.
	System.Timers	Contains classes for programming events to occur on re-occurring intervals.
Net	System.Net	Contains classes providing an interface for programming targeted toward network protocols.

Table 4.2: Namespaces and Their Related Classes (continued)

Category	Namespace	Description
Programming Basics	System.Collection	Contains classes for building and manipulating a variety of data structures including lists, queues, arrays, hash tables and dictionaries.
	System.IO	Contains classes for manipulating data streams and files.
	System.Text	Contains classes for manipulating and converting text data.
	System.Threading	Contains classes for building multi-threaded applications.
Reflection	System.Reflection	Contains classes for reading and manipulating component or assembly metadata or manifests.
Rich Client Side GUI	System.Drawing	Contains classes for accessing GDI+ functionality.
	System.Windows.Forms	Contains classes for building Windows applications.
Runtime Infrastructure Services	System.Runtime.Remoting	Contains classes for building distributed applications.
	System.Runtime.Serialization	Contains classes for converting data into a searialized byte stream.
.NET Framework Security	System.Security	Contains classes for supporting .NET Framework Security.
Web Services	System.Web	Contains classes for communication between browsers and servers.

NOTE *A Class Browser application is provided by the .NET Framework. You can find the application in the* c:\Program Files\Microsoft.NET\FrameworkSDK\Sample\. *After it is installed you can run this application from http://localhost/clsview/Default.aspx. This application allows you to navigate through all classes that are provided by the .NET Framework.*

Summary

The .NET Framework is the heart of Microsoft's .NET initiative. Development issues are addressed by components of the .NET Framework:

- Managed code is code that is written to target the .NET Framework.
- The Common Language Runtime (CLR) is an execution engine that provides all the .NET Framework services.
- Visual Studio .NET compiles code into a Microsoft Intermediate Language (MSIL) that is processor-independent.
- Microsoft provides a set of just-in-time (JIT) compilers for each supported platform.
- The assembly is a collection of one or more files that maintain a developer's code and all the information that is required by the CLR execution environment.
- A manifest is the part of the assembly which holds information about the assembly.
- Developers can determine the versioning rules of assemblies by specifying the assembly version that your component is allowed to use.
- Assemblies that are designated as "shared" are stored in the Global Assembly Cache.
- Application Domains improve both performance and scalability because the high overhead that is required to communicate across processes is eliminated.
- Common Type System provides a common set of classes from which all .NET languages can create data types.
- The Runtime Host that is provided by the CLR creates and maintains the actual environment in which .NET applications run.
- Namespaces provide access to objects within the object hierarchy, which you can import to provide easier access to component classes.
- The .NET Class Framework is a set of object models that provides easy access to base functionality through a common namespace.

5

VISUAL STUDIO . NET TOOLS

Visual Studio .NET provides a wealth of tools to aid in the development of new applications and the support of delivered applications. Some of these tools have been around in the Microsoft development environment for several years and have improved; others are completely new.

The Event Log that was introduced with Microsoft's Windows NT 3.1 remains an important component of Microsoft Windows 2000 and Microsoft Windows XP. Nearly all applications that run on the Microsoft platform use the Event Log to record application performance data, and, with the introduction of Microsoft Windows 2000, your application can have an Event Log dedicated to it. We will be building an application that will create an application Event Log and allow you to save informational, warning, or error messages to it. We'll also discuss a variety of debugging tools for inspecting your application while in development.

Many .NET Framework applications can technically be deployed using a simple XCopy command, while others require packaging and deployment, which can be a messy experience if a set of good packaging and deployment tools are not available. Visual Studio .NET provides several packaging and deployment wizards and project types. We will package and deploy our Event Log application, then follow-up with a walkthrough of the installation.

The Event Log

The Event Log is a central location for system and application events to be recorded. Events can be defined as anything that happens to any system resource or application, and recording every event will quickly fill up the Event Log in its default configuration. You should keep in mind the following:

- The Event Log is not included with Visual Studio .NET. However, it is provided by the Windows operating system.
- The Event Log is a central location for system and application events.
- The Event Log is a tool that must be managed to take full advantage of it on behalf of your application.
- Filters can be placed on the Event Log for ease of use.
- The Event Log is helpful when tracking your applications performance after deployment.

The Event Log should be used to record useful information only, although what you consider useful will depend on the environment's security needs and the application's security and reliability needs. Most applications require errors to be logged to the Event Log while secure environments require logging of all resource usage or denied access attempts.

Accessing the Event Log

You can access the Event Log in several ways. The most common way is by selecting Event Viewer in the Administrative Tools folder. The Event Viewer (Figure 5-1) displays and manages event logs.

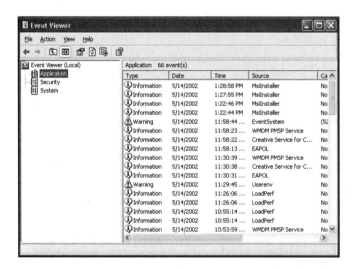

Figure 5-1: The Event Viewer application used to view and manage event logs.

While Visual Studio .NET does not provide the Event Log, the new Visual Studio .NET IDE provides access to it through the Server Explorer window as shown in Figure 5-2.

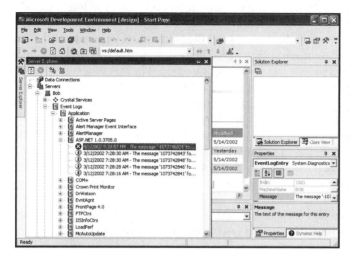

Figure 5-2: The Server Explorer as implemented in Visual Studio .NET.

Event Types

The Event Log supports five types of events and not all information in it indicates a problem.

- *Information* events: Indicate the successful completion of a task.
- *Warning* events: Indicate that a task completed successfully but a problem or potential problem may exist.
- *Error* events: Indicate a problem that should be addressed (a task may have been interrupted or failed all together).
- *Success* and *Failure* audit events: Indicate successful or unsuccessful attempt to access system resources. (These two events are used in the Security Log.)

Event Log Types

By default, there are three log types available when either Windows NT or Windows 2000 are installed:

- Application Log: Records events for all applications programmed to use it.
- Security Log: Records all information concerned with access to resources where auditing is turned on.
- System Log: Stores information about all system level events.

Managing Event Logs

To manage an application's event log, right-click the log and select Application Properties to open a dialog box (Figure 5-3) where you can view or modify its properties. Here you can find information on the log size and set the properties that determine how information is logged and made available.

By default, the log is configured to overwrite events that have been logged more than seven days ago. The problem with this default configuration is that its maximum log size is easily exceeded before seven days have passed. When this occurs, you will receive a dialog box indicting that the log file is full.

To keep the log from filling up, you can select the Overwrite events as needed option, although when selected the oldest events will be overwritten, which may be undesirable in a production environment. Another option is to increase the maximum log size, which will immediately resolve the problem of having a full event log; however, though the log file may still fill up before events are overwritten. Finally, the event log can be configured to require manual intervention to clear the log. This is the desired option for production environments because it enables you to save the log to a file before clearing it. All logs for a production system should be kept for troubleshooting.

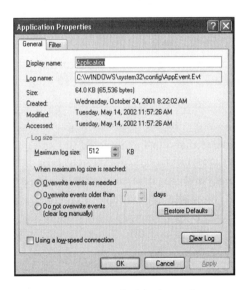

Figure 5-3: The General tab in the Application Properties dialog box.

Filtering the Log Viewer

The Event Viewer can be configured to filter out events to make the log easier to view and scan for specific kinds of events. Figure 5-4 shows the Filter tab that includes options for selecting the log viewer's settings.

Another way to make it easier and less time consuming to view logs is to copy an existing log and customize it for viewing specific kinds of information.

Figure 5-4: The Filter tab in the Application Properties dialog box.

For example, to create a new log, follow these steps:

1. Open the Event Viewer from the Administrative Tools folder of the start menu.

2. Right-click the Application Log event log and select New Log View.

3. Right-click on the new log view and select Rename. Rename this log view Application Log (Errors).

4. Right-click the Application Log (Errors) event log and select properties. Select the Filter tab.

5. Deselect all Event Types except the Error event type.

6. Press OK.

The result is an Application log that you can quickly and easily reference for all error events, as shown in Figure 5-5.

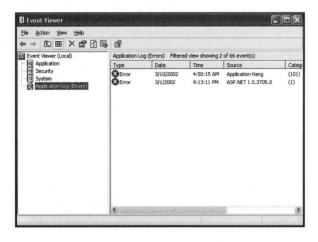

Figure 5-5: The new Application log created for viewing errors.

Logging Application Events

Application events help to debug applications and track their status. While events for applications can use the Application Log, it can be beneficial to create an event log specific to your application.

For example, to build a simple application that will allow you to create and manage an event log and add each type of event to it including additional information that may be helpful for debugging and monitoring and applications performance, do the following:

1. Open up Visual Studio .NET and create a new Windows Form application named `EventLogApp`.

2. Now import the `System.Diagnostic` namespace.

```
Imports System.Diagnostics
```

3. Drag six buttons, three text labels, and three text boxes onto the form and arrange, as shown in Figure 5-6.

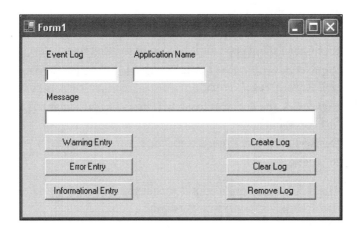

Figure 5-6: The Event Log Sample applications user interface.

4. Name your controls and captions based on Table 5-1.

Table 5-1: Controls and Captions

Control	Caption	Name
Form	Event Log Sample App	Form1.vb
Command Button	Create Log	cmdCreateLog
Command Button	Clear Log	cmdClearLog
Command Button	Remove Log	cmdRemoveLog
Command Button	Warning Entry	cmdWarning
Command Button	Error Entry	cmdError
Command Button	Informational Entry	cmdInfo
Label	Event Log	lblEventLog
Label	Application Name	lblAppName
Label	Message	lblMessage
TextBox		txtLogName
TextBox		txtAppName
TextBox		txtMessage

5. Copy the following code into the Form1.vb form or open the EventLogApp:

```
    Protected Sub cmdClearLog_Click(ByVal sender As Object, ByVal e _
                                        As System.EventArgs) _
Handles cmdClearLog.Click
        Try
            Dim Eventlog As New EventLog(txtLogName.Text)
            Eventlog.Clear()
        Catch
            MessageBox.Show(Err.Description)
        End Try
    End Sub


    Protected Sub cmdInfo_Click(ByVal sender As Object, ByVal e _
                                        As System.EventArgs) _
Handles cmdInfo.Click
        Try
            Dim Eventlog As New EventLog()
            Eventlog.WriteEntry(txtAppName.Text, txtMessage.Text, _
                        EventLogEntryType.Information)
```

(continued on next page)

```
            Catch
                MessageBox.Show(Err.Description)
            End Try
        End Sub


    Protected Sub cmdError_Click(ByVal sender As Object, ByVal e _
                                            As System.EventArgs) _
    Handles cmdError.Click
            Try
                Dim Eventlog As New EventLog()
                Eventlog.WriteEntry(txtAppName.Text, txtMessage.Text, _
                                        EventLogEntryType.Error)
            Catch
                MessageBox.Show(Err.Description)
            End Try
        End Sub


    Protected Sub cmdWarning_Click(ByVal sender As Object, ByVal e _
                                            As System.EventArgs) _
    Handles cmdWarning.Click
            Try
                Dim Eventlog As New EventLog()
                Eventlog.WriteEntry(txtAppName.Text, txtMessage.Text, _
                                        EventLogEntryType.Warning)
            Catch
                MessageBox.Show(Err.Description)
            End Try
        End Sub


    Protected Sub cmdRemoveLog_Click(ByVal sender As Object, ByVal e _
                                            As System.EventArgs) _
    Handles cmdRemoveLog.Click
            Try
                EventLog.Delete(txtLogName.Text)
            Catch
                MessageBox.Show(Err.Description)
            End Try
        End Sub


    Protected Sub cmdCreateLog_Click(ByVal sender As Object, ByVal e _
                                            As System.EventArgs) _
    Handles cmdCreateLog.Click
            Try
                EventLog.CreateEventSource(txtAppName.Text, txtLogName.Text)
            Catch
                MessageBox.Show(Err.Description)
            End Try
        End Sub
```

The EventLogApp is an easy application to use and is by no means the last word on how to take full advantage of the event log. After all, every application's needs are different.

Before you can add any event log messages you must create a new log and specify an application to use it. Once created you can add error, informational, or warning messages. Once you've had enough you can clear or remove the log altogether.

Debugging

Once upon a time, debugging an application meant running the code and hoping to get an error message that would tell you the line number on which your application failed. The next step was to print your application code on that wide green and white striped paper with holes on each side and take it home. Then you would spend the rest of the evening reading through the code with a marker, circling different variables and making notes. Finally, you might have had a few ideas to try and headed into work. The next day was much of the same.

For the last decade we've had a number of debuggers with several tools for investigating different aspects of the problem. These tools speed up the process of debugging applications and allow the developer to spend more time addressing business problems and less time mired in code searching of a simple syntax error.

As programming techniques have advanced and the interaction and coordination with a variety of different platforms has increased, there has been a need for more advanced debugging tools. Visual Studio .NET provides numerous debugging tools (shown in Figure 5-7), including windows for viewing internal aspects of your application while it runs, advanced tools for managing breakpoints, and the ability to quickly and easily access code which may reside in a number of different components:

- The Locals window displays all variables in the current procedure.
- The Autos window displays all variables in the current and previous statements.
- The Watch window displays values for selected variables.
- The Quick Watch dialog allows for quick viewing of any variable and works closely with the Watch Window.
- The Call Stack window displays the names of functions used to the point of current execution.
- The Command window is a replacement of the immediate window provided by Visual Studio 6.
- Breakpoints stop execution while you examine your applications state.

The following sections will talk about these tools in more detail.

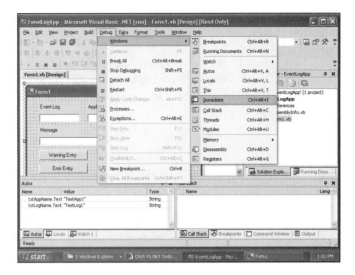

Figure 5-7: The many debugging tools available at runtime.

Locals Window

The Locals window (Figure 5-8) displays all variables in the current procedure.
All values in the Locals window are updated only when a breakpoint is reached.
During execution, the values displayed become outdated until the next break-
point; during a breakpoint you can modify these values.

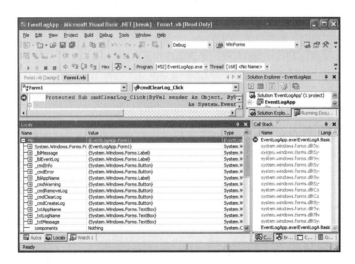

Figure 5-8: The Locals window.

Autos Window

The Autos window (Figure 5-9), in break mode, displays all the variables and their values for the current and previous statements. The values of the variables can be modified while in break mode by double-clicking them in the Autos window and inputting new ones.

The Watch window, which is discussed in the following section, is similar to the Autos window except that all values are automatically tracked in the Autos window while only selected values are tracked if you specifically add them to them to the Watch window.

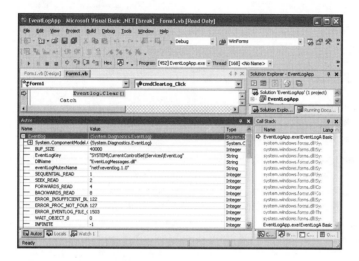

Figure 5-9: The Autos window.

Watch Window

Like the Locals window, the Watch window (Figure 5-10) displays information about variables including the variable name, value, and type. The Watch window differs from the Locals window because it displays values for variables specifically requested while the Locals Window displays all variables in the current procedure. Another significant difference is that values in the Watch window are always current, which means that you can trust the values they display while your application is running.

To add a variable to the Watch window, simply right-click the variable in the code window and select Add Watch. To remove a variable from the Watch window, right-click the variable in the Watch window, and select Delete Watch. To change a value in the Watch window, double-click the Value column and enter the new value.

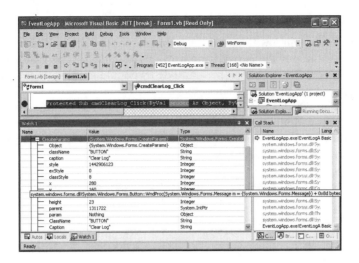

Figure 5-10: The Watch window.

QuickWatch Dialog Box

The QuickWatch window (Figure 5-11) works closely with the Watch window. This dialog allows you to take a quick look at variables rather than adding them to the Watch window then later having to remove them.

Before committing to using any variable in the Watch window, you can right-click the variable and select QuickWatch. From here, you can quickly evaluate the variable value, then decide whether or not to add it to the Watch window for future use.

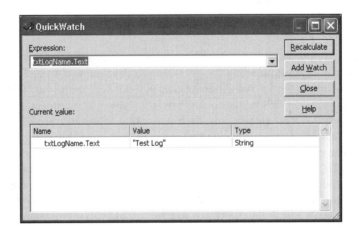

Figure 5-11: The QuickWatch dialog box.

Call Stack Window

The Call Stack window, shown in Figure 5-12, displays the names of functions used up to the current point of execution. You can add, disable, or remove breakpoints simply by right-clicking on the desired procedure name and selecting a breakpoint option.

Double-click a procedure name in the Call Stack window to view the code behind that procedure. If you happen to double-click a procedure name for which the code is not available, a Disassembly window is displayed. If the Disassembly window has the focus when double-clicking a procedure name, your code is disassembled and displayed.

The Call Stack window also provides easy access to SQL Server Stored Procedures. Stored procedures show up in the Call Stack window just like any other procedure and can be treated as such. Breakpoints can also be added to stored procedures, which will display the stored procedures source code for debugging purposes.

Figure 5-12: The Call Stack window.

Command Window

In Chapter 3, "Visual Studio.NET Walkthrough," you learned about the various uses and functions that are provided by the Command window. It is important to note, however, that in the context of debugging, the Command Window has assumed the functionality of the Immediate window from Visual Studio 6.

Breakpoints

Breakpoints determine when to pause the execution of code and are useful when debugging or testing a code segment. This is often handy when skipping through code to a specific point where heavy scrutiny is needed. At this point, other debugging windows can be used, such as the Locals, Watch, Autos, or Command window.

The Breakpoints window (Figure 5-13) provides a central location for managing all breakpoints throughout the application. Select Windows from the Debug menu and then select Breakpoints to access the Breakpoints window.

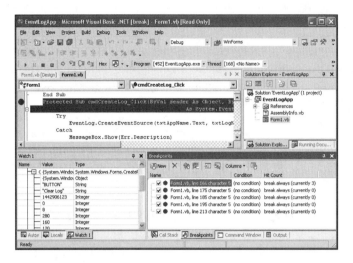

Figure 5-13: The Breakpoints window.

The Breakpoint window provides a variety of configuration settings for breakpoints including the ability to create new breakpoints. The source code behind a breakpoint can be displayed by right-clicking the breakpoint and selecting Go To Source Code or by double-clicking the breakpoint in the Breakpoint window.

Right-clicking any breakpoint in the Breakpoint window and selecting properties displays the Breakpoint Condition dialog box (Figure 5-14). Here you are able to set properties that determine when a breakpoint is executed such as Hit Count and when a value is true or has changed.

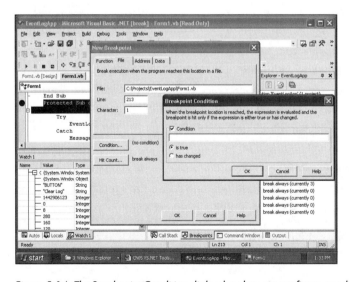

Figure 5-14: The Breakpoint Condition dialog box lets you configure conditions for a Breakpoint.

Package and Deployment

Packaging and deploying applications has had its own fair share of challenges over the years. When discussing application deployment in the workplace, it is difficult to avoid terms such as "DLL Hell," interface compatibility, and registering class GUIDs. Before the .NET Framework, the most significant challenge in deploying applications was registering and un-registering different versions of DLLs. COM implemented a binary standard where all interfaces of a component must be registered in the registry of the operating system.

Whenever an interface, which is defined by its methods, properties, events, and enumerations, changes, the binary compatibility is said to have been broken. The impact of broken compatibility means that the old DLL is unregistered, a new interface, including a new set of GUIDs, is registered, and all client links to the DLL become invalid. You must recompile and deploy all clients to the changed DLL to correct the broken compatibility.

With Visual Studio.NET, keep in mind the following:

- All .NET Framework applications can be installed using a simple XCopy command.
- Visual Studio .NET provides a variety of installation options including Package and Deployment Project and Package and Deployment Wizards employing intelligence into your deployment package.

Visual Studio .NET Wizards

Visual Studio 6 provided a simple wizard for deploying applications called the Package and Deployment Wizard. Visual Studio .NET provides a set of setup and deployment project types. To create a new setup project, simply create a new project from the Setup and Deployment Projects folder (Figure 5-15).

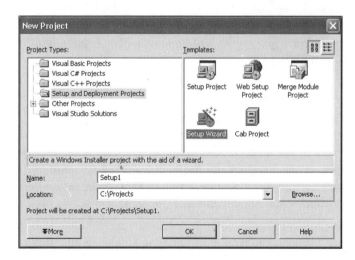

Figure 5-15: The New Project dialog box with Package and Deployment templates.

The Cab Project

The Cab Project allows you to add files or applications for deployment. Once the Cab files are created, users can run them by double-clicking or they can be downloaded through a browser. For installations that are intended to be run directly by the user, it may be preferable to use the Setup Wizard to create an msi (Windows Installer Files).

The Deployment Wizard

The Deployment Wizard walks you through the process of deploying a .NET application. For example, you can build a deployment package for the EventLogApp, and then run the installation. To create the package, follow these steps:

1. Create a new project by selecting Deployment Wizard from the Setup Wizard of the New Project dialog box.

2. Name the project EventLogAppSetup and press OK. A wizard appears to walk you through creating the deployment package, as shown in Figure 5-16. Press Next.

Figure 5-16: The initial dialog box displayed in a deployment wizard.

3. This screen requests information about your application (Figure 5-17). A web application includes ASP.NET and Web Services applications. Because the Event Log application is a rich client application, select Deploy a Rich Windows Application and click Next.

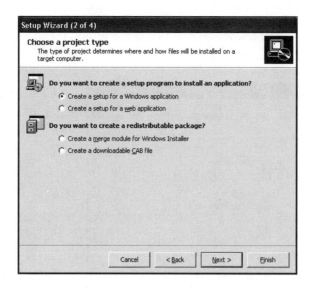

Figure 5-17: Choosing a package configured for a web or Windows application.

4. The next wizard page allows you to include any additional files your application may require or files that may add value to your installation, such as readme.txt files (Figure 5-18). You could go ahead and include all of your application files here but we will not. Click Next to continue.

Figure 5-18: Adding additional files to you deployment package.

5. The final deployment wizard dialog box displays all of the choices that you selected so you can verify them before the project is created (Figure 5-19). Select Finish.

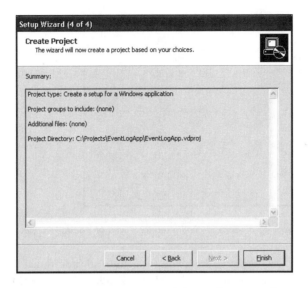

Figure 5-19: Viewing a summary of choices that you made.

6. Now it is time to add the EventLogApp application files to the setup package. Right-click on the EventLogApp deployment package and select File from the Add menu.

7. Browse your system and find the EventLogApp application we built earlier in this chapter. Navigate to the bin directory and select the EventLogApp.exe file, then click Open. The application's dependencies are displayed in the Detected Dependencies folder of the deployment package.

8. Right-click on the deployment project and select Build to create the msi installation file.

9. To run the installation, navigate to the Debug folder of your deployment project and double- click on the EventLogApp.msi file to load the Setup Wizard (Figure 5-20). Select Next.

Figure 5-20: The Event Log sample installation program.

10. Now you can select the application folder to which you want to install your application (Figure 5-21). You can also choose to install this application for all users of the system or only yourself. Press Next to continue.

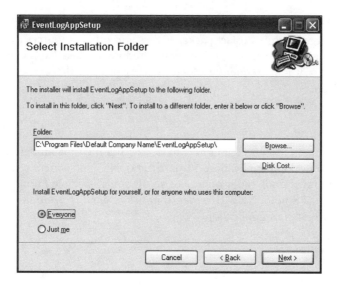

Figure 5-21: Selecting the directory for the Event Log application.

11. The next screen lets you know the installation is ready to begin. Click Next to begin the installation. A progress bar should appear briefly, followed by a status screen that indicates a successful installation (Figure 5-22).

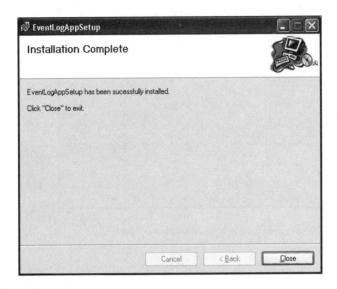

Figure 5-22: Completing the installation.

The Merge Module Project

The Merge Module Project packages files and other resources that will be used by multiple applications. The file generated by this installation package is an .msi file that is subsequently added to other projects that rely on these shared resources.

Summary

Development tools go a long way to decreasing the time and effort required to deliver a working application. Visual Studio .NET introduces a few new tools and improves upon older ones. Not all the tools available for applications come with Visual Studio .NET. However, they are available for monitoring the performance of your application.

6

DESIGNERS, DATABASE AND MONITORING TOOLS

In Chapter 5, "Visual Studio .NET Tools," you learned about various Visual Studio .NET tools that aid in the development, debugging, and deployment of .NET applications. This chapter covers a variety of designers for windows forms, web forms, .NET components, XML, and user controls. You'll examine Visual Database Tools and related database object designers while examining the potential impact of poor database object implementation. Finally, you'll learn about the tools that are available only with Visual Studio .NET Enterprise Edition, including tools for performance monitoring (Visual Studio Analyzer), reporting (Crystal Reports), and Application Boundary enforcement (Enterprise Templates).

The Windows Form Designer

The Windows Forms Designer is used for building rich windows based applications. Classic Windows applications are based on the Win32 API, the Visual Basic 6.0 windows designer that included most Win32 functionality, effectively shielding the developer from the details of implementation.

Visual Studio .NET's Windows Forms Designer differs from classic Windows development in two significant areas. First, Windows applications that are based on the .NET Class Framework, not on the Win32 API, as evident when viewing the implementation details. The second difference lies in the implementation details, all of which are exposed to the developer. Not surprisingly, this can confuse classic Windows developers who are accustomed to Visual Basic 6.0's hidden implementation.

Figures 6-1 and 6-2, respectively, show the difference between the classic (Figure 6-1) and the .NET (Figure 6-2) way of implementing applications. All code was generated by the Visual Basic 6 and Visual Studio .NET IDE. You'll notice the implementation code that appears in the .NET window in Figure 6-2.

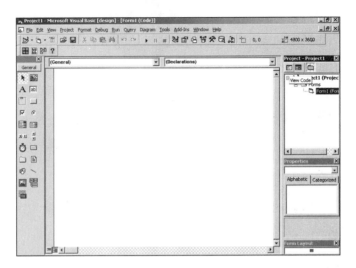

Figure 6-1: The Visual Basic 6 code window for a new form.

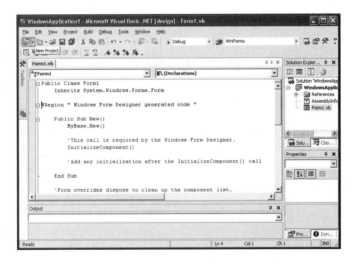

Figure 6-2: The Visual Basic .NET code window for a new form. Notice the implementation code.

Web Form Designer

Web forms are HTML-based user interfaces that allow developers to implement code behind a form; they are dynamically created by IIS when requested by a web browser. Before IIS gives the requested page to the browser, the page's programming logic and processing are performed, and the result is formatted and returned as pure HTML. Consequently, Web Forms are compatible with all HTML-based browsers including most browsers today.

The Web Form Designer allows web page development to replace much of what Visual Interdev (in previous versions of Visual Studio) handled. Visual Interdev provided the ability to build ASP and HTML web pages as well as client and server side scripting, but failed to separate the presentation layer from programming logic. The end result was complex spaghetti-like code with all the makings of bug-prone and hard-to-modify applications.

Unfortunately, ASP required this type of implementation. ASP.NET, on the other hand, when it interprets compiled code, transforms ASP from a late-binding interpreted language to a strongly-typed compiled language with the ability to take full advantage of the same development environment as Visual Basic, Visual C++, or C#. This effectively eliminates the need for a separate development environment and makes the Web Form Designer possible (Figure 6-3). Chapter 8, "Building Forms," covers the Web Form Designer in more detail.

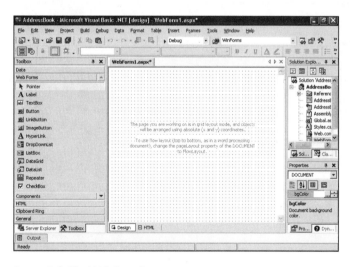

Figure 6-3: The Web Form Designer.

The Component Designer

The Component Designer makes it easier to develop components than in previous versions of Visual Studio. Many common tasks such as programming events log tasks, message queuing, and reporting components can be dragged onto the Component Designer. The code that is necessary to instantiate the components is added automatically and all programming tasks can be completed and tested using the code viewer.

When creating a component in Visual Studio .NET, you will notice that certain implementations are generated automatically. This is partly due to the fact that .NET components require a container.

Components are classes that implement the System.ComponentModel.IComponent class interface. When creating a new component, the System.ComponentModel.Component class is inherited, and it, in turn, implements the System.ComponentModel.IComponent interface for use by the component. This interface allows the component to be wrapped a within a container, thus providing services such as memory cleanup with access to the Dispose method. All resources allocated to a container are released when the container is torn down.

To access the Component Designer, right-click on a component or class and select View Designer. The Component Designer initially shows a blank screen and a single instruction stating how to proceed. To design your component, drag controls from the Server Explorer and Toolbox to the designer interface—a visual way to build non-visual components. The designer shows a visual representation of non-visual components as shown in Figure 6-4.

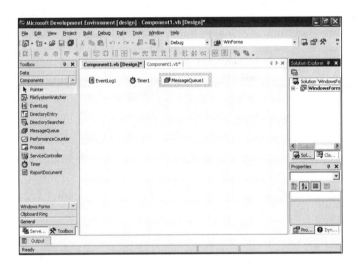

Figure 6-4: The Component Designer.

The XML Designer

The XML Designer helps to implement XML by providing three views.

Schema View

The Schema view (Figure 6-5) is a design interface for creating and editing XML Schemas, which can be as simple as dragging and dropping a table from the Server Explorer onto the designer. Aside from allowing you to add several types of XML properties, the XML Schema designer can be used to generate ADO.NET DataSets (as discussed in Chapter 9, "Retrieving Data").

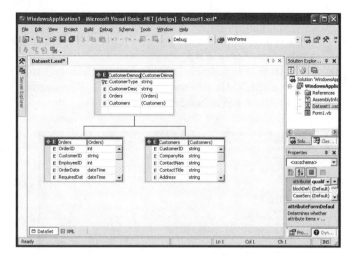

Figure 6-5: Modifying an XML Schema with drag and drop using the Schema view.

Data View

When an XML data file is added to a project, the Data view (Figure 6-6) can be used to view tables and their relationships to each other. You can modify tables, data, and create new schemas. The Data view can only be displayed if the XML contains actual data.

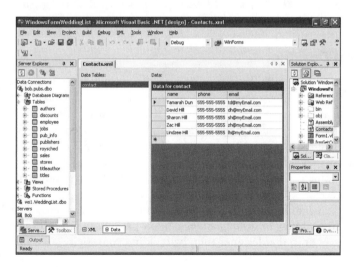

Figure 6-6: The Data View Designer.

Source View

The XML Source view is similar to the Windows and Web Designers when it comes to XML development because it provides Intellisense and statement completion.

To add XML files to a project, right-click the desired project, select Add Item, and choose the XML Schema file. The XML Schema view lets you begin modifying the XML Schema, as shown in Figure 6-7.

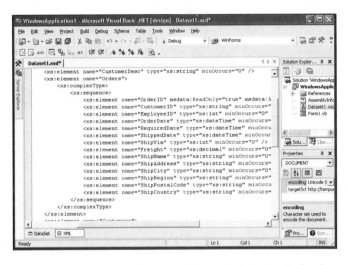

Figure 6-7: An XML Schema generated by Visual Studio .NET after dragging the employee table of the Pubs database onto the Schema view.

The User Control Designer

Visual Studio .NET provides a host of controls, allowing a drag-and-drop style development environment for building feature rich applications. While these controls provide a base functionality that, in many cases, meets development requirements, a custom solution is sometimes required.

The User Control Designer (Figure 6-8) provides a visual interface for creating custom controls called *user controls*. User controls are controls based on the functionality of more than one control; when they are compiled into a DLL, they are called *composite controls*.

To begin building user controls, simply open or create a new Windows Control Library or Web Control Library project. Begin by dragging the desired controls onto the designer then by building your logic.

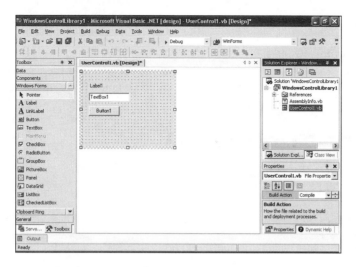

Figure 6-8: The User Control Designer.

Visual Database Tools

Visual Studio .NET arrives with a set of visual tools for creating and modifying database objects and schemas, such as diagrams, indexes, triggers, and stored procedures. These database tools offer a single interface to multiple database server backbends. At the time of this writing, only SQL Server and Oracle databases are supported; however, support for additional databases is expected in the near future.

Tracking changes and coordinating versions of database objects within an application can become quickly overwhelming. Before Visual Studio .NET, database objects, which were created within SQL Server's SQL Enterprise Manager, could be added to a source control application only after generating scripts for all the objects and then saving them to a file. This made script generation time consuming. Fortunately, Visual Studio .NET's IDE lets you create database objects and queries then check them into source control. (You learn about source control in Chapter 9.)

Database Projects

When creating a new application, it is often necessary to create a new database. By creating a database project, you can build a new database while tracking stored procedure changes for version control of database objects. Versioning of database objects is possible because all Visual Studio .NET projects, including database projects, can be added to Source Control.

You can create a database project in Solution Explorer to organize your database references, scripts, and queries. This allows you to work with an application's database aspects without having to recreate database references or cluttering up other projects in a solution with data related objects because while your presentation resides in one project, the database exists in another. This separation helps the application to be more modularized and easier to manage.

To create a new database project, follow these steps:

1. From the File menu, choose New • Project.

2. Expand Other Projects and Database Projects and then select Database Projects. You can create a new database connection or select an existing one as shown in Figure 6-9.

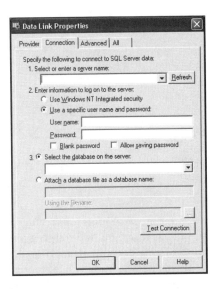

Figure 6-9: The Add Database Reference dialog box.

The end result is a database project (as shown in Figure 6-10) with everything you need in order to begin adding and manipulating database schemas and objects.

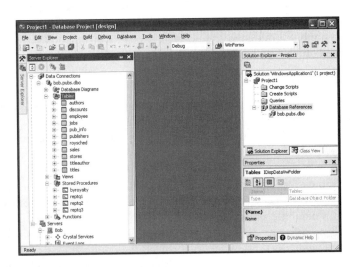

Figure 6-10: A database project.

Database Designer

The Database Designer is a visual database schema editor for Microsoft SQL Server and Oracle databases, which enables developers to add, modify, and delete database objects. These objects include tables, views, indexes, and stored procedures.

Creating a database table is as simple as right-clicking on the Tables icon of the database connection in Server Explorer and selecting New Table. A designer (shown in Figure 6-11) is provided for entering the new table's attributes. Follow the same process to create or modify views, indexes, and stored procedures.

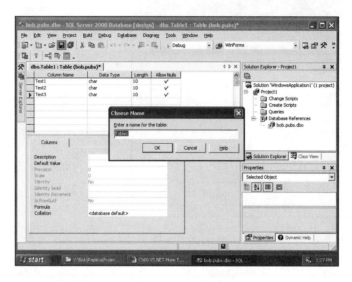

Figure 6-11: The Database Designer's table design page.

Query Designer

The Query Designer allows developers to build queries visually. Using a visual view of tables and columns, developers can decide what data will be returned and how that data will relate to other tables.

Selecting tables and columns in the Query Designer is a quick and dirty way to select data for retrieval, but most applications require queries that do more than just return data. Often the data returned must be sorted by a specific column or other criteria that limit the returned data. Because the visual configuration and design of queries can never meet all application requirements for data retrieval, the Query Designer allows for complete control over the development of queries through direct editing of queries.

No query is complete until it has been tested to verify that it meets your application's requirements and that it is bug free. To test your query, once you are finished building it, simply execute it in the Query Designer and examine the results for errors.

To create a query with the Query Designer, follow these steps:

1. Select Add Query . . . from the Project menu. The Database Query item is automatically selected. Give your query file the desired name and press Open.

2. You are presented with the Add Table dialog box that is shown in Figure 6-12, allowing you to select the tables involved in your query. Select authors then press Add then Close.

Figure 6-12: The Add Table dialog box.

3. Select fields by checking boxes next to the columns as shown in Figure 6-13. The columns you select will be listed so that you can select sort options and filtering criteria. Also, you can see the SQL query syntax automatically generated each time you select or configure an option.

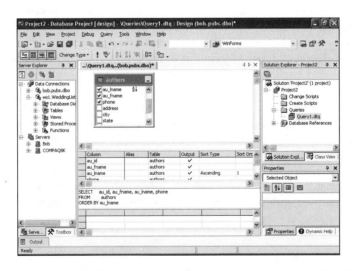

Figure 6-13: The Query Designer, including selected fields and a selected sort order.

4. Select a sort option. If you select more than one sort option, you can modify the sort order to determine the order in which columns are sorted. Notice that the au_lname field is selected for Ascending sort order in Figure 6-13.

To run the new query, right-click anywhere in the Query Designer and select Run (Figure 6-14).

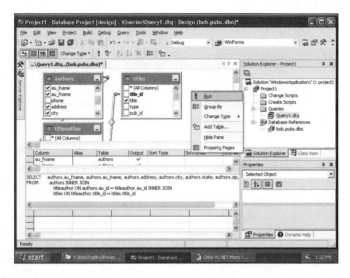

Figure 6-14: The Query Designer as the query is executed.

Once a tested query has been idle for some time, Visual Studio .NET will attempt to save SQL Server resources by releasing what it considers to be an unnecessary connection or lock on data resources. You'll see the dialog box shown in Figure 6-15.

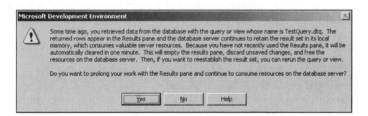

Figure 6-15: The warning that server resources will be released.

Script Editor

The Script Editor allows you to edit any script including SQL Server stored procedures and triggers and Oracle PL/SQL. Color-coding is available; however, no Intellisense is provided. (Look for this feature in future releases of Visual Studio.)

The Script Editor breaks SQL code into logical blocks of execution. These blocks are not always executed linearly because in T-SQL (Transact-SQL, the language of SQL Server stored procedures), conditional criteria can be specified before it is evaluated. When you debug a stored procedure, you will notice that breakpoints are not enforced at the line level. This is the same reason why SQL code is broken into logical blocks; each block of code is allowed a single breakpoint.

Stored Procedures

Stored procedures are precompiled database objects that contain code for implementing business rules, data retrieval, and data modification.

With that said, there is a distinct difference between precompiled stored procedures and compiled components. Components, such as .NET components and windows forms, are compiled into byte code, which is a lower-level machine language. Stored procedures are not compiled in the same way, although the path that is required to execute the stored procedure (the query plan) is compiled and stored in memory.

With regard to business rules, there is no speed or language advantage to building business rules into a stored procedure. Business rules in the database should be built into database constraints or triggers, effectively preventing an application from bypassing the rule.

Visual Studio .NET provides for the creation, modification, and deletion of stored procedures through the Server Explorer toolbox. Once a stored procedure is created, it must be tested and debugged if necessary, which is historically a difficult and time-consuming proposition. SQL Server did not provide a means of stepping through stored procedures until the release of SQL Server 2000.

Unfortunately, developers must use a separate tools set, SQL Query Analyzer, to step through a stored procedure. Visual Studio .NET allows developers to continue using a single tool set for developing all aspects of an application including stepping through and debugging stored procedures.

Right-clicking on a stored procedure in the Server Explorer exposes a set of functions that can be performed against the stored procedure including running and debugging. When running a stored procedure the Visual Studio .NET IDE will prompt for the parameter values the stored procedure is expecting, as shown in Figure 6-16.

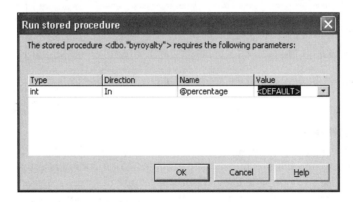

Figure 6-16: The Run stored procedure dialog box.

To save time, the IDE saves values that you've entered for the stored procedure parameters for use as default values the next time you run the stored procedure. The execution results are displayed in the output window.

Debugging a stored procedure is the same as running a stored procedure except that while debugging occurs, breakpoints can be added to blocks of code in the stored procedure as shown in Figure 6-17. While stepping through a stored procedure, you can change the values of local variables, allowing you to test a wider range of possible situations.

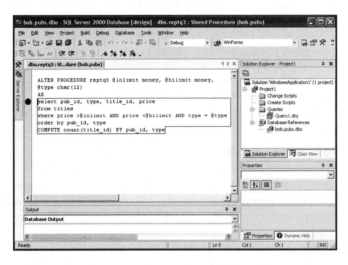

Figure 6-17: Displays a stored procedure in debug mode.

Database Objects

Let's look at a few objects that are most often abused or forgotten because the proper use of database objects can make or break an application. Two of the more significant problems application developers tend to have is a poor understanding of indexes and the implementation of business rules (constraints) in a database. This is partially Microsoft's fault because developers are able to get by during development with visual tools to aid in the implementation of database objects without a clear understanding of certain design issues. The result is a database that seems to perform with relatively few records, but which causes panic when the application fails to perform or scale in production.

Index Objects

Indexes are the single most important and overlooked database object when it comes to performance. Indexes organize data in tables so that the database query engine does not need to scan the entire table searching for your application's data. Table scans should be avoided at all costs because they cause a serious performance hit that may not manifest itself until several thousand records are added to the table. That cost is associated with the support of indexes. Indexes should be used on columns in which query criteria are determined, such as columns that are referenced in the WHERE clause or columns that are referenced in an ORDER By or sort option.

Indexes are set up as a subset of data from the column it is created in an index table and a set of pointers to the physical table itself. The index tables are updated when data is inserted, updated, or deleted. This can actually have a negative performance impact if indexes are unnecessarily created. The overuse of indexes can become as much a burden to the application as not having indexes.

The type of index that is used can also impact performance. Clustered indexes physically reorder a table on the column they are created on, and searches on columns that are physically ordered yield the fastest results. Because the table's data is physically reordered, only a single clustered index can be defined per table, and only the most searched column should have the clustered index. In most cases, this is the *primary key*. A primary key index enforces uniqueness on the column it is defined on.

NOTE *It is a little misleading to say that you are adding a primary key index. A truer statement would be that you are defining a primary key constraint, which in turn implements a unique index. A unique index enforces uniqueness within the column for which it is defined.*

You only touched the tip of the iceberg here. Your next step will be to find out what the pad index and fill factor are—two index properties that are often overlooked and likely misunderstood. Similar to tables scans, improperly configured pad index and fill factor settings can prove a significant performance hit through page splitting. For more information, see MSDN online.

Constraints: The Implementation of Business Rules

As you learned in Chapter 2, "Evolution of Tier Development," all data-specific rules that can be easily enforced in the database should be. Constraints are a way to implement simple business rules at the database level; you cannot bypass a business rule that is implemented as a constraint.

Table triggers are like constraints except that triggers allow you to implement more complex business rules than constraints. However, constraints offer a performance gain over triggers because in order for a trigger to fire, data must have already been inserted or modified. Constraints, on the other hand, implement business rules before data modification can occur, which increases overall database performance.

Types of Constraints

Database constraints are database objects that aid in the enforcement of business rules. More specifically, they enforce data specific business rules.

Check constraints define the type and format expected by the column receiving data. Default constraints are useful for defining the value to be saved if a value is not supplied. (This can be very handy when using the NewId() function of SQL Server to create GUIDs in a column for a record that may be used for replication to diverse systems.)

Unique constraints enforce column uniqueness on columns that are defined with a unique constraint and by primary key columns. Foreign key constraints enforce referential integrity between the column defined with the foreign key and the primary key it is related to. Primary keys will usually be defined on a different table; however, a recursive relationship can exist between two columns in the same table. That means the same column can be both a primary key and foreign key. This type of relationship can be useful when defining hierarchical data such as a company organizational chart.

Visual Studio Analyzer

The Visual Studio Analyzer (VSA) tool allows developers to dig into their application to evaluate component interactions and detect performance bottlenecks. Detection of potential bottlenecks is essential for creating scalable distributed applications. Applications are expected to use resources when running, of course, but we must avoid having an application or a component of a distributed application abuse resources or take longer than necessary to perform a task.

Bottlenecks

For purposes of our discussion, a "bottleneck" is the area of an application that runs so slowly that it holds up other processes. In a monolithic application, a bottleneck was considered the process in a set of processes that took the longest to run. In today's distributed application architectures, a bottleneck is more complex. Not only is a bottleneck a slow-running process, in a distributed environment it can be a network resource. To build a scalable distributed application you must monitor processor usage, network usage, system resources, and input/output (I/O).

VSA allows us to monitor an application with a client-server approach through its client and server components (shown in Figure 6-18) in which each component of VSA resides on a single machine. This may often be the scenario the developer employees while in development; however, often application components are distributed among multiple machines. The scenario, as shown in Figure 6-18, is one in which the VSA Server collects information from IIS, COM+ services, and the data source.

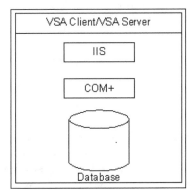

Figure 6-18: A single server application and VSA Client Server components.

VSA's client and server components are not the same as your application's client or server; they are VSA components used to collect and analyze information from VSA server components. The VSA Server resides on any machine where distributed application components exist (including presentation, business, or data access layers).

In a single server environment in which the user services, business services, and data services tiers exist on the same server machine, the VSA client and server components are installed on the same computer. This is often typical in a development environment.

In a production environment it is best, for scalability sake, to separate each tier and distribute the tiers among multiple servers when appropriate. Often your average application will not require this level of distribution of processes. When a distributed architecture is required, a VSA Server component can be installed on each of the tier servers and the VSA Client on a development workstation where the distributed application can be monitored as shown Figure 6-19. In this scenario the application is distributed requiring careful thought to where each VSA component is distributed. The VSA Servers that collect performance data are placed on the IIS, COM+, and Database machines; these are the locations of the components that we wish to monitor. The VSA Client, used to view the performance data, is placed on the workstation.

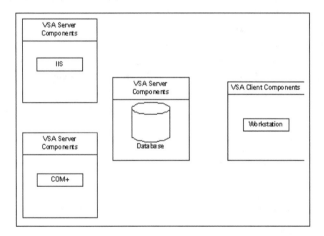

Figure 6-19: VSA components spread among a distributed application.

As you can see in this diagram, only VSA Server components are required on machines with our distributed application components. In this case, the IIS server, COM+ server, and database servers have VSA Server installed while the workstation that is used for collecting and analyzing performance information requires only the VSA Client components.

Visual Studio Analyzer Architecture

The VSA Server consists of three server components that must be installed on all machines in which collection occurs. A logical view is shown in Figure 6-20.

- Event Sources: Components registered to VSA that generate events.

- In-process event creator (IEC): Called by the event source. The IEC provides a method for generating VSA events.

- Local Event Concentrator (LEC): Collects all events of the server machine. One LEC component must exist on each computer generating events.

The Visual Studio Analyzer Client consists of two components as shown in Figure 6-20.

- Primary Event Collector (PEC): Also referred to as Public in Event Generation in some MSDN documentation. The PEC collects all events generated by all VSA Servers through each VSA Server's LEC.

- User Interface (UI): Provides a number of interfaces for viewing performance data and storing events in a log for future analysis.

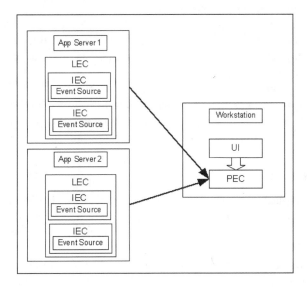

Figure 6-20: The complete Visual Studio Analyzer architecture.

Crystal Reports

Visual Studio .NET Enterprise Edition includes the Crystal Reports object model and designer for creating professional quality reports. The report object model provides programmatic access to reports built in the Crystal Reports Designer, making the implementation of reports easier than ever. It has never been easier to connect to a variety of data sources that include directly accessing databases taking advantage of recordsets and datasets. The Crystal Reports Designer will be familiar to users of previous versions of Crystal Reports.

Once a Crystal Report file is created with the designer, the report is complete, although displaying the report file in an application is another issue. Report files must be contained in a report container called the Crystal Reports Viewer, which is a container for report files that are available both to Web Forms and Windows Forms. During runtime, a single Crystal Reports Viewer can satisfy the use of several reports. Programmatic access to this viewer enables the user to select from a list of available reports to be displayed in the viewer.

In the spirit of delivering software as a service, the version of Crystal Reports that is available with Visual Studio .NET can be displayed as a Web Service. (The client requesting the report must support XML because it is how the Web Service report is transmitted.)

As with most reporting applications, a Crystal Report in Visual Studio .NET can be previewed and then printed. It can also be exported to a variety of formats, including HTML, PDF, XLS, DOC, and RTF formats, as well as a Crystal Report format (RPT).

Reporting can be a critical component of an application's functionality; in fact, some applications, such as analytical applications, can be useless without them. Visual Studio .NET and Crystal Reports have made great strides to ease the pains of report development and delivery.

Enterprise Templates

Enterprise application development provides a set of logistical challenges. Not the least of these is the result of a large number of developers from a diverse set of backgrounds with different ideas as to how an enterprise application should be delivered.

Large application development efforts often employ application architects to provide guidance. Once a framework and approach are defined, that information is disseminated to developers through various documents and workshops.

Enterprise Templates that are included with Visual Studio .NET provide a means for defining and enforcing Application Layer Boundaries, which describe the scope of each layer of an applications model. For example, a Microsoft Windows DNA style model describes five layers of distinct functionality.

As mentioned earlier it is not always necessary to physically divide these layers, although it can certainly help to logically divide applications. The presentation layer displays information to the end user and provides a means for data entry. Just below this layer is the facades layer that shields the presentation layer and developer from the complexity of the application implemented in the

Business Level Layer (BLL). The Business Level Layer provides all of the application's functionality including most business rules, validation, and control of application-specific functionality such as credit card transactions. The Data Access Layer (DAL) provides all data access to application data while the database in the data services tier provides data storage and implements simple data specific business rules.

Application architects provide guidance to developers through naming conventions, standards, and guidelines, and until now, these guidance measures were nearly impossible to enforce without a code review for all developers. For application architects, Enterprise Templates will become the tool of choice for physical enforcement of Application Boundaries.

Enterprise Templates allow architects to actually define a set of templates that warn developers from certain actions such as trying to add a Windows Form to a component in the business services tier or an attempt to access data directly from the presentation layer. There are too many possibilities to discuss in this overview of Enterprise Templates so this chapter will conclude with a description of where Enterprise Templates fit into the Microsoft Windows DNA style model.

Visual Studio .NET comes with a set of predefined Enterprise Templates. Figure 6-21 shows the Enterprise Template projects that are available, and Figure 6-22 provides a chart of the Windows DNA style model and the Enterprise Templates that it supports. The chart in Figure 6-22 represents a separation of application functionality. Figure 6-21 shows Enterprise Template projects that aid in the development of whatever model is decided.

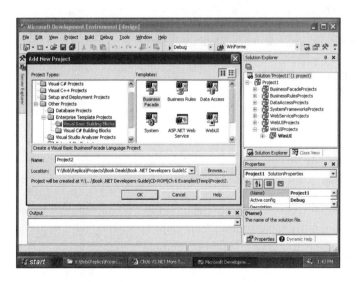

Figure 6-21: The Visual Basic .NET Enterprise Templates supporting DNA or whatever architecture that is chosen.

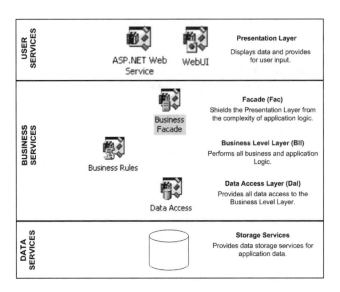

Figure 6-22: A chart of the Windows DNA style model showing where Enterprise Templates fit in.

Summary

As you have learned in this chapter, nearly every aspect of .NET development offers some type of designer or wizard to aid in the rapid development of .NET applications. However, with regards to database objects, even with the designers and wizards that are available the improper implementation of technology, specifically in the case of database objects such as indexes, can lead to poor application performance. The tools that are provided by Visual Studio .NET can aid in rapid application development, but are not a replacement for good programming practices.

7

A VISUAL BASIC .NET
CRASH COURSE

Visual Basic (VB), for all intensive purposes, has arrived, and it's just as powerful and flexible as any other .NET language, although this may well be due more to the strength of the .NET Framework than to Visual Basic as a programming language.

All versions of VB prior to Visual Basic .NET (let's refer to these versions as "classic" VB) were criticized as being non-object oriented programming languages not worthy of enterprise level or mission critical applications. However, while earlier versions lacked true full inheritance, they have been widely used to deliver mission critical applications successfully.

The fact is, a well-written Visual C++ application will nearly always out perform a Visual Basic application. But Visual Basic, while lacking in some flexibility and power, is easier to implement than Visual C++. Furthermore, because VB lacks flexibility and power, developers are less likely to create multithread problems or memory leaks at the cost of performance and stability.

This chapter provides an overview of many new Visual Basic .NET features and concepts. (For a detailed language reference, see the MSDN library online or *The Book of VB .NET, .NET Insight for VB Developers.*)

What's New in Visual Basic .NET?

The number of language enhancements in Visual Basic. NET nearly justifies the creation of a new language. Let's look at a few of the more visible changes.

Option Explicit

Forcing the explicit declaration of all variables reduces potential bugs. Classic VB required an Option Explicit statement in the declaration section of code if we wanted the Visual Basic compiler to enforce variable declaration which held the potential for problems because variables were often misspelled. When using Option Explicit, an entirely new variable is created if not already declared. Unlike classic VB, Visual Basic .NET implements Option Explicit by default, preventing the accidental creation of new variables and protecting the use of declared ones.

Option Strict

Option Strict is similar to Option Explicit in that it tells the compiler to require a variable declaration and requires all data conversions to be explicit. In classic Visual Basic, implicit conversions are not possible when Option Strict is on. (This setting is off by default.)

Option Compare

Option Compare, as you might guess, determines how strings will be evaluated. The two possible parameter values are binary and text. Binary compares the literal binary values of the two values being compared. A binary compare would mean the upper- and lower-case values cannot be equal, in effect enforcing case-sensitive compares. Text allows the evaluation of two variables to be case-insensitive.

Your application requirements will determine which Option Compare option you will use.

Option Base

Option Base is a retired option of classic Visual Basic that allowed developers to determine whether or not arrays will be 0 or 1 based. Visual Basic .NET no longer recognizes this option and sets all arrays to base 0.

Variables

Variables in .NET come in two flavors: value types and reference types. All primitive data types with the exception of the string data type are value type variables. All classes including the string data type are reference types.

The most significant difference between the types is in how they are stored in memory. Value types are stored in a stack (which requires a smaller memory footprint), while reference types are stored in a heap.

Boxing

Boxing occurs when a value type is converted to a reference type and recreated on the heap. Boxing should be used sparingly as the ability to move values from the stack to the heap is performance intensive.

The most common occurrence of boxing is when a value type variable is passed to a procedure that accepts the System.Object data type. System.Object is the equivalent of the classic Visual Basic variant data type.

ReDim

The ReDim statement, available in classic Visual Basic, is still available in Visual Basic .NET. Classic Visual Basic not only allowed developers to rediminish an array, but also initialize the array. Visual Basic .NET allows the use of ReDim to rediminish an array but not to initialize an array.

StringBuilder

The StringBuilder class is an impressive class optimizing string manipulation. You'll better understand its advantages once you understand how string manipulation has historically worked.

Classic Visual Basic hid the actual implementation code supporting functions available in the Visual Basic library, and string manipulation was no exception.

One common string function is the concatenation of two strings. Unfortunately, Visual Basic doesn't simply add the two strings together; instead, the windows system determines the space required for the new string, allocates memory, and places the new concatenated value into the newly allocated memory.

The StringBuilder class is implemented as an array of characters. This allows it to implement methods to manipulate what appears to be a string without the overhead incurred by an actual string. The Insert method of the StringBuilder class is used to add to the character array in a way that is much more efficient than classic string manipulation, increasing performance of many common programming scenarios. (You'll find the StringBuilder class in the System.Text namespace.)

Using the StringBuilder

This example will show you how to use the StringBuilder class and will compare its performance against the performance of classic Visual Basic string concatenation. To begin, follow these steps:

1. Create a windows project and build a window that looks the same as Figure 7-1, using the parameters in Table 7-1.

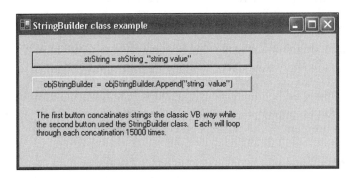

Figure 7-1: Using the StringBuilder class.

Table 7-1: Parameters for the StringBuilder Class

Control	Property	Value
Button	Name	btnString
	Text	strString = strString & "string value"
Button	Name	BtnStringBuilder
	Text	objStringBuilder = objStringBuilder.Append("string value")
Label	Name	lblStringDisplay
Label	Name	lblStringBuildingDisplay
Label	Text	The first button concatinates strings the classic VB way while the second button used the StringBuilder class. Each will loop through each concatination 15000 times.

2. Add the following code segment to the click event of the btnString button.

```
        Dim dateStart As Date
        Dim strString As String
        Dim i As Integer

        dateStart = DateAndTime.TimeOfDay

        For i = 1 To 15000
            strString = strString & "string value "
        Next i
lblStringDisplay.Text = DateAndTime.DateDiff(DateInterval.Second, _
dateStart, DateAndTime.TimeOfDay) & " Seconds"
```

3. Add the following code segment to the click event of the btnStringBuilder button.

```
        Dim dateStart As Date
        Dim objString As New System.Text.StringBuilder()
        Dim i As Integer

        dateStart = DateAndTime.TimeOfDay

        For i = 1 To 15000
            objString = objString.Append("string value ")
        Next i
            lblStringBuilderDisplay.Text = DateAndTime.DateDiff( _
DateInterval.Second, dateStart, _
DateAndTime.TimeOfDay) & " Seconds"
```

4. Now run the example and press each button. You will see a significant difference between the performances of the two methods of string concatenation.

NOTE *Previously, strings were built by simply adding one onto the end of another. This only seems to be what is happening. What is actually occurring is something different. When adding one string to another, you begin with the original string in memory, then a new string is allocated in memory for the string being added. Next, a new string representing the new concatenated string is created and the new string placed into it, and finally, the original string and the added string are de-allocated, leaving only the newly concatenated string in memory.*

As you might imagine, this is a very inefficient process for simply adding two string values together. The StringBuilder class is a collection of characters. The StringBuilder character collection can allow values to be added and removed without the need to re-allocate and de-allocate memory blocks. As you will see, the performance difference is significant.

Structures

Classic Visual Basic allowed developers to create their own data types called User Defined Data Types or UDTs, which were implemented using the Type keyword. Visual Basic .NET has retired the Type keyword and replaced it with the keyword Structure, like so:

```
Public Structure Person
    Dim strFirstName as String
    Dim strLastName as String
End Struct
```

Variable Scope

All variables have a predefined scope that is assigned during initialization. Listed below are a few of the most common scope declarations and their definitions.

- *Private scope:* Defines a variables scope as restricted to the current method. A variable defined as having *private scope* is referred to as a member variable and is commonly prefixed with an "m".
- *Public scope:* Allows the parent class, or calling class, access to the data held by a public variable or method.
- *Friend scope:* Similar to public scope as far as all code within a project is concerned. The difference between the *public scope* and *friend scope* is that variables or methods that are defined with the *friend scope* cannot be accessed by a parent class outside of the project.
- *Protected scope:* A new scope declaration that allows access to classes that inherit from the variables class.

Regions

The #Region directive allows you to organize your code into collapsible blocks which help to make the code window easier to work with by displaying only those functions you are working with. Each region can be defined with a name helping each region to be more easily identifiable, as shown here

```
#Region "MyRegion"
    'some code
#End Region
```

When you are done writing "some code," you can collapse the region and begin working on the next segment of code.

Windows Forms

Visual Basic .NET implements Windows Forms as classes that inherit windows functionality from the Form class found in the System.Windows.Forms namespace. Developing Win32 applications in Visual Basic .NET is still very similar to classic Visual Basic windows development in that windows controls can be dragged and dropped onto the form designer. The difference is that none of the implementation code is hidden.

For example, here's the implementation code for the Windows Form discussed in the previous example of the StringBuilder class. While this type of code must be implemented in classic Visual Basic forms, it is hidden. As you can see, the code is no longer hidden; however, I would strongly recommend leaving this code alone unless you really know what you are doing and have a specific need to fill. Take a look at the code below and notice that the entire form is actually a class that inherits the System.Windows.Forms.form class. As mentioned earlier in this book, everything in .NET is a class. There are no exceptions.

```
Public Class Form1
    Inherits System.Windows.Forms.Form

#Region " Windows Form Designer generated code "

    Public Sub New()
        MyBase.New()

        'This call is required by the Windows Form Designer.
        InitializeComponent()

        'Add any initialization after the InitializeComponent() call

    End Sub

    'Form overrides dispose to clean up the component list.
    Protected Overloads Overrides Sub Dispose(ByVal disposing As Boolean)
        If disposing Then
            If Not (components Is Nothing) Then
                components.Dispose()
            End If
        End If
        MyBase.Dispose(disposing)
    End Sub

    'Required by the Windows Form Designer
    Private components As System.ComponentModel.IContainer
```

(continued on next page)

```
'NOTE: The following procedure is required by the Windows Form Designer
    '

    End Sub

#End Region
End Class
```

The implementation code for all the controls on the form were stored in the "Windows Form Designer generated code" region. (This information has been removed so you won't be distracted from the Windows Form's own implementation.)

Project Structure

While the Visual Basic compiler used a file's extension to determine what type of project file it was, Visual Basic .NET implements all code through classes. All Visual Studio .NET needs to know is the language the file is written in.

Project groups in Visual Studio have proved to be a powerful tool for managing, building, and debugging multiple project solutions. Visual Studio .NET replaces the Group Project with a Project Solution, which is one or more projects and the supporting files. Because solutions actually contain projects and items, they are often referred to as Solution Containers. And, because projects also contain files, it should come as no surprise that projects are referred to as Project Containers.

Solutions and project files each have their own extensions so that Visual Studio .NET knows what kind of container they are:

.sln: The file extension of a solution file which maintains all solution specific information.

.suo: The file extension of all Solution User Options files which maintains all of the user's preference information for the solution.

.vbproj: The file extension of all Visual Basic project files.

.vb and **.cs**: The file extensions of Visual Basic .NET and C# files, respectively. This is a significant improvement from previous versions of Visual Studio when forms, classes, and other components were given component specific file which offered no clue as to the language used to build the file. Project items built using a specific language will always have that language's file extension, thus allowing Visual Studio .NET to know which compiler it must use. (For additional information on file extensions of project items, refer to the MSDN article entitled, "File Types and File Extensions in Visual Basic and Visual C#".)

ErrorProvider

One of the more interesting Windows and Web Form improvements is the ability to alert the user of exceptions without interrupting them until they press a button that performs validation, providing better overall user experience. The ErrorProvider component is a non-visual component that allows you to perform data validation on form controls. If a data violation occurs, you can set a message to be displayed as a tool tip near the offending control.

Ideally, you should implement data validation, a type of business rule enforcement, at the lowest common layer. The most ideal place to do so is at the database level because this is the only application layer that cannot be bypassed. Furthermore, rules enforced here are not duplicated as they would be if you implemented business rules in the presentation layer. For example, if a name can be equal to or less than 20 characters and the rule is implemented in the presentation layer, then every form that supports the use of the name must implement the same rule. If the rule is changed, it must be changed in every form that uses the name. This is both sloppy and error prone.

Current technology does not lend itself to this level of data validation very easily; however, over time Microsoft will devise better validation schemes and developers will build custom solutions. The challenge is to provide solid data validation without compromising user experience. To implement data validation in the presentation layer means that we are duplicating business rule enforcement because the same rules are surely implemented in the database as well. Of course the risk is that when the database schema changes, we may miss making the same changes in the presentation layer.

If all business rules are implemented in the Component layer, it is possible to bypass the rules by ignoring the Component layer or building another one that does not implement the rule. In such a case, you have the potential of corrupting data that will be more expensive to repair then it would have cost to devise a sound business rules enforcement schema.

NOTE *The XML Schema is excellent place to begin looking for sound business rule implementation. By pulling the database schema from the database and persisting it in memory, you can leverage XML Schema to enforce data types and constraints. Also, when building your web page dynamically you can enforce these data specific rules through the ErrorProvider. In this case, you are implementing rules at the business level layer, which were defined in the database at design time; the violation can be made known through the ErrorProvider at the presentation layer. This is the ideal way to enforce data specific business rules; all other programmatic business rules should be implemented in the business level layer. Never enforce business rules in the presentation layer.*

Implementing Namespaces

Namespaces make it easy to organize classes, functions, data types, and structures into a hierarchy. Namespaces allow you to quickly access classes and methods buried in the .NET Framework Class Library or any other application that provides a namespace. The .NET Framework Class Library provides hundreds of classes and thousands of functions as well as data types and structures.

Use the Imports statement to import a namespace for easy access to its classes and methods. Once imported it is no longer necessary to use a fully qualified path to the desired class or method. For example:

```
Imports system.text ' Give access to the StringBuilder class
```

Table 7-2 lists the namespaces that are used most commonly and their general functionality.

Table 7-2: Commonly Used Namespaces

Namespace	Functionality
Microsoft.VisualBasic	Contains the Visual Basic .NET runtime, classes, and methods used for compiling Visual Basic code.
Microsoft.VSA	Provides a host of scripting functionality, allowing you to give users the ability to customize of your application.
Microsoft.Win32	Provides access to the Windows Registry and the ability to handle events raised by the operating system.
System	Provides basic classes and methods commonly used by all .NET languages. Includes data types, arrays, exception classes, Math functions, Garbage collector, conversion classes, console access, and the Object class along with many more commonly used components.
System.Collection	Provides interfaces and classes used for creating a variety of collection types. Collection types are • ArrayList: Basic collection object. • BitArray: A collection of bits. (0 and 1 values) • DictionaryBase: Implements base class for strongly typed collections supporting key (name) value pairs. • HashTable: High performing collection of key (name) value pairs. • Queue: FIFO (First-in First-out) collection. • SortedList: A collection of key (name) value pairs sorted by the key (name). • Stack: LIFO (Last-in First-out) collection. • Specialized.ListDictionary: A faster collection than a HashTable for 10 items or less. • Specialized.HybridDictionary: Acts as a ListDictionary until the collection gets larger where it converts to a HashTable. • Specialized.StringCollection: A collection of strings.

Table 7-2: Commonly Used Namespaces (continued)

Namespace	Functionality
System.ComponentModel	Provides classes and interfaces for runtime and design time behavior including the ability to contain or to be contained. The Container interface allows the Visual Studio .NET development environment to provide a graphical interface when developing a component.
System.Data	Provides classes and interfaces to support data access including ADO.NET, XML, OLEDB, and SQL Server access.
System.Diagnostics	Provides classes, allowing access to • Event Log: A mechanism employed by the operating systems providing a common area to record application and system events. Events can include errors, warnings, and informational data. • Processes: Provides the ability start and stop processes as well as monitor processes on remote machines. • Performance Counters: Provides the ability to monitor performance of local and remote machines including the ability to define and create customer performance counters.
System.DirectoryServices	Provides the ability to search and interact with Active Directory services providers: • Active Directory is a hieratical mean for logically organizing network and system resources. • Active Directory providers include IIS, LDAP (Lightweight Directory Access Protocol), NDS (Novel NetWare Directory Service), and WinNT directory services.
System.EnterpriseService	Provides the ability to employ COM+ functionality for building enterprise applications.
System.Globalization	Provides classes supporting multiple languages and cultures including date formats, calendars, and currencies.
System.IO	Provides read and write access to data streams and files. Additional access is provided to related tasks including: • Manipulation of the creation, modification, and deletion or file directories. • Manipulation of files through creation, modification, deletion, coping, and moving. • Provides information about files and directories, such as the existence of a file or directory, the extension of files, and the full path of files. • Allows access to system events including file system changes.

(continued on next page)

Table 7-2: Commonly Used Namespaces (continued)

Namespace	Functionality
System.Management	Provides access to information provided by WMI (Windows Management Instrumentation) including information about a systems drive space and CPU Utilization. Please refer to WMI for additional information concerning data that can be derived from the System.Management namespace.
System.Messaging	Provides classes for managing Message Queues.
System.Net	Provides classes for commonly used network protocols.
System.Reflection	Provides classes for access to component metadata stored in an assemblies manifest.
System.Runtime.Remoting	Provides classes designed for building distributed applications similar to classic DCOM (Distributed Component Object Model).
System.Runtime.Serialization	Provides classes designed to serialize objects into a sequence of bits for storage or transfer to another system.
System.Security	Implements the CLR's (Common Language Runtime) security components.
System.ServiceProcess	Provides classes required for building Windows Services.
System.Text	Provides classes for manipulating string data. Most notable is the StringBuilder class defining a modern approach to string manipulation.
System.Tread	Provides classes for building multi-threaded applications.
System.Timer	Provides classes for implementing non-visual timed events allowing actions to be taken on a given interval.
System.Web	Provides classes and additional subordinate namespaces encompassing all aspects of web development including ASP .NET, Web Services, and web controls and more.
System.Windows.Forms	Provides classes required for developing windows form applications.
System.XML	Provides classes for manipulating and using XML.

Structured Exception Handling

One of the more complex and important aspects of application development is error handling. Errors that are not handled can have devastating effects on the success of any application because, in most cases, the application will not be able to recover or shut down gracefully. Among the challenges is the lack of comprehensive error handling across languages and platforms.

To complicate matters further, handling errors is only the tip of the proverbial iceberg. As important as error handling is, an application must be able to handle unacceptable application level events or exceptions that are not necessarily system generated error. Now, the term "error handling" is no longer sufficient.

Exception handling deals with any system or application generated error, what we now refer to as an exception. This ability to handle all exceptions, both system and application generated, goes a long way toward giving the user a stable application and a better overall user experience.

The CLR is a language independent means for exception handling that places all raised or thrown errors into an exception object that can be manipulated like any other object. In addition, the exception object can be created and used, programmatically, anywhere within an application.

The CLR implements exception handling with the Try/Catch/Throw model. This model of exception handling, while foreign to Visual Basic programmers, is well known by C++ programmers. This is a structured exception handling model that is time tested and proven as a solid means for handling or dealing with thrown exceptions.

Throwing an exception is similar to raising an error in Visual Basic. The simplest exception structure is as follows:

```
Public Sub MySub()
    Try
    'Some code
    Catch
    'Deals with any exception that may occur.
    End Try
End Sub
```

In its most basic form, all application and exception code goes into what is called a Try block. In this example, the Try block is the area between the Try and the End Try statements.

The Try block can be divided into three clauses. The area between the Try and Catch statements is where you place your applications code. The area between the Catch and, in this case, the End Try statements are where your exception handling code resides. Another section, defined as the finally clause, is available in the last clause where the Try blocks code executes. Our simple exception handling example does not use the finally clause as it is not required when a Catch statement is available.

Exception Handling Rules

A set of rules governs how the Try block can be used. But before we have a look at these rules, let's take a quick look at some of the classes that support exception handling.

Table 7-3 lists several common exception classes you can look forward to using. Exception classes are thrown when a related exception is thrown; when looking for exceptions look for the following:

Table 7-3: Exception Classes

Exception Class	Reason Exception Class Is Thrown
System.AppDomainUnloadedException	Thrown when attempting to use an unloaded application domain.
System.ApplicationException	Thrown when a non-fatal application error has occurred.
System.ArgumentException	Thrown when an argument passed is not valid.
System.ArgumentNullException	Thrown when a null is passed as a method parameter that does not accept null values.
System.ArgumentOutOfRangeException	Thrown when a passed value is outside the range of a methods parameter.
System.ArithmeticException	Thrown when an error occurs while performing arithmetic and conversion operations.
System.ArrayTypeMismatchException	Thrown when adding a value of the incorrect data type to an array.
System.DivideByZeroException	Thrown whenever a value is divided by zero.
System.DllNotFoundException	Thrown when a DLL referenced as imported is not available.
System.IndexOutOfRangeException	Thrown when trying to access an invalid index in an array.
System.InvalidCaseException	Thrown when an invalid conversion attempt is made.
System.NullReferenceException	Thrown when attempting to dereference a null object reference.
System.OutOfMemoryException	Thrown when memory is not available to perform the specified task.
System.OverflowException	Thrown when an operation overflow occurs.
System.RankException	Thrown when an array with the wrong number of dimensions is passed to a methods parameter.
System.SystemException	Is the base class for all exception classes in the System namespace.
System.Data.ConstraintException	Thrown when a constraint is violated.
System.Data.DataException	Thrown when an ADO.NET component generates an error.
System.Data.DBConcurrencyException	Thrown when the number of rows affected in an update procedure is zero.
System.Data.DeletedRowInaccessibleException	Thrown when attempting to perform data manipulation operations on a data row that has been deleted.
System.Data.InvalidConstraintException	Thrown when a data relationship is violated.

Table 7-3: Exception Classes (continued)

Exception Class	Reason Exception Class Is Thrown
System.Data. NoNullAllowedException	Thrown when inserting a null value where one is not accepted.
System.IO. DirectoryNotFoundException	Thrown when a specified directory cannot be found.
System.IO.FileLoadException	Thrown when a file cannot be loaded.
System.IO.IOException	Thrown when an I/O error occurs.
System.IO.PathToLongException	Thrown when a path or file name are too long.
System.Runtime.Remoting. RemotingException	Thrown when an error occurs during a remote operation.
System.Runtime.Remoting. RemotingTimeoutException	Thrown when the response of a server or client exceed a predefined interval.
System.Runtime.Remoting. ServerException	Thrown when an error occurs while working with a remote component that is an unmanaged application incapable of throwing an exception.
System.Runtime.Serialization. SerializationException	Thrown when an error occurs during the serialization or deserialization of a component.
System.Web.HttpException	Allow an http exception to be thrown.
System.XML.XmlException	Provides exception information about the last XML exception.

Basic Rules

Basic rules govern the use of a Try block. (They will quickly become obvious after using Try blocks a few times.)

- All Try blocks must employ at least one catch or finally clause.
- A Catch clause with no other parameters will catch all unhandled exceptions.
- The finally clause always executes when available except when an Exit Try occurs. As such, the finally clause is a good place to perform component cleanup. If an Exit Try statement is used anywhere in the Try block then it is better to perform cleanup after the End Try block statement.
- Developers familiar with the On Error statement may still perform error handling as they did in Visual Basic only when a Try block does not exist in the procedure.

Exception Handling Examples

For the following examples we will create a single Windows Form and add a button for each example. To begin, create a new project and name it "Exception Handler".

Try . . . Catch

One popular and easy way to understand an example of error handling has always been the divide by zero error, or in .NET terms "exception." You will use the divide by zero exception wherever possible so as to not distract you from what the chapter is trying to convey. (You will examine a few other specific exception conditions later in this chapter.)

This example demonstrates the simplest of all exception structures:

1. Drag a button onto your Windows Form and label it "Try... Catch".

2. Change the buttons name to "btnTryCatch".

3. Apply the following code in the click event of the button.

```
Dim intResult as Integer"
Dim int1 as Integer = 5
Dim int2 as Integer = 0
Try
     intResult = int1 / int2
Catch objException as System.OverflowException
    Messagebox.Show("Divide by zero has occurred")
End Try
```

The preceding example evaluates the exception object by using the catch clause. The catch clause checks to see if the exception object contains an "OverflowException" exception. If so, and in this case it will, the code in the catch clause executes.

The Finally Clause

This example employs the same code as the one previously, except it demonstrates that the Finally clause always executes:

1. Drag another button onto your Windows Form and label it "Finally".

2. Change the buttons name to "btnFinally".

3. Apply the following code in the click event of the button.

```
Dim intResult as Integer
Dim int1 as Integer = 5
Dim int2 as Integer = 0
Try
     intResult = int1 / int2
Catch objException as System.OverflowException
```

```
        Messagebox.Show("Divide by zero exception has occurred")
Finally
        Dim obj As New System.Text.StringBuilder()
    obj = obj.Append("Regardless of whether or not an ")
    obj = obj.Append("exception occurs, the Finally clause ")
    obj = obj.Append("will execute.")
   MessageBox.Show(obj.ToString)
    obj = Nothing
End Try
```

Feel free to remove the errant code with "intResult = int1 / 1" and observe that the finally clause still executes.

The Exit Try Statement

This example demonstrates the Exit Try statement. You could simply add the Exit Try statement to a previous example: however, go ahead and create a new button to keep each example separate for future reference.

1. Drag another button onto your Windows Form and label it "Exit Try".

2. Change the button name to "btnExitTry".

3. Cut and paste code from the Finally button to the Exit Try button.

4. In the Catch clause, place the "Exit Try" statement after the messagebox statement:

```
Dim intResult as Integer
Dim int1 as Integer = 5
Dim int2 as Integer = 0
Try
     intResult = int1 / int2
Catch objException as System.OverflowException
    Messagebox.Show("Divide by zero exception has occurred")
    Exit Try
Finally
        Dim obj As New System.Text.StringBuilder()
    obj = obj.Append("Regardless of whether or not an ")
    obj = obj.Append("exception occurs, the Finally clause ")
    obj = obj.Append("will execute.")
   MessageBox.Show(obj.ToString)
    obj = Nothing
End Try
```

You will notice when the exception occurs, the exceptions message is displayed and the Try block is exited. In this case, the Finally block does not execute and is not a good place to clean up objects in memory.

Multiple Catch Statements

It is often preferable to use Multiple Catch statements in a single Try block, although the placement of Catch statements can impact performance.

Once an exception is caught, the processing of the remaining Catch statements is aborted. Subsequently, once the Catch clause completes processing, the Finally clause is processed if available. To increase the performance of your Try blocks, place the most likely one to error or more common exceptions in the first Catch blocks while placing the least likely errors toward the end.

Here's how to use Multiple Catch statements:

1. Drag another button onto your Windows Form and label it "Multiple Catch".
2. Change the button name to "btnMultipleCatch".
3. Cut and paste code from the Finally button to the Multiple Catch button.
4. Make the following changes as highlighted in the code below:

```
Dim intResult As Integer
Dim int1 As Integer = 5
Dim int2 As Integer = 0
Dim str1 As String

Try
    str1 = int1 / int2
    Throw (New Exception("A different exception"))
Catch objException As System.OverflowException
    MessageBox.Show("Divide by zero exception has occurred")
Catch
    MessageBox.Show("Some other exception has occured.")
Finally
    Dim obj As New System.Text.StringBuilder()
    obj = obj.Append("Regardless of whether or not an ")
    obj = obj.Append("exception occurs, the Finally clause ")
    obj = obj.Append("will execute.")
    MessageBox.Show(obj.ToString)
obj = Nothing
End Try
```

As you step through the procedure you will notice that you no longer receive an overflow exception. You will also notice that the string value receiving the results of the calculation has the value "infinity" when dividing a number by zero. The overflow exception does not occur, however, when we threw an exception to the calling method. The first Catch clause is completely ignored, but the second Catch clause is not looking for any specific exception; as a result, the second Catch clause catches all exceptions not already caught.

NOTE *Historically, when you were building COM components, the best practice was to ensure that all methods and components handled their own exceptions. The best practice with .NET components is to pass the exception to the client and allow the client to determine the next course of action. This is due in part because all languages now understand how to deal with each other's languages exceptions, therefore, it is no longer critical for the language catching the exception to also deal with the exception. Also, exceptions don't always correlate to an error that occurred. Often an exception simply indicates an application state that is not what the method requires. This could be as simple as the database is not available. In this care, no error has occurred in the code; however, because the database is unavailable, the method cannot complete its assigned task.*

Getting Exception Information

The exception class has several properties and methods. You'll learn about a few of the more notable ones here and then examine an example of each:

- **Source property:** The Source property of the exception class is intended to hold the application or object name generating the exception. It can also be programmatically set, but if it is not set, the property returns the assembly name where the exception occurred.

- **Message property:** The Message property is a string containing a description of the current exception.

- **TargetSite property:** The TargetSite property is a string containing the name of the procedure where the exception occurred.

- **GetType method:** The GetType method is inherited from the System.Object class and returns the type of exception that has occurred.

- **ToString method:** The ToString method returns a string describing the current exception including information provided by several other exception class properties and methods.

Exception Class Properties and Methods Example

This example demonstrates the use of some exception class properties and methods:

1. Drag another button onto your Windows Form and label it "Properites/Methods."
2. Change the button name to "btnPropMeth."

3. Cut and paste code from the Finally button to the Properties/Methods button.4. Add the following code to the newly pasted code:

```
Dim intResult as Integer
Dim int1 as Integer = 5
Dim int2 as Integer = 0
Try
    intResult = int1 / int2
Catch objException as System.OverflowException
    Messagebox.Show("Divide by zero exception has occurred")

    'Source, Message, TargetSite, GetType, ToString
MessageBox.Show("Source: " & objException.Source())
MessageBox.Show("Message: " & objException.Message())
MessageBox.Show("TargetSite: " & objException.TargetSite.Name)
MessageBox.Show("GetType.Name: " & objException.GetType.Name)
MessageBox.Show("ToString: " & objException.ToString())
Finally
    Dim obj As New System.Text.StringBuilder()
    obj = obj.Append("Regardless of whether or not an ")
    obj = obj.Append("exception occurs, the Finally clause ")
    obj = obj.Append("will execute.")
    MessageBox.Show(obj.ToString)
    obj = Nothing
End Try
```

Object-Oriented Programming (OOP)

As mentioned earlier, Visual Basic did not meet the test as a true object-oriented language that implements true object-oriented programming as defined by abstraction, encapsulation, polymorphism, and inheritance. Visual Basic .NET not only supports inheritance, but also supports a variety of inheritance implementations including interface, forms, and implementation or polymorphism inheritance.

Before you continue any further, let's briefly discuss the four main concepts of object orientation and the implementation code for each. Each brief discussion is followed with an example that demonstrates the discussed OOP concept.

Abstraction

Abstraction is the easiest of the OOP concepts to understand and is often something we implement naturally without realizing it. In short, abstraction is the implementation of code to mimic the actions and characteristics of any real-world entity.

The most commonly-used example for describing abstraction is the abstraction of a person. Imagine that we want to create an object from a class that represents a person. A person class will need to describe its characteristics through the implementation of properties. Actions of the person class are performed by methods.

Encapsulation

Encapsulation is the programmatic equivalent of a black box. An actual black box may have a switch and dials. Inside the box would be the mechanisms to perform the actions provided by the black box.

We expose properties and methods through abstraction, but we implement the actual workings of our component through encapsulation. A few encapsulated actions might include data access, data validation, calculations, adding data to an array or collection, or calling other methods or other components.

Exposing our components interface while hiding the component's implementation code effectively separates interface implementation from our black box implementation. This separation helps to modularize components to perform a more specific task while requiring minimal knowledge of how the black box actually works.

One of the more useful applications of encapsulation is in making a complex component. For example, your program may require interaction with a third party system, but interaction with this system can only be achieved through a complex API. Rather than requiring all developers on a project to spend valuable time figuring out how to correctly use the third party API or even find ways to misuse it, one developer could study the API then encapsulate it in a component that exposes a less complex interface. This is a common practice that saves time and reduces potential bugs.

Like abstraction, encapsulation isn't as much a technology as it is a method of code implementation. In the case of encapsulation, our method of implementation separates the exposed interface from the actual implementation code.

Polymorphism

Abstraction is an interface implemented to represent a real-world object; encapsulation is the implementation of a black box through interface and implementation separation; and polymorphism is the ability to implement the interface of another class into multiple classes or to implement multiple interfaces on a single class. This method of implementation is referred to as *interface-based programming*.

A vehicle is a good example of polymorphism. A vehicle interface would only have those properties and methods that all vehicles have, a few of which might include paint color, number of doors, accelerator, and ignition. These properties and methods would apply to all types of vehicles including cars, trucks, and semi-trucks.

Polymorphism will not implement code behind the vehicle's properties and methods. (That's the job of inheritance covered in the next section.) Instead, polymorphism is the implementation of an interface. If the car, truck, and semi-truck all implement the same vehicle interface, then the client code for all three classes can be exactly the same.

Implementing the vehicle interface only requires the declaration of properties and methods. To create a new interface, use the Interface keyword in place of the Class keyword. The client implementing the new interface can do so by using the Implements keyword as shown in the example:

```
Implements IVehicle
```

After using the Implements keyword, you will notice that Intellisense displays the properties and methods of the IVehicle interface. Using the Implements keyword will only give access to the properties and methods of the IVehicle interface; however, you must provide your own code behind the methods and property declarations to match the interface.

Inheritance

Inheritance is the ability to apply another class's interface and code to your own class. Remember, with polymorphism, you got the interface; however, you must apply your own code. The power of inheritance is the ability to inherit code, saving developers time. This type of inheritance is called *implementation inheritance*. To inherit another class, use the Inherits keyword.

Visual inheritance is the ability to inherit another form's look and feel onto another. Remember, everything in .NET is a class, including forms. If you create a project that exists in the MyApp namespace, create a form name MyBaseForm. The following code will inherit the MyBaseForm within our new form:

```
Public Class MyNewForm
      Inherits MyApp.MyBaseForm
End Class
```

Properties

Properties are part of a program's interface and describe the characteristics of a class. These properties hold information about a class or, when loaded into memory, an object. Properties, as they exist in classes, are often referred to as "data." When a reference is made to a class's data, you will know that the reference is actually directed toward a class's property.

To create a property, use the Property keyword and then define the type of property you are implementing. Properties can be read-only, write-only, or read and writable. To define the characteristics of properties, use the keywords ReadOnly, WriteOnly, or supply no definition at all to implement both read and write ability.

Visual Studio .NET makes properties easier to implement by adding the basic shell of property code based on the property's scope definition. Unlike Visual Basic, Visual Basic .NET automatically supplies code for both read and write functionality: "Get" for read ability method and "Set" for write access to a property.

Create a new class, type the following code, and press ENTER:

```
Public Property FName() As String
```

Visual Studio .NET will automatically fill in the rest of the code that is required by the FName property:

```
Get
Return m_FName
End Get
    Set(ByVal Value As String)
        m_FName = Value
    End Set
End Property
```

Methods

Methods are the actions exposed by a class in the form of either functions or sub-procedures. Sub-procedures and functions both execute code on behalf of the calling application, but sub-procedures simply execute code while functions execute code, then return a value.

The .NET Framework provides at least two new changes to how you can use procedures. In Visual Basic, you could call a procedure without the use of parameters, including procedures that required no parameters at all. The .NET Framework requires parenthesis to follow all methods even when parameters are not required. For example:

- Visual Basic 6 method call:

```
intResult = DoSomething
```

- Visual Basic .NET method call:

```
intResult = DoSomething()
```

Another change is the addition of the Return keyword. When returning a value for a function in Visual Basic, you set the function's name equal to the value being returned. With Visual Basic .NET, you can set the keyword Return equal to a value and the value will be returned with the function. This is very useful when making code more generic. For instance, you can easily cut and past a method's code without regard to another method's function name because the keyword Return is used for setting the method equal to a return value. Examples of the old versus new method for returning values of a function are:

- Visual Basic 6 method call:

```
Public Function DoSomething() as Int32
    DoSomething = 10
End Function
```

- Visual Basic .NET method call:

```
Public Function DoSomething() as Int32
    Return = 10
End Function
```

If you look closely at a function's supporting properties you will find that the Return keyword is used by default. You can set the function name equal to a given value.

The third significant change is in how parameters are passed. Visual Basic passed a parameter value ByRef by default. The preferred method for passing parameter values is to explicitly define whether a value is passed by ByRef or ByVal. Finally, when using the Option keyword, you must define a default value similar to how C has worked for many years now.

Declaration Options

We have covered a few of the most common declaration methods including those that describe the scope of a property or method. Several description options will extend or restrict scope.

Here is a list of the most commonly-used declaration options with brief descriptions of each:

Private: The Private keyword defines a variable or method as accessible only by code within the context of where the declaration occurred; outside code is not permitted access. Variables and methods defined as private are often referred to as member variables or methods, and commonly prefixed with an "m".

Public: The Public keyword declares a property or method as accessible by anyone within the calling application or within the class itself.

Friend: The Friend keyword defines a property or method as accessible by members within the class it is declared in.

Protected: The Protected keyword defines a property or method as accessible only by members of its class or by members of an inheriting class.

Default: A Default property is a single property of a class that can be set as the default. This allows developers that use your class to work more easily with your default property because they do not need to make a direct reference to the property. Default properties cannot be initialized as Shared or Private and all must be accepted at least on argument or parameter. Default properties do not promote good code readability, so use this option sparingly.

Overloads: The Overloads property allows a function to be described using deferent combinations of parameters. Each combination is considered a signature, thereby uniquely defining an instance of the method being defined. You can define a function with multiple signatures without using the keyword Overloads, but if you use the Overloads keyword in one, you must use it in all of the function's Overloaded signatures.

Shared: The Shared keyword is used in an inherited or base class to define a property or method as being shared among all instances of a given class. If multiple instances of a class with shared properties or methods are loaded, the shared properties or methods will provide the same data across each instance of the class. When one class alters the value for a shared property, all instances of that class will reflect the change. Shared properties of all instances of the class point to the same memory location.

Overridable: The Overridable keyword is used when defining a property or method of an inherited class, as overridable by the inheriting class.

Overides: The Overides keyword allows the inheriting class to disregard the property or method of the inherited class and implements its own code.

NotOverridable: The NotOverridable keyword explicitly declares a property or method as not overridable by an inheriting class, and all properties are "not overridable" by default. The only real advantage to using this keyword is to make your code more readable.

MustOverride: The MustOverride keyword forces the inheriting class to implement its own code for the property or method.

Shadows: The Shadows keyword works like the Overloads keyword except that with shadows we do not have to follow rules such as implementing the same signature. The Shadows keyword does not require the consent (override ability) of the inherited class to replace the property or method's implementation code. A method does not have to be defined as overridable for the Shadows keyword to work.

Object Instantiation

When you drag and drop controls onto a Windows Form, you are using objects. When you observe your code, you are looking at a class; when that code is loaded into memory, at runtime, it is considered an object. The importance of the distinction is simply to describe that a class is a template, while an object is an instance of that template in memory. Also, many copies of the template can exist in memory at the same time as objects.

Fortunately, we do not have to depend on the component designer to work with classes; we can build our own classes and components. This is nothing new for a moderately experienced developer; what is new is how Visual Basic .NET permits us to instantiate classes.

Classic COM relied on the Windows Registry to store its exposed properties, methods, events, and enumerations; a client application could only access these exposed interfaces through the Registry. As a result, the way you instantiate classes when using classic COM components in COM+ is very important. Visual Basic .NET accepts a number of instantiation methods without performance impacts, although all variables must first be diminished and then instantiated before they can be used.

The two methods for instantiating classic COM are the CreateObject and New keywords. CreateObject uses the Windows Registry to obtain the interface of the class being instantiated. Because CreateObject depends on windows for access to the register, COM+ can apply a context for use by the COM+ services.

The New keyword in classic COM also depends on Windows for access to the Windows Registry. The catch is that it doesn't always have to access the Windows Registry to discover a class's interface if the class resides inside the same component as the calling class. Because the New keyword has no problem accessing a class's interface within the same component, a class can be instantiated by passing COM+ services that would normally add a context or other component service. While this will not prevent you from loading a class into COM+, to take full advantage of COM+ services you should use the CreateObject keyword.

Having said all that, the CreateObject keyword cannot be used to instantiate .NET classes, although it can be used to instantiate classes that exist within classic COM components. Because .NET components don't rely on the Windows Registry, the New keyword is used when loading all .NET components.

Here are several examples of how you might define and load classes into memory. First, the variable is diminished as MyClass:

```
Dim obj As MyClass
```

Second, you load the class "MyClass" into memory. An instance of a class loaded into memory is referred to as an object. Notice there is no "Set" keyword used.

```
Obj = New MyClass
```

Another method is to declare and instanciate an object in a single line:

```
Dim obj2 As MyClass = New MyClass()
```

Finally, you can implicitly diminish a variable with a class you are attempting to load. This is the shortest method and is perfectly acceptable:

```
Dim obj3 As New MyClass
```

Early and Late Binding

Binding is something we do when diminishing a variable, though many developers may not realize the importance of how they bind a class.

Early binding, often referred to as strong typing, refers to explicitly declaring the class used to define a variable. Early binding has several benefits. For example, when programming, Visual Studio .NET can give access to the class's interface with Intellisense which greatly reduces potential for typos and promotes rapid development. Also, when early binding a class, the Visual Basic compiler can enforce the proper use of a class's interface by providing warnings and refusing to complete the compile until the error is resolved. But performance gains are probably the most important reason to bind early: Early binding allows your program to access your class's interface directly, rather than through the Windows Registry or at runtime. If the compiler knows ahead of time which classes you will be using in your application, it can make the appropriate compilation optimizations.

Late binding can be useful when developing against non-existent components or ones that are being developed. Late binding allows you to continue compiling your code until the component is available; once the class is available, you can modify your code to early bind. You might also use late binding when you truly don't know the object type that will be passed to your function, in which case it is perfectly acceptable to accept any type of object.

Before late binding can occur, the Option Strict option must be set to off. Option strict is off by default:

```
Option Strict Off
```

To declare a variable as late bound, simply diminish the variable as type object:

```
Option Strict Off
Dim obj As Object
'or
Dim obj As System.Object
```

The System.Object class is the class from which all other classes are derived. While it has no specific characteristics that prevent it from acting as any other class, it is used for late binding.

Components

A class defines something that can exist in memory. It defines an object's interface including properties, methods, events, and enumerations as well as implementation code. An object is an instance of a class in memory; while a class may exist only once, multiple instances of that class may reside in memory as objects.

When adding items to a project, you can add a "class" or a "component class". In essence, these are the same thing with one exception: a component class implements the IComponent interface, enabling Visual Studio .NET to drag non-visual controls, such as the timer control, onto a component designer.

Visual Studio .NET provides a designer for building components, which allows you to drag visual controls onto your class or component, and begin coding. For example, if you want to program a delay into your class, you can use a component item with the designer to drag the timer control onto your component. The implementation of a graphical designer (IE Component Designer) and container are available to you when you selected "component class" as a new item. Visual Studio creates your class by adding a line of code that inherits everything your class needs to be a component, as follows:

```
Inherits System.ComponentModel.Component
```

Then the designer creates a components object using the IContainer interface so that the designer can allow drag and drop capabilities:

```
Private components As System.ComponentModel.IContainer
```

Simple OOP Examples

Now you'll build an example application that employs abstraction, encapsulation, polymorphism, and inheritance:

1. Create a new class library project named "PersonProj".
2. Rename the Class1.vb file to "Person.vb".
3. Add a new Windows Application project to the solution named "TestClient".
4. Right-click on the TestClient project and select Set as StartUp Project.

Adding Abstraction

Now add abstraction:

1. Replace the default class in Person.vb with the following code:

```
Public Class clsPerson
    Public FName As String
    Public LName As String
    Public FullName As String
    Public BirthDate As Date
    Public Age As Integer
    Public TotalHours As Integer

    Public Sub Work(ByVal intHours As Integer)
        TotalHours += intHours
    End Sub
End Class
```

2. Create a form that looks like Figure 7-2, and name it "frmAbstraction.vb." Use the parameters in Table 7-4 to build the new Windows Form.

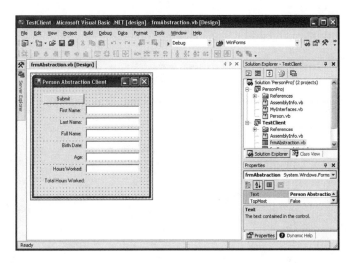

Figure 7-2: Creating a new Windows Form.

Table 7-4: Form Parameters

Control	Property	Value
Button	Name	btnSubmit
	Text	Submit
Textbox	Name	txtFName
Textbox	Name	txtLName
Textbox	Name	txtFullName
Textbox	Name	txtBirthDate
Textbox	Name	txtAge
Textbox	Name	txtHoursWorked
Label	Name	lblTotalHoursWorked

3. Right-click on the TestClient project and select Properties. Change the Startup object to "frmAbstraction.vb".

4. Add a reference to the PersonProj. Right-click on the TestClient project and select Add Reference. Select the Projects tab and press the "Select" button then press OK.

5. Add the following object declaration to the initialization of frmAbstraction form:

```
' Here we are initializing the Person class. Normally this would be done
' when the class was needed for data access but in this case we are using
' the Person class to maintain our data.
Dim objPerson As New PersonProj.clsPerson()
```

6. Add the following code to the submit buttons click event:

```
        objPerson.FName = txtFName.Text
        objPerson.LName = txtLName.Text
        objPerson.FullName = txtFullName.Text

        If IsDate(txtBirthDate.Text) Then
            objPerson.BirthDate = CDate(txtBirthDate.Text)
        End If

        If IsNumeric(txtAge.Text) Then
            objPerson.Age = CInt(txtAge.Text)
        End If

        If IsNumeric(txtHoursWorked.Text) Then
            objPerson.Work(CInt(txtHoursWorked.Text))
        End If

        lblTotalHoursWorked.Text = "Total Hours Worked: " _
& objPerson.TotalHours.ToString
```

7. Now run the application.

You should be able to place any value you wish into the First and Last name fields, then completely contradict yourself when filling in your full name. The same should hold true for entering your birth date and age. This example abstracts a person but does not hide any implementation; each time you press the Submit button, the Total Hours Worked is summed and displayed.

Adding Encapsulation

The encapsulation example implements the clsPerson class and encapsulated code, hiding the implementation code for all the properties and methods.

In the abstraction example, the user has to enter both their birthday and age. As you encapsulate the implementation for the Person object, you will hide the implementation of their age. Age will be derived from the person's birth date, thus preventing a user from creating an invalid age and birth date values. Properties are also encapsulated, allowing the class to derive the full name from the first and last names that have been entered.

1. Add a new Windows Form item named "frmEncapsulation.vb".

2. Add the controls and parameters listed in Table 7-5 to the frmEncapsulation.vb form.

Table 7-5: Controls for the Form

Control	Property	Value
Button	Name	btnSubmit
	Text	Submit
Textbox	Name	txtFName
Textbox	Name	txtLName
Label	Name	lblFullNameDisplay
Textbox	Name	txtBirthDate
Label	Name	lblAgeDisplay
Textbox	Name	txtHoursWorked
Label	Name	lblTotalHoursWorked

3. Create a new class in the Person class using the following code:

```
Public Class clsPerson2
    Private m_FName As String
    Private m_LName As String
    Private m_BirthDate As Date
    Private m_TotalHours As Integer

    Public Property FName() As String
        Get
            Return m_FName
        End Get
        Set(ByVal Value As String)
            m_FName = Value
        End Set
    End Property

    Public Property LName() As String
        Get
            Return m_LName
        End Get
        Set(ByVal Value As String)
            m_LName = Value
        End Set
    End Property

    Public ReadOnly Property FullName() As String
        Get
            Return m_FName & " " & m_LName
        End Get
    End Property
```

```
    Public Property BirthDate() As Date
        Get
            Return m_BirthDate
        End Get
        Set(ByVal Value As Date)
            If IsDate(Value) Then
                m_BirthDate = Value
            End If
        End Set
    End Property

    Public ReadOnly Property Age() As Integer
        Get
            If DatePart(DateInterval.Year, m_BirthDate) = 1 Then
Exit Property
            End If
            Return DateDiff(DateInterval.Year, m_BirthDate, Now)
        End Get
    End Property

    'Method for adding hours to m_TotalHours worked.
    Public Sub Work(ByVal intHours As Integer)
        m_TotalHours += intHours
    End Sub

    Public ReadOnly Property TotalHoursWorked() As Integer
        Get
            Return m_TotalHours
        End Get
    End Property

End Class
```

4. Add the following object declaration to the initialization of frmAbstraction form:

```
' Here we are initializing the Person class. Normally this would be done
' when the class was needed for data access but in this case we are using
' the Person class to maintain our data.
Dim objPerson As New PersonProj.clsPerson2()
```

5. Right-click and select Properties then change the StartUp object to "frmEncapsulation".

6. Add the following code to the Submit button:

```
objPerson.FName = txtFName.Text
objPerson.LName = txtLName.Text

If IsDate(txtBirthDate.Text) Then
    objPerson.BirthDate = CDate(txtBirthDate.Text)
Else
    MsgBox("Please provide a valid Birth Date.")
End If

If IsNumeric(txtHoursWorked.Text) Then
    objPerson.Work(CInt(txtHoursWorked.Text))
    txtHoursWorked.Text = ""
End If

lblFullNameDisplay.Text = objPerson.FullName.ToString
lblAgeDisplay.Text = objPerson.Age.ToString

lblTotalHoursWorked.Text = "Total Hours Worked: " _
                & objPerson.TotalHoursWorked.ToString
```

7. Now run the application and enter the information.

You'll notice that your age is calculated for you so that it cannot contradict what the age should be based on the birth date, and the full name is derived from the first and last name.

Adding Polymorphism or Interface-based Inheritance

This example features an interface called IPerson and a class named Employee that uses the IPerson interface:

1. First create a new Windows Form with the same controls as used in the encapsulation example and name it "frmPolymorphism".

2. Add a new Module to the PersonProj project and name it "MyInterfaces.vb".

3. Apply the following code to the MyInterface.vb module. The code defines the interface.

```
Public Interface IPerson
    Property FName() As String
    Property LName() As String
    ReadOnly Property FullName() As String
    Property BirthDate() As Date
    ReadOnly Property Age() As Integer

'Method for adding hours to m_TotalHours worked.
    Sub Work(ByVal intHours As Integer)
    ReadOnly Property TotalHoursWorked() As Integer
End Interface
```

4. Right-click and select Properties, then change the StartUp object to "frmPolymorphism".

5. Create a new class to the Person.vb module. You will use it to inherit the new interface:

```
Public Class clsPerson3
    Implements IPerson
    Private m_FName As String
    Private m_LName As String
    Private m_BirthDate As Date
    Private m_TotalHours As Integer
    Private m_HrRate As Integer
    Private m_TotalPay As Double
    Public Property FName() As String _
Implements IPerson.FName
        Get
            Return m_FName
        End Get
        Set(ByVal Value As String)
            m_FName = Value
        End Set
    End Property

    Public Property LName() As String _
Implements IPerson.LName
        Get
            Return m_LName
        End Get
        Set(ByVal Value As String)
            m_LName = Value
        End Set
```

```vb
    End Property

    Public ReadOnly Property FullName() As String _
Implements IPerson.FullName
        Get
            Return m_FName & " " & m_LName
        End Get
    End Property

    Public Property BirthDate() As Date _
Implements IPerson.BirthDate
        Get
            Return m_BirthDate
        End Get
        Set(ByVal Value As Date)
            If IsDate(Value) Then
                m_BirthDate = Value
            End If
        End Set
    End Property

    Public ReadOnly Property Age() As Integer _
Implements IPerson.Age
        Get
            If DatePart(DateInterval.Year, _
m_BirthDate) = 1 Then Exit Property
            Return DateDiff(DateInterval.Year, _
m_BirthDate, Now)
        End Get
    End Property

    'Method for adding hours to m_TotalHours worked.
    Public Sub Work(ByVal intHours As Integer) _
Implements IPerson.Work
        m_TotalHours += intHours
    End Sub

    Public ReadOnly Property TotalHoursWorked() As Integer _
Implements IPerson.TotalHoursWorked
        Get
            Return m_TotalHours
        End Get
    End Property

    'Additional Properties:
    'HrRate
```

(continued on next page)

```
Public WriteOnly Property HrRate()
    Set(ByVal Value)
        m_HrRate = Value
    End Set
End Property

'TotalPay
Public ReadOnly Property TotalPay() As Double
    Get
        Return m_HrRate * m_TotalHours
    End Get
End Property

End Class
```

6. Now run this example just as you ran the previous ones.

You will not notice a difference in how the application runs, although the plumbing has changed quite a bit.

With this simple example, it is easy to question the usefulness of polymorphism. However, if you were to continue building an application that dealt with several aspects of a person, you might find polymorphism more helpful to use if you had to deal with Employees, Customers, Managers, and Contractors.

Working with Inheritance

This inheritance example inherits the interface and implementation code of the clsPerson3 class:

1. Add a new Windows Form item named "frmInheritance.vb". Use the same controls as we used in the encapsulation example.

2. Add the following code to the initialization section of the form:

```
' Here we are initializing the Person class. Normally this would be done
' when the class was needed for data access but in this case we are using
' the Person class to maintain our data.
Dim objPerson As New Person.clsEmployee()
```

3. Add the following class to the Person.vb module of the PersonProj project:

```
Public Class clsEmployee
    Inherits clsPerson3
End Class
```

4. Right-click and select Properties, then change the StartUp object to "frmInheritance".

5. Now Run the inheritance example as you did the previous ones.

Notice that the clsEmployee class inherits the functionality of the clsPerson3 class, which in turn implements the IPerson interface. This example demonstrates both polymorphism and inheritance that have been combined to form a single solution.

Summary

In this chapter, you learned that Visual Basic has come a long way from a reduced featured-set language that promoted RAPID application development to a full featured language. Now employing full inheritance, Visual Basic promises to aid in the delivery of enterprise level applications that may previously have been better delivered in another OOP language.

8

ASP.NET

ASP (Active Server Pages), Microsoft's solution for building dynamic web applications, has come a long way in a short time. ASP.NET was designed to address the scalability and reliability of mission critical enterprise applications not addressed by ASP.

This chapter will introduce you to web development using ASP.NET. Many of the programming topics of the previous chapter on VB .NET also apply to ASP.NET as scripting is no longer supported and has been replaced by .NET languages. This chapter will introduce ASP.NET while walking you through a fully functional application.

ASP Versus ASP.NET

ASP.NET is much more than an upgrade from ASP. In fact, it's entirely different from ASP in terms of platform and implementation. The only thing ASP and ASP.NET seem to have in common is they both are used for building web-based applications and are supported by IIS services.

Table 8-1 compares a few features of ASP and ASP.NET.

Table 8-1: ASP versus ASP.NET

Feature	ASP	ASP.NET
Application State	Limited scalability	Multiple scalability options
Data Types	Late-Binding	Strong Typing (All variables must be explicitly declared)
End Product	Interpreted Script	Compiled Code
Extensions	.asp	.aspx
Implementation	Presentation and scripted logic are maintained in the same physical file.	Presentation and programmatic logic are stored in separate physical files.
Language support	Java script and VB script	Scripting languages are not supported. All .NET languages are supported for web development with ASP.NET.

Compiled Code

ASP supports only scripted languages though it can still instantiate and utilize COM. While using COM to implement all business logic and data access greatly improves performance, the remaining ASP script is still interpreted rather than compiled, as it is with ASP.NET. This causes a performance hit because interpreted code is much slower than compiled code.

If you're building an enterprise application, your goal should be to place as much of your code as possible into COM components. The only way to place all your code into COM components is to return a string from your COM layer that represents the HTML you want to display on the client. The only action taken by your ASP page is performing a "`Response.Write`" on the returned string. The Response.Write command will actually imbed the returned string into the HTML. The downside to placing all code in COM components is that, because Visual Interdev is not built to support this type of development, debugging and testing are very difficult.

Here's a quick example of how you might place all your code in compiled COM components while using ASP for "`Response.Write`".

ASP Page

The following code will reside in the calling ASP page. This page effectively loads up an instance of a class stored in a compiled COM component. The Response.Write command takes the result of the myObject.myFunction method and inserts it into the HTML code that is sent to the client browser.

```
<%
    Dim myObject
    set myObject = Server.CreateObject("myComponent.myClass")
    Response.Write(myObject.myFunction)
    Set myObject = Nothing
%>
```

Function of myComponent.myClass

This is the code placed in the myComponent component. This code effectively builds the HTML string and passes it back to the calling application which in this case is an ASP page. The advantage is the code normally reserved for scripting and interpretation is now compiled into a COM component that will perform better than interpreted code.

```
Option Explicit
Public Function myFunction() As String
On Error GoTo ErrorHandler
Dim strResult as string
strResult = strResult & "<%@ Language=VBScript %>"
strResult = strResult & "<HTML>"
strResult = strResult & "<HEAD><META name='VI60_DefaultClientScript'"
strResult = strResult & " Content='VBScript'><META NAME='GENERATOR'"
strResult = strResult &." Content='Microsoft Visual Studio 6.0'>"
strResult = strResult & "</HEAD>"
strResult = strResult & "<BODY>"
strResult = strResult & "<FORM ACTION='UserLoginProcess.asp' METHOD='post'"
strResult = strResult & " id=form1 name=form1>"
strResult = strResult & "<FONT face=Arial><P>"
strResult = strResult & "<TABLE cellSpacing=1 cellPadding=1 width=750"
strResult = strResult & " height=425 align=center"
strResult = strResult & " border=1 borderColorDark=#06767d>"
strResult = strResult & "<TBODY><TR height=50 ><TD>"
strResult = strResult & "<TABLE cellSpacing=1 cellPadding=1 width='100%'"
strResult = strResult & " border=0>"
strResult = strResult & "<TR><TD style='WIDTH: 225px' align=top width=225>"
strResult = strResult & "</TD><TD width=100></TD>"
strResult = strResult & "<TD align=top style='WIDTH: 250px' width=250>"
strResult = strResult & "<STRONG>User Login</STRONG></TD>"
strResult = strResult & "<TD align=top></TD></TR></TABLE></TD></TR><TR>"
strResult = strResult & "<TD vAlign=top align=middle>"
strResult = strResult & "<TABLE cellSpacing=1 cellPadding=1 width='100%'"
strResult = strResult & " border=0>"
strResult = strResult & "<TR><TD style='WIDTH: 325px' align=top width=325"
strResult = strResult & " height=50>"
```

(continued on next page)

```
strResult = strResult & "<P align=left><A href='../default.asp'>"
strResult = strResult & "<FONT size=2></FONT></A> </P></TD>"
strResult = strResult & "<TD align=top><P align=left> </P>"
strResult = strResult & "</TD><TD align=top></TD></TR><TR>"
strResult = strResult & "<TD align=top><P align=right>User ID:</P>"
strResult = strResult & "</TD><TD align=top><INPUT id=text1 "
strResult = strResult & " style='LEFT: 229px; TOP: 153px' name=txtUserId>"
strResult = strResult & "</TD><TD align=top></TD></TR>"
strResult = strResult & "<TR><TD align=top height=15></TD><TD align=top>"
strResult = strResult & "</TD><TD align=top></TD></TR>"
strResult = strResult & "<TR><TD align=top><P align=right>Password:</P>"
strResult = strResult & "</TD><TD align=top><INPUT id=password1"
strResult = strResult & " style='LEFT: 229px; TOP: 191px' type=password"
strResult = strResult & " name=password1></TD>"
strResult = strResult & "<TD align=top></TD></TR><TR><TD height=10></TD>"
strResult = strResult & "<TD></TD><TD></TD></TR><TR>"
strResult = strResult & "<TD align=top><P align=right> </P></TD>"
strResult = strResult & "<TD align=top><INPUT id=submit1 style='LEFT: 229px;"
strResult = strResult & " WIDTH: 107px; TOP: 225px; HEIGHT:"
strResult = strResult & " 24px' type=submit size=33 value='Log in'"
strResult = strResult & " name=submit1></TD>"
strResult = strResult & "<TD align=top></TD></TR></TABLE></TD></TR><P></P>"
strResult = strResult & "<P></P></FONT></TBODY>"
strResult = strResult & "<P></P><P></P><P></P><P></P><P></P></FORM>"
strResult = strResult & "<P></P><P></P><P></P><P></P><P></P><P></P></P> "
strResult = strResult & "</BODY>"
strResult = strResult & "</HTML>"
myFunction = strResult
Exit Function
ErrorHandler:
Set oCn = Nothing
App.LogEvent vbObjectError + 1001 & ' ' _
    & strErrorDescription, vbLogEventTypeError
Err.Raise vbObjectError + 1001, 'DBConnection.objNewConnection', _
    strErrorDescription
Err.Clear
End Function
```

Placing your presentation code in COM components, as you would with ASP, gives the best possible performance and promotes scalability but is very difficult to implement and support.

With ASP.NET you get the performance and scalability advantages of compiled code with none of ASP's disadvantages. ASP.NET completely separates presentation and business logic into different physical files during development; then, once the project is built, the logic files are compiled into a single DLL. When a web page is requested, the DLL sends the appropriate HTML code to the client. Since ASP.NET was developed with compiled code in mind, Visual Studio .NET can easily debug and test your ASP.NET application.

HTML and Server Controls

One of the more impressive features of ASP.NET is programmatic access to server controls. Server controls are controls available at design time that can be referenced at runtime, though at runtime the client receives the HTML equivalent of the server control. Server controls are more flexible than HTML controls because they can be accessed programmatically, but using server controls when no programmatic access is required hurts performance. For example, if you have a page that uses labels, text controls, and buttons, consider using an HTML label control for all your labels, and server controls for the text boxes and buttons. HTML controls are fine to use except when programmatic access is required.

Server controls must be placed within an HTML form object so that they can be posted back to the server for manipulation. You will take a closer look at the implementation of server controls when building the sample application.

Postback

All server controls must be placed within a form object so they can be posted back to the server, which is called *postback*. Postback introduces event-driven programming, previously only enjoyed by Win32-based applications, to the Web. Each server control has a number of events that can be fired when the page is posted back to the server.

Application State (_ViewState)

Application state management is the persistence of values the application requires to function properly. This may include the user's id, password, and the values of other controls. A hidden text control named _ViewState holds the contents of all the controls on a page so that the page can be generated during a postback. View state can be turned on or off at the page level or for each individual control.

Turning Off View State at the Page Level

```
<% Page Language="vb" SmartNavigation="True" EnableViewState="False" %>
```

The preceding code snippet displays three individual page directives: The first specifies the language used, the second enables smart navigation, and the third sets view state. View state is demonstrated with other page directives because more often than not, several page directives will be required. No more than one set of page directives can be used. The following code segment will fail:

```
<% Page Language="vb" SmartNavigation="True" %>
<% Page EnableViewState="False" %>
```

SmartNavigation

ASP.NET allows web applications to be event driven, similar to what we are used to with Win32 applications; however, Win32 applications have no need to reload. Web applications are connectionless and therefore, each web page must be rebuilt each time the page is submitted or when an event is fired.

SmartNavigation is a new feature available in IE versions 5 and greater that allows your page to refresh in a way that does not flash, flicker, or reset your scroll position. Using this feature allows you to build applications that provide a good user experience. The SmartNavigation page directive was shown in the previous directives example for view state.

ASP.NET Address Book Walkthrough

Rather than read about the theoretical implementation of ASP.NET, you are going to build a fully functional application. You will walk through the creation of a simple address book application using several ASP.NET facilities.

System Requirements

Before you begin building the address book application, take a quick look at the applications required by the example.

Visual Studio .NET

Visual Studio .NET is not required to build ASP.NET applications; however, you are taking advantage of Visual Studio .NET for rapid application development. Therefore, Visual Studio .NET is a requirement of this example.

IIS Server

Because the web pages need a web server, you will need to install Microsoft's Internet Information Server (IIS). This can easily be installed by selecting Control Panel from the Settings menu option under the Start bar. Then select Add/Remove Programs and finally select Add/Remove Windows Components.

SQL Server 2000

The address book data will be stored in SQL Server 2000. You could just as easily use an Access database, Oracle, or any other version of SQL Server. The examples in this chapter demonstrate the application using SQL Server 2000 because while you will not be taking advantage of SQL Server's support for XML or Stored Procedures, these features will be implemented into the address book later in the book.

Building the Address Book Database

Creating our address book database involves two steps. First, you'll use SQL Server Enterprise Manager to create the database. Next, you'll run a script to build the address book table.

Creating the Database

To create the database, follow these steps:

1. Open SQL Server's Enterprise Manager by selecting Programs from the Start menu and clicking Enterprise Manager from the Microsoft SQL Server menu.
2. Expand the Microsoft SQL Servers group then the SQL Server group. You should be able to see your server in the list. Expand your server's icon.
3. Right-click on the Databases folder and select New Database. The database properties page appears and allows you to enter your new database's name, "AddressBook", and click OK.

Creating the Table

To create the table, follow these steps:

1. From Enterprise Manager, select SQL Query Analyzer from the Tools menu.
2. Select Open from the File menu and navigate to the "Ch09 Examples" directory on the CD-ROM that accompanies the book. Select the AddressBook.sql file and choose Open.
3. The following T-SQL script is loaded:

```
--********************************************************
USE AddressBook
if exists (select * from dbo.sysobjects where id = object_id(N'[dbo].[AddressBook]')
and OBJECTPROPERTY(id, N'IsUserTable') = 1)
drop table [dbo].[AddressBook]
GO
CREATE TABLE [dbo].[AddressBook] (
    [id] [int] IDENTITY (1, 1) NOT NULL ,
    [FName] [varchar] (20) COLLATE SQL_Latin1_General_CP1_CI_AS NOT NULL ,
    [MName] [varchar] (20) COLLATE SQL_Latin1_General_CP1_CI_AS NULL ,
    [LName] [varchar] (20) COLLATE SQL_Latin1_General_CP1_CI_AS NOT NULL ,
    [NName] [varchar] (20) COLLATE SQL_Latin1_General_CP1_CI_AS NULL ,
    [SpouseName] [varchar] (50) COLLATE SQL_Latin1_General_CP1_CI_AS NULL ,
    [Address] [varchar] (50) COLLATE SQL_Latin1_General_CP1_CI_AS NULL ,
    [City] [varchar] (50) COLLATE SQL_Latin1_General_CP1_CI_AS NULL ,
    [State] [varchar] (2) COLLATE SQL_Latin1_General_CP1_CI_AS NULL ,
    [Zip] [varchar] (10) COLLATE SQL_Latin1_General_CP1_CI_AS NULL ,
    [HomePhone] [varchar] (14) COLLATE SQL_Latin1_General_CP1_CI_AS NULL ,
    [CellPhone] [varchar] (14) COLLATE SQL_Latin1_General_CP1_CI_AS NULL ,
    [EMail] [varchar] (100) COLLATE SQL_Latin1_General_CP1_CI_AS NULL ,
    [Comments] [varchar] (7500) COLLATE SQL_Latin1_General_CP1_CI_AS NULL ,
    [Child1] [varchar] (20) COLLATE SQL_Latin1_General_CP1_CI_AS NULL ,
    [Child2] [varchar] (20) COLLATE SQL_Latin1_General_CP1_CI_AS NULL ,
```

(continued on next page)

```
        [Child3] [varchar] (20) COLLATE SQL_Latin1_General_CP1_CI_AS NULL
) ON [PRIMARY]
GO
ALTER TABLE [dbo].[AddressBook] WITH NOCHECK ADD
        CONSTRAINT [DF_AddressBook_FName] DEFAULT ('') FOR [FName],
        CONSTRAINT [DF_AddressBook_MName] DEFAULT (' ') FOR [MName],
        CONSTRAINT [DF_AddressBook_LName] DEFAULT ('') FOR [LName]
GO
--******************************************************
```

4. Select Execute from the Query menu and your table is created. If you expand the AddressBook database and then select the Tables icon, you should see your AddressBook table. Go ahead and close both Query Analyzer and Enterprise Manager. For the purpose of this example, you will not need them any longer.

Creating a New ASP.NET Application

The next few steps will walk you through creating your AddressBook project:

1. Start up Visual Studio .NET and select New Project.

2. Select the ASP.NET Web Application in the Visual Basic Projects folder as shown in Figure 8-1.

3. Type http://localhost/Ch09/AddressBook into the location text box and press OK. Visual Studio .NET creates all the necessary files needed for both the new project and solution.

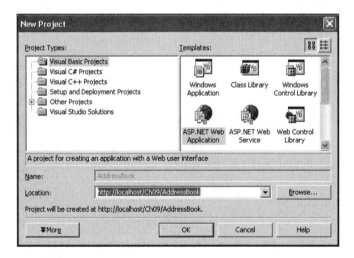

Figure 8-1: The New Project dialog screen.

4. The default aspx file created by Visual Studio .NET is WebForm1.aspx. Right-click on this file and select Rename. Rename the file to "AddressBook.aspx".

Laying Out the Page

Laying out the page includes the placement and organization of controls on the page. You will be using a combination of HTML and server controls. First, you will determine what the layout should be, then you'll use HTML tables to hold the controls. Next, you will drag the controls onto the appropriate table cells and finally set the controls properties. This will take a little time, so please sit back and follow these instructions carefully.

Setting Up the Background

To set up the background, follow these steps:

1. Right-click on the AddressBook.aspx design view page and select Properties. This will bring up a properties page to assist you in modifying the page properties.
2. Select the Browse button to find and select image file of your choice.
3. Using the drop box, change Page Layout to FlowLayout and press OK.

Border and Application Title

To set the border and application title, follow these steps:

1. Select Insert and Table from the Table menu.
2. Set the following Table attributes:

- Rows = 1
- Columns = 1
- Width = 700 pixels
- Alignment = center
- Highlight Color = #330066

3. Press OK.
4. Create another new table by left-clicking inside our new table then selecting Table, Insert, and Table again.
5. Right-click on the table, select Properties, and set the following Table attributes:

- Rows = 1
- Columns = 1
- Width = 100 percent
- Alignment = center
- Border size = 0

6. Set the following Cell attributes:
- Alignment = left

7. The new table is difficult to see because the border property is set to 0; however, if you look close enough you can see a lightly blurred border. Drag Web Forms Label from the Toolbox, drop it inside the new table, and set the following label properties.

Text = My Address Book Listings

Name = Comic Sans MS

Datagrid Control

To create a Datagrid control, follow these steps:

1. Drag a DataGrid control from the Web Forms Toolbar and drop it just below the new table that is inside the outer table.
2. Right-click on the grid control and select Properties.
3. Rename the grid to "DataGridAddressList."
4. Right-click on the grid and select AutoFormat.

The AutoFormat feature of the DataGrid is a powerful tool for quickly creating a presentable look and feel for you application's DataGrid controls. Feel free to play around with the available grid formats.

5. Select Professional 3 and press OK. We will come back and format the columns when we bind data to our DataGrid control.
6. Set the DataGrids width property to 690px.

Button Links

Next, you are going to add the button links the application will use for creating new contacts, editing contacts, and deleting old contacts. Before you continue, you will need room to create another table to hold the control. As you will observe, there seems to be no room at the bottom of the outer table, which serves as our application's border, to insert another table.

1. Move your cursor immediately to the right of the DataGrid control and press enter to insert a new space.
2. Click inside the new space and select Table, Insert, and then Table to create a new table.
3. Set the following Table attributes:

Rows = 1

Columns = 4

Width = 100 percent

Alignment = center

Border size = 1 (You will set this back to 0 once we are finished dropping controls into the cells. This should make our job just a little easier.)

4. Press OK.

5. Right-click in each first three cells of the new table and select Properties. Change the width property of this cell to 200 pixels.

6. Drag-and-drop the LinkButton from the Web Form toolbox into the first three cells of the new table.

7. Set the following properties of the first LinkButton control.

ID = lbtnNew
Bold = True
Name = Courier New
Size = X-Small
Text = New Contact

8. Set the following properties of the second LinkButton control.

ID = lbtnEdit
Bold = True
Name = Courier New
Size = X-Small
Text = Edit Contact

9. Set the following properties of the third LinkButton control.

ID = lbtnDelete
Bold = True
Name = Courier New
Size = X-Small
Text = Delete Contact
Change the table's border size property to 0.

Validation Summary Control

The Validation Summary control will serve as a single location for all business rule violations to be displayed. A description of each violation will help the user to determine what fields need to be changed before they can continue. Classic ASP forced the page to be submitted back to the server for validation, which did not lend itself to delivering a good user experience. Validation control helps to implement simple data validation without forcing a round trip to the server.

1. Drag the ValidationSummary control and drop it onto the space at the bottom of the border table, click just to the right of the new validation control, then hold SHIFT and press ENTER to create a space for adding another table.

2. Set the following properties of the ValidationSummary control.

ID = ValidationSummary1 (This will be the default.)

DisplayMode = BulletList

EnableClientScript = False (This allows the validation to be posted back to the server because some browsers cannot support validation script.)

HeaderText = The following validation errors have occured:

Height = 66px

ShowMessageBox = False

ShowSummary = True

Width = 733px

Contact Information Controls

You are going to create a table to hold the labels and controls for viewing, modifying, and creating contact information:

1. Click in the available space at the bottom of the border table and create a new table with the following properties:

Rows = 11

Columns = 4

Width = 700 pixels

Alignment = Left

Border size = 1 (Again, you will change this back to 0 when we are done adding new controls.)

2. Press OK.
3. Right-click inside each cell of the first row and select properties. Change the Width property to 200 pixels.
4. Right-click in the cell at Row 8 and Column 3 then select Properties. Under Span set Columns to 2.
5. Right-click in the cell at Row 10 and Column 1 then select Properties. Under Span set Columns to 4. Under Horizontal set Alignment to left.

Placing Controls into the Table

Place each Web Form control into the new table as indicated in Table 8-2. The "Placement" property isn't an actual property of the control. "Placement" property is where the control is to be physically placed. The placement of a label control that is to be placed into the first cell of the first row of the table will have a value of "Row = 1; Column = 1". After the control is placed, right-click on the control and set the remaining property values.

Table 8-2: Web Form Controls

Control	Property	Value
Label	Placement	Row = 1; Column = 1
	ID	lblFName
	EnableViewState	False
	Text	First:
TextBox	Placement	Row = 1; Column = 1
		(Just to the right of lblFName inside the same table cell)
	ID	txtID
	Visible	False
	Width	56px
Label	Placement	Row = 1; Column = 2
	ID	lblMName
	EnableViewState	False
	Text	Middle:
Label	Placement	Row = 1; Column = 3
	ID	lblLName
	EnableViewState	False
	Text	Last:
Label	Placement	Row = 1; Column = 4
	ID	lblNName
	EnableViewState	False
	Text	Nick Name:
TextBox	Placement	Row = 2; Column = 1
	ID	txtFName
	MaxLength	20
TextBox	Placement	Row = 2; Column = 2
	ID	txtMName
	MaxLength	20
TextBox	Placement	Row = 2; Column = 3
	ID	txtLName
	MaxLength	20
TextBox	Placement	Row = 2; Column = 4
	ID	txtNName
	MaxLength	20

(continued on next page)

Table 8-2: Web Form Controls (continued)

Control	Property	Value
Label	Placement	Row = 3; Column = 1
	ID	lblSName
	EnableViewState	False
	Text	Spouse's Name:
Label	Placement	Row = 3; Column = 2
	ID	lblChildren
	EnableViewState	False
	Text	Children:
TextBox	Placement	Row = 4; Column = 1
	ID	txtSName
	MaxLength	50
TextBox	Placement	Row = 4; Column = 2
	ID	txtChild1
	MaxLength	20
TextBox	Placement	Row = 4; Column = 3
	ID	txtChild2
	MaxLength	20
TextBox	Placement	Row = 4; Column = 4
	ID	txtChild3
	MaxLength	20
Label	Placement	Row = 5; Column = 1
	ID	lblAddress
	EnableViewState	False
	Text	Street Address:
Label	Placement	Row = 5; Column = 2
	ID	lblCity
	EnableViewState	False
	Text	City:
Label	Placement	Row = 5; Column = 3
	ID	lblState
	EnableViewState	False
	Text	State:

(continued on next page)

Table 8-2: Web Form Controls (continued)

Control	Property	Value
Label	Placement ID EnableViewState Text	Row = 5; Column = 4 lblZip False Zip Code:
TextBox	Placement ID MaxLength	Row = 6; Column = 1 txtAddress 50
TextBox	Placement ID MaxLength	Row = 6; Column = 2 txtCity 50
TextBox	Placement ID MaxLength	Row = 6; Column = 3 txtState 2
TextBox	Placement ID	Row = 6; Column = 4 txtZip
Label	Placement ID EnableViewState Text	Row = 7; Column = 1 lblHomePhone False Home Phone:
Label	Placement ID EnableViewState Text	Row = 7; Column = 2 lblCellPhone False Cell Phone:
Label	Placement ID EnableViewState Text	Row = 7; Column = 3 lblEmail False Email Address:
TextBox	Placement ID MaxLength	Row = 8; Column = 1 txtHomePhone 14
TextBox	Placement ID MaxLength	Row = 8; Column = 2 txtCellPhone 14

(continued on next page)

Table 8-2: Web Form Controls (continued)

Control	Property	Value
TextBox	Placement	Row = 8; Column = 3
	ID	txtEmail
	MaxLength	100
	Width	353px
Label	Placement	Row = 9; Column = 1
	ID	lblComments
	EnableViewState	False
	Text	Comments:
TextBox	Placement	Row = 10; Column = 1
	ID	txtComments
	MaxLength	8000
Label	Placement	Row = 11; Column = 1
	ID	lblStatus
	EnableViewState	False
	Bold	True
	Name	Arial
	ForeColor	DarkSlateBlue (Web tab)
	Text	Status =
	Width	126px
Label	Placement	Row = 11; Column = 2
	ID	lblMode
	EnableViewState	False
	Name	Arial
	ForeColor	DarkSlateBlue
	Text	Mode
LinkButton	Placement	Row = 11; Column = 3
	ID	lbtnEnter
	Bold	True
	Name	Courier New
	Size	X-Small
	Text	Enter

Table 8-2: Web Form Controls (continued)

Control	Property	Value
LinkButton	Placement	Row = 11; Column = 4
	ID	lbtnCancel
	Bold	True
	Name	Courier New
	Size	X-Small
	Text	Cancel
RequiredField Validator	Placement	Row = 2; Column = 1 (Just to the right of the textbox) valRequiredFName
	ID	txtFName
	ControlToValidate	Dynamic
	Display	False
	EnableClientScript	The 'First' name field is required.
	ErrorMessage	*
	Text	
RequiredField Validator	Placement	Row = 2; Column = 3 (Just to the right of the textbox) valRequiredLName
	ID	txtLName
	ControlToValidate	Dynamic
	Display	False
	EnableClientScript	The 'Last' name field is required.
	ErrorMessage	*
	Text	
RegularExpression Validator	Placement	Row = 6; Column = 4 (Just to the right of the textbox) valExpressionZip
	ID	txtZip
	ControlToValidate	Dynamic
	Display	False
	EnableClientScript	The Zip code must be in (#####-####) format.
	ErrorMessage	*
	Text	
	ValidationExpression	\d{5}(-\d{4})?

(continued on next page)

Table 8-2: Web Form Controls (continued)

Control	Property	Value
RegularExpression Validator	Placement	Row = 8; Column = 1
		(Just to the right of the textbox)
		valExpressionHomePhone
	ID	txtHomePhone
	ControlToValidate	Dynamic
	Display	False
	EnableClientScript	Must use a valid phone number for the 'Home Phone'.
	ErrorMessage	*
	Text	((\(\d{3}\) ?)|(\d{3}-))?\d{3}-\d{4}
	ValidationExpression	
RegularExpression Validator	Placement	Row = 8; Column = 2
		(Just to the right of the textbox)
		valExpressionCellPhone
	ID	txtCellPhone
	ControlToValidate	Dynamic
	Display	False
	EnableClientScript	Must use a valid phone number for the 'Cell Phone'.
	ErrorMessage	*
	Text	((\(\d{3}\) ?)|(\d{3}-))?\d{3}-\d{4}
	ValidationExpression	
RegularExpression Validator	Placement	Row = 8; Column = 3
		(Just to the right of the textbox)
		valExpressionEmail
	ID	txtEmail
	ControlToValidate	Dynamic
	Display	False
	EnableClientScript	Must use a valid 'Email Address'.
	ErrorMessage	*
	Text	\w+([-+.]\w+)*@\w+([-.]\w+)*\.\w+([-.]\w+)*
	ValidationExpression	

This concludes the control layout for the application. You will revisit some of the control properties as you build more advanced functionality. Figure 9-2 represents the AddressBook page as displayed in the ASP.NET designer.

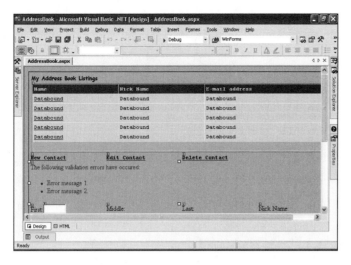

Figure 8-2: The AddressBook page displaying book listings.

Behavior Functions

The AddressBook web page supports multiple functions from viewing, editing, and creating contacts. When viewing contact information, the text controls should be read-only and certain link buttons should not be available. Each mode or function of the application will have similar situations in which some controls are set to read or write, and some link buttons are available while others are not.

The following functions should be placed into the Visual Basic portion of the web application. Double-click on the web page in Design view to bring up the AddressBook.aspx.vb page and build the following functions:

```
Private Sub SetControlsReadOnly()

    txtFName.ReadOnly = True
    txtMName.ReadOnly = True
    txtLName.ReadOnly = True
    txtNName.ReadOnly = True
    txtSName.ReadOnly = True
    txtChild1.ReadOnly = True
    txtChild2.ReadOnly = True
    txtChild3.ReadOnly = True
    txtAddress.ReadOnly = True
    txtCity.ReadOnly = True
    txtState.ReadOnly = True
    txtZip.ReadOnly = True
    txtHomePhone.ReadOnly = True
    txtCellPhone.ReadOnly = True
    txtEmail.ReadOnly = True
```

(continued on next page)

```
          txtComments.ReadOnly = True

      End Sub

      Private Sub SetControlsWritable()

          txtFName.ReadOnly = False
          txtMName.ReadOnly = False
          txtLName.ReadOnly = False
          txtNName.ReadOnly = False
          txtSName.ReadOnly = False
          txtChild1.ReadOnly = False
          txtChild2.ReadOnly = False
          txtChild3.ReadOnly = False
          txtAddress.ReadOnly = False
          txtCity.ReadOnly = False
          txtState.ReadOnly = False
          txtZip.ReadOnly = False
          txtHomePhone.ReadOnly = False
          txtCellPhone.ReadOnly = False
          txtEmail.ReadOnly = False
          txtComments.ReadOnly = False

      End Sub

      Private Sub ResetControls()

   txtFName.Text = ""
          txtMName.Text = ""
          txtLName.Text = ""
          txtNName.Text = ""
          txtSName.Text = ""
          txtChild1.Text = ""
          txtChild2.Text = ""
          txtChild3.Text = ""
          txtAddress.Text = ""
          txtCity.Text = ""
          txtState.Text = ""
          txtZip.Text = ""
          txtHomePhone.Text = ""
          txtCellPhone.Text = ""
          txtEmail.Text = ""
          txtComments.Text = ""

      End Sub
```

```
Private Sub SetControlsVisibleTrue()

    lblFName.Visible = True
    lblMName.Visible = True
    lblLName.Visible = True
    lblNName.Visible = True
    lblSName.Visible = True
    lblChildren.Visible = True
    lblAddress.Visible = True
    lblCity.Visible = True
    lblState.Visible = True
    lblZip.Visible = True
    lblHomePhone.Visible = True
    lblCellPhone.Visible = True
    lblEmail.Visible = True
    lblComments.Visible = True

    txtFName.Visible = True
    txtMName.Visible = True
    txtLName.Visible = True
    txtNName.Visible = True
    txtSName.Visible = True
    txtChild1.Visible = True
    txtChild2.Visible = True
    txtChild3.Visible = True
    txtAddress.Visible = True
    txtCity.Visible = True
    txtState.Visible = True
    txtZip.Visible = True
    txtHomePhone.Visible = True
    txtCellPhone.Visible = True
    txtEmail.Visible = True
    txtComments.Visible = True

End Sub

Private Sub SetControlsVisibleFalse()

    lblFName.Visible = False
    lblMName.Visible = False
    lblLName.Visible = False
    lblNName.Visible = False
    lblSName.Visible = False
    lblChildren.Visible = False
    lblAddress.Visible = False
    lblCity.Visible = False
```

(continued on next page)

```
                    lblState.Visible = False
                    lblZip.Visible = False
                    lblHomePhone.Visible = False
                    lblCellPhone.Visible = False
                    lblEmail.Visible = False
                    lblComments.Visible = False

                    txtFName.Visible = False
                    txtMName.Visible = False
                    txtLName.Visible = False
                    txtNName.Visible = False
                    txtSName.Visible = False
                    txtChild1.Visible = False
                    txtChild2.Visible = False
                    txtChild3.Visible = False
                    txtAddress.Visible = False
                    txtCity.Visible = False
                    txtState.Visible = False
                    txtZip.Visible = False
                    txtHomePhone.Visible = False
                    txtCellPhone.Visible = False
                    txtEmail.Visible = False
                    txtComments.Visible = False

                 End Sub
```

Page_Load

The Page_Load function is the first function to execute after the controls are initialized, giving you programmatic access to the properties.

Double-clicking anywhere on the Web Form loads the Visual Basic form and creates the Page_Load function. Place the following code into the Page_Load function:

```
SetControlsVisibleFalse()
    SetControlsReadOnly()
    lblMode.Text = "List View"
    lbtnNew.Visible = True
    lbtnEdit.Visible = False
    lbtnEnter.Visible = False
    lbtnCancel.Visible = False
    lbtnDelete.Visible = False
```

Page.IsPostBack

ASP.NET allows access to server control properties and events through the use of PostBack. When the page is posted back to the server, the event associated with the action that posted the page back is executed and so is the Page_Load function. It may not be desirable to execute code in the Page_Load function after the page is initially loaded. You can use the Page.IsPostBack page property to determine if this is the first time the page has loaded or if the Page_Load function is executing as a result of a PostBack.

Add an If Not Page.IsPostBack to the Page_Load function. The end result should look like the following:

```
If Not Page.IsPostBack Then
        SetControlsVisibleFalse()
        SetControlsReadOnly()
           lblMode.Text = "List View"
        lbtnNew.Visible = True
        lbtnEdit.Visible = False
        lbtnEnter.Visible = False
        lbtnCancel.Visible = False
        lbtnDelete.Visible = False
End If
```

Adding Data to the DataGrid

The first thing you need to do is import the namespaces of the data classes that you plan on using. Place these imports statements above the AddressBook class declaration at the top of the page. Be sure to place the sa password after "pwd=" if it is not blank.

```
Imports System.Data
Imports System.Data.SqlClient
Imports System.Text


Public Class AddressBook
```

Add the following code to the AddressBook class to create the PopulateAddressBook function:

```
    Private Sub PopulateAddressBook()

        Dim objConn As SqlConnection
        Dim objCmd As SqlCommand
        Dim objDataAdapter As New SqlDataAdapter()
        Dim objDataSet As New DataSet()
```

(continued on next page)

```
Dim strSQL As String
Dim strConn As String

strSQL = "SELECT id, FName + ' ' + MName + ' ' + LName as [Name], NName,"
strSQL += " Email FROM AddressBook"

strConn = "server=localhost;uid=sa;pwd=;database=addressbook"

objConn = New SqlConnection(strConn)
objConn.Open()

objCmd = New SqlCommand(strSQL, objConn)

objDataAdapter.SelectCommand = objCmd
objDataAdapter.Fill(objDataSet, "AddressBook")

DataGridAddressList.DataSource = objDataSet
DataGridAddressList.DataBind()

End Sub
```

Now that this function is available, go ahead and add it to the Page_Load function. It should look something like this:

```
'Put user code to initialize the page here

If Not Page.IsPostBack Then

    SetControlsVisibleFalse()

    SetControlsReadOnly()

    PopulateAddressBook()

    lblMode.Text = "List View"

    lbtnNew.Visible = True
    lbtnEdit.Visible = False
    lbtnEnter.Visible = False
    lbtnCancel.Visible = False
    lbtnDelete.Visible = False

End If
```

Jazzing up our DataGrid

In design view, right-click on the DataGrid and select Property Builder. Select Columns and you will see the screen that's shown in Figure 9-3.

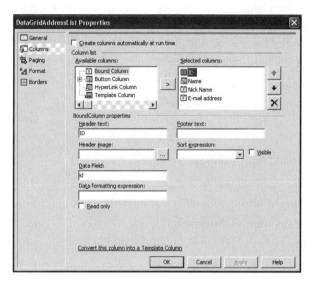

Figure 8-3: The Property Builder of the DataGrid control.

You are going to use this interface to build one nonvisible and three visible columns. You could allow the DataGrid to determine what columns to display automatically, although it is a better practice to control the columns you wish to display.

ID Column

To set the ID, follow these steps:

1. Deselect the "Create columns automatically at run time" checkbox.

2. Select Bound Column and use the ">" symbol to move it into the Selected Columns list box.

3. Deselect the Visible check box.

4. Set Header Text to "ID".

5. Set Data Field to "ID".

Name

To add the name, follow these steps:

1. Add another item to the Selected Columns list box, but this time, expand the Button Column item and select and move the Select item to the Selected Columns list box.

2. Set Header Text to "Name".

3. Set Text Field to "Name".

4. Set Command name to "Select".

5. Set ButtonType to "LinkButton".

Nickname

To add the nickname, follow these steps:

1. Select Bound Column and use the ">" symbol to move it into the Selected Columns list box.

2. Set Header Text to "Nickname".

3. Set Data Field to "NName".

Email Address

To set the email address, follow these steps:

1. Select Bound Column and use the ">" symbol to move it into the Selected Columns list box.

2. Set Header Text to "Email address".

3. Set Data Field to "Email".

Configure Paging

To configure the page, follow these steps:

1. Select the Paging tab.

2. Select the Allow Paging check box.

3. Change page size to 5.

4. Press OK.

SelectedIndexChanged Function

To modify the SelectedIndexChanged function, follow these steps:

1. Switch to the presentation design view and double-click on the DataGrid. This will bring up the SelectedIndexChanged function of the DataGrid.

2. Add the following code to the DataGridAddressList_SelectedIndexChanged. This function is executed when the Name link is selected at runtime. You will notice that some of the functions, for instance "GetContactDetail(strID)", are

not yet defined. Ignore this for now. If you still have functions that are not defined when this exercise is complete, double-check all spellings:

```
Private Sub DataGridAddressList_SelectedIndexChanged(ByVal sender As _
System.Object, ByVal e As System.EventArgs) Handles _
DataGridAddressList.SelectedIndexChanged

SetControlsVisibleTrue()

Dim strID As String

strID = DataGridAddressList.Items(sender.selecteditem.itemIndex).Cells(0).Text
GetContactDetail(strID)

SetControlsReadOnly()

lblMode.Text = "View"

lbtnNew.Visible = True
lbtnEdit.Visible = True
lbtnEnter.Visible = False
lbtnCancel.Visible = True
lbtnDelete.Visible = True

    End Sub
```

ChangedGridPage

When configuring the DataGrid, you allowed paging. Paging is the ability to show only a subset of records in the grid, while allowing for additional records to be displayed when requested by the user. The user can request additional pages by selecting a page number hyperlink at the bottom of the grid. Unfortunately, there is not a property for setting the name of the function to run when the page change event occurs. For the grid control to know what to do, you will need to set the following grid control property within the declaration of the grid control in HTML. The statement you need to add is OnPageIndexChanged="ChangeGridPage". Your HTML page should look something like this:

```
..."<asp:datagrid id="DataGridAddressList" OnPageIndexChanged="ChangeGridPage""...
```

When this page is selected, the ChangedGridPage event occurs.
Build the ChangedGridPage using the following code:

```
Public Sub ChangeGridPage(ByVal sender As Object, ByVal args As _
        DataGridPageChangedEventArgs)

    DataGridAddressList.CurrentPageIndex = args.NewPageIndex

    PopulateAddressBook()

    'The following code is same as lbtnCancel()
    SetControlsVisibleFalse()
    ResetControls()
    SetControlsReadOnly()

    lblMode.Text = "Canceled"

    lbtnNew.Visible = True
    lbtnEdit.Visible = False
    lbtnEnter.Visible = False
    lbtnCancel.Visible = False
    lbtnDelete.Visible = False

End Sub
```

Update Page_Load
It's time to add initialization code for the DataGrid control:

```
Private Sub Page_Load(ByVal sender As System.Object, ByVal e As _
                            System.EventArgs) Handles MyBase.Load
    'Put user code to initialize the page here

    If Not Page.IsPostBack Then

        SetControlsVisibleFalse()

        SetControlsReadOnly()

        DataGridAddressList.CurrentPageIndex = 0
        DataGridAddressList.PageSize = 3
        DataGridAddressList.PagerStyle.Mode = PagerMode.NumericPages
        DataGridAddressList.PagerStyle.NextPageText = "Next"
        DataGridAddressList.PagerStyle.PrevPageText = "Prev"
        PopulateAddressBook()

        lblMode.Text = "List View"
```

```
            lbtnNew.Visible = True
            lbtnEdit.Visible = False
            lbtnEnter.Visible = False
            lbtnCancel.Visible = False
            lbtnDelete.Visible = False

        End If

    End Sub
```

Detailed View

When an address is selected, the detailed contact information will be displayed for view or modification. The function that populates this data is the GetContactDetail function.

Use the following code to create the GetContactDetail function:

```
Private Sub GetContactDetail(ByVal strID As String)

    Dim objConn As SqlConnection
    Dim objCmd As SqlCommand
    Dim objReader As SqlDataReader
    Dim strSQL As String
    Dim strConn As String

    txtID.Text = strID

    strSQL = "SELECT * FROM AddressBook WHERE id=" & strID

    strConn = "server=localhost;uid=sa;pwd=;database=addressbook"

    objConn = New SqlConnection(strConn)
    objConn.Open()

    objCmd = New SqlCommand(STRSQL, objConn)

    objReader = objCmd.ExecuteReader
    objReader.Read()

    If Not IsDBNull(objReader.Item("FName")) Then txtFName.Text = _
        objReader.Item("FName") Else txtFName.Text = ""
    If Not IsDBNull(objReader.Item("MName")) Then txtMName.Text = _
        objReader.Item("MName") Else txtMName.Text = ""
    If Not IsDBNull(objReader.Item("LName")) Then txtLName.Text = _
        objReader.Item("LName") Else txtLName.Text = ""
```

(continued on next page)

```
If Not IsDBNull(objReader.Item("NName")) Then txtNName.Text = _
    objReader.Item("NName") Else txtNName.Text = ""
If Not IsDBNull(objReader.Item("SpouseName")) Then txtSName.Text = _
    objReader.Item("SpouseName") Else txtSName.Text = ""
If Not IsDBNull(objReader.Item("Child1")) Then txtChild1.Text = _
    objReader.Item("Child1") Else txtChild1.Text = ""
If Not IsDBNull(objReader.Item("Child2")) Then txtChild2.Text = _
    objReader.Item("Child2") Else txtChild2.Text = ""
If Not IsDBNull(objReader.Item("Child3")) Then txtChild3.Text = _
    objReader.Item("Child3") Else txtChild3.Text = ""
If Not IsDBNull(objReader.Item("Address")) Then txtAddress.Text = _
    objReader.Item("Address") Else txtAddress.Text = ""
If Not IsDBNull(objReader.Item("City")) Then txtCity.Text = _
    objReader.Item("City") Else txtCity.Text = ""
If Not IsDBNull(objReader.Item("State")) Then txtState.Text = _
    objReader.Item("State") Else txtState.Text = ""
If Not IsDBNull(objReader.Item("Zip")) Then txtZip.Text = _
    objReader.Item("Zip") Else txtZip.Text = ""
If Not IsDBNull(objReader.Item("HomePhone")) Then txtHomePhone.Text = _
    objReader.Item("HomePhone") Else txtHomePhone.Text = ""
If Not IsDBNull(objReader.Item("CellPhone")) Then txtCellPhone.Text = _
    objReader.Item("CellPhone") Else txtCellPhone.Text = ""
If Not IsDBNull(objReader.Item("Email")) Then txtEmail.Text = _
    objReader.Item("Email") Else txtEmail.Text = ""
If Not IsDBNull(objReader.Item("Comments")) Then txtComments.Text = _
    objReader.Item("Comments") Else txtComments.Text = ""


objReader.Close()


End Sub
```

Data Access Functions

Now you are going to implement the data access function along with functions for building insert, update, and delete queries:

```
Private Sub ExecuteQuery(ByVal strSQL As String)

    Dim objConn As SqlConnection
    Dim objCmd As SqlCommand
    Dim strConn As String

    strConn = "server=localhost;uid=sa;pwd=;database=addressbook"

    objConn = New SqlConnection(strConn)
    objConn.Open()
```

```
        objCmd = New SqlCommand(strSQL, objConn)

        objCmd.ExecuteNonQuery()

End Sub
Private Sub InsertRecord()

    Dim strSQL As String

    strSQL = "INSERT AddressBook (FName, MName, LName, " _
        & "NName, SpouseName, Address, City, State, Zip, HomePhone, " _
        & "CellPhone, EMail, Comments, Child1, Child2, Child3) " _
        & "VALUES ('" & txtFName.Text & "', '" & txtMName.Text _
        & "', '" & txtLName.Text & "', '" & txtNName.Text _
        & "', '" & txtSName.Text & "', '" & txtAddress.Text _
        & "', '" & txtCity.Text & "', '" & txtState.Text _
        & "', '" & txtZip.Text & "', '" & txtHomePhone.Text _
        & "', '" & txtCellPhone.Text & "', '" & txtEmail.Text _
        & "', '" & txtComments.Text & "', '" & txtChild1.Text _
        & "', '" & txtChild2.Text & "', '" & txtChild3.Text & "')"

    ExecuteQuery(strSQL)

End Sub

Private Sub UpdateRecord()

    Dim strSQL As String

    strSQL = "UPDATE AddressBook SET " _
            & "FName = '" & txtFName.Text _
            & "', MName = '" & txtMName.Text _
            & "', LName = '" & txtLName.Text _
            & "', NName = '" & txtNName.Text _
            & "', SpouseName = '" & txtSName.Text _
            & "', Address = '" & txtAddress.Text _
            & "', City = '" & txtCity.Text _
            & "', State = '" & txtState.Text _
            & "', Zip = '" & txtZip.Text _
            & "', HomePhone = '" & txtHomePhone.Text _
            & "', CellPhone = '" & txtCellPhone.Text _
            & "', EMail = '" & txtEmail.Text _
            & "', Comments = '" & txtComments.Text _
            & "', Child1 = '" & txtChild1.Text _
            & "', Child2 = '" & txtChild2.Text _
            & "', Child3 = '" & txtChild3.Text _
```

(continued on next page)

```
                            & "' WHERE ID = " & txtID.Text

          ExecuteQuery(strSQL)

    End Sub

    Private Sub DeleteRecord()

        Dim strSQL As String

        strSQL = "DELETE FROM AddressBook WHERE ID = " & txtID.Text

        ExecuteQuery(strSQL)

    End Sub
```

Click Events

The following code is for the click events for the New, Edit, Delete, Enter, and Cancel clicks:

```
    Private Sub lbtnNew_Click(ByVal sender As System.Object, ByVal e As _
                System.EventArgs) Handles lbtnNew.Click

        SetControlsVisibleTrue()
        SetControlsWritable()
        ResetControls()

        'Need to set focus to the txtFName control.

        lblMode.Text = "New"

        lbtnNew.Visible = False
        lbtnEdit.Visible = False
        lbtnEnter.Visible = True
        lbtnCancel.Visible = True
        lbtnDelete.Visible = False

    End Sub

    Private Sub lbtnEdit_Click(ByVal sender As System.Object, ByVal e As _
    System.EventArgs) Handles lbtnEdit.Click

        SetControlsWritable()

        lblMode.Text = "Edit"
```

```
            lbtnNew.Visible = False
            lbtnEdit.Visible = False
            lbtnEnter.Visible = True
            lbtnCancel.Visible = True
            lbtnDelete.Visible = False

    End Sub

    Private Sub lbtnDelete_Click(ByVal sender As System.Object, ByVal e As _
System.EventArgs) Handles lbtnDelete.Click

            SetControlsVisibleFalse()
            SetControlsReadOnly()

            lblMode.Text = "Deleted"

            DeleteRecord()

            PopulateAddressBook()
            ResetControls()

            lblMode.Text = "List View"

            lbtnNew.Visible = True
            lbtnEdit.Visible = False
            lbtnEnter.Visible = True
            lbtnCancel.Visible = True
            lbtnDelete.Visible = False

    End Sub

    Private Sub lbtnEnter_Click(ByVal sender As System.Object, ByVal e As _
System.EventArgs) Handles lbtnEnter.Click

            If Page.IsValid Then

                SetControlsVisibleFalse()
                SetControlsReadOnly()

                If lblMode.Text = "New" Then InsertRecord()
                If lblMode.Text = "Edit" Then UpdateRecord()

                PopulateAddressBook()
                ResetControls()
```

(continued on next page)

```
            lbtnNew.Visible = True
            lbtnEdit.Visible = False
            lbtnEnter.Visible = False
            lbtnCancel.Visible = False

            lblMode.Text = "List View"

        End If

    End Sub

    Private Sub lbtnCancel_Click(ByVal sender As System.Object, ByVal e As _
    System.EventArgs) Handles lbtnCancel.Click
        'Complete

        SetControlsVisibleFalse()
        ResetControls()
        SetControlsReadOnly()

        lblMode.Text = "Canceled"

        lbtnNew.Visible = True
        lbtnEdit.Visible = False
        lbtnEnter.Visible = False
        lbtnCancel.Visible = False
        lbtnDelete.Visible = False

    End Sub
```

SmartNavigation

As you learned earlier in this chapter, SmartNavigation allows you to build applications that seem more like Win32 form applications than a web site.

Add SmartNavigation="True" to the Page declaration of the HTML page. Your end result should look something like this, except it will all be on a single line:

```
<%@ Page Language="vb" SmartNavigation="True" AutoEventWireup="false"
Codebehind="AddressBook.aspx.vb" Inherits="AddressBook.AddressBook"%>
```

Summary

This chapter served only as an introduction that allowed for some hands-on experience. Using what you learned in Chapter 7, "A Visual Basic .NET Crash Course," Visual Basic .NET and the hands-on experience that you gained in this chapter, bundled with tools that are available in Visual Studio .NET should help you get started in building web applications. For a more in-depth look at ASP.NET, take a look at MSDN articles that are available with Visual Studio .NET and at http://msdn.microsoft.com.

9

PROMOTING APPLICATION SCALABILITY

Accessing data is fundamental to the information world; however, the techniques for accessing data can vary depending on an application's specific requirements. Some applications run on a single machine and access data only on that machine, while others are distributed and require a data access model to promote scalability.

This chapter will address the technologies available in .NET that promote application scalability. You'll learn about ADO.NET first, Microsoft's classes for accessing data for .NET applications. Then you'll look at SQL Server 2000 and how to extend the scalability of an application using stored procedures. Finally you'll examine how XML can be used with SQL Server 2000 stored procedures to apply an additional layer of scalability.

The sample code in this chapter is dependent on your completion of the AddressBook sample of Chapter 8, "ASP.NET"; however, you will find this sample application in the Chapter 8 folder of your CD-ROM.

ADO.NET: An Introduction

ADO.NET represents the classes and methods made available by the .NET framework when accessing data. ADO.NET provides all the functionality you need to connect to, retrieve, and modify a data source. ADO.NET's functionality is divided into a set of classes that perform specific data services as follows:

Connection Object: Establishes a connection to a data source.

Command Object: Executes commands against the data source connected to by the connection object.

DataReader Object: Returns data in a read-only/forward-only fashion.

DataAdapter Object: Populates a DataSet with the fill method and can resolve changes to the DataSet back to the data source.

DataSet Object: Holds data in a relational data structure. The DataSet achieves this through collections of objects that define relational data. These collections include table, column, row, and relationship objects.

Probably the most significant difference between ADO.NET's and its predecessor, ADO 2.6, is the plumbing. ADO 2.6 is based on classic COM technology that requires all components using it to enforce binary compatibility. For components to take advantage of ADO.NET they need only understand XML, which is leveraged by ADO.NET to define its data schema, as well as the format used for the storage and transmission of data. Any component that understands XML can receive data from ADO.NET and ADO.NET can understand data transmitted by other platforms as XML.

This separation of data access functionality in ADO.NET allows for data manipulation of the returned DataSet while not actually connecting to the data source. Not only can a DataSet object work independently of a connection, it has no knowledge of a connections existence. The concept will be better explained later in this chapter. Classic ADO could work with record sets independently of a connection; however, this is not the default configuration. Classic ADO 2.6 is a connected model.

The advantage of working with disconnected data is scalability. More concurrent users are able to use an application written in ADO.NET because of its disconnected nature requires less database resources and a reduction in the number of concurrent connections to the database. One scalability killer of the past has been an application's need to remain connected to the data source. Database connections are expensive resources to use, in terms of client and server memory, processing time and network usage.

Performance is another benefit of ADO.NET. Classic ADO converted all data to and from a variant data type. ADO.NET understands how to support data in its original data type and does not require the overhead of data type conversion.

Implementing ADO.NET

Like everything else in the .NET Framework, you must either import the appropriate namespaces or use the fully qualified name of the class you want to create. For example, a fully qualified name of the SqlCommand class is System.Data.SqlClient.SqlCommand while the short name, if the System.Data.SQLClient namespace is imported, is SqlCommand.

The following are the namespaces used to access ADO.NET:

System.Data: Holds ADO.NET data components.

System.Data.OleDb: Holds ADO.NET data classes for the OleDb .NET data provider.

System.Data.SqlClient: Holds ADO.NET data classes for Microsoft SQL Server 7.0 or later. These classes access the Microsoft SQL Server TDS (Tabular Data Stream), thus removing a complete layer of data abstraction and COM interoperability, and greatly improving performance. COM interoperability is used with OleDb because OleDb drivers are COM based.

System.Data.odbc: Holds ADO.NET classes for using ODBC.

Connection Object

The Connection object is a class provided by the .NET Framework that connects the requesting application to the data source. There are currently two flavors of the connection object with a beta for Oracle on the way.

The OleDbConnection class, found in the System.Data.OleDb namespace, supports all OleDb Data Providers. Use the following imports statement and OleDBConnection object when using the OleDb Data providers.

```
Imports System.Data.OleDb
Public Class MyClass
     Dim objConn As OleDbConnection
```

You can also use the class's fully qualified name rather than importing the namespace. (You can access any class in the .NET Framework this way to make your code more readable, especially when classes with the same name exist.)

```
Public Class My Class
     Dim objConn As System.Data.OleDb.OleDbConnection
```

Setting OleDbConnection Properties

The OleDbConnection object's properties can be set or retrieved in code, but they are usually set these through a string passed to the ConnectionString property. Here is an example of a connection string for the OleDbConnection.ConnectionString property. (This connection string will connect you to the AddressBook database we created in Chapter 8, "ASP.NET.")

```
Dim strConn As String
strConn = "Provider=SQLOLEDB;Data Source=localhost;" & _
"Initial Catalog=AddressBook;User Id=sa;Pwd=;"
```

The connection object's required properties are now stored in the strConn string. While there are several other connection properties, you'll learn about the required ones:

Provider: Name of the OleDb data provider, which is a fancy way of saying database driver.

Data Source: This is the name of the server's name where the database resides. This could just as easily be the IP address of the database server.

Initial Catalog: This is the name of the database you want to connect to.

User ID: The User Id for the database you wish to connect with.

Pwd or Password: The user's password of the User Id provided.

Once you set all the required properties you can Open the connection. Following are few ways to build a connection object, then open a database connection.

Building a Connection Object

Let's build a quick and dirty application that won't actually do anything interesting. You'll simply open a database connection and then close it. You'll also use the connection object to extract a database schema.

1. Create a new Visual Basic windows application named "Connection Objects".

2. Add two buttons and a data grid control onto the form. Set the properties of each control, as listed in Table 9-1.

Table 9-1: Control Properties for Connection Objects

Control	Property	Value
Button	ID	btnConnections
	Text	Connection Objects
Button	ID	btnGetOleDbSchemaTable
	Text	GetOleDbSchemaTable
DataGrid	ID	DataGrid1

3. Add the "Imports System.Data.OleDb" statement before the "Public Class Form1 statement" of the Windows Form.

4. Double-click the btnConnections button and build the connection string for each of our connection examples:

```
' These are only a few options for creating and opening a connection
'object.
Dim strConn As String
strConn = "Provider=SQLOLEDB;Data Source=localhost; & _
    "Initial Catalog=AddressBook;User Id=sa;Pwd=;"
```

5. The first connection example creates a new connection by first declaring an object as type OleDbConnection then instantiating it with the connection string:

```
' Option 1
Dim objConn As OleDbConnection
objConn = New OleDbConnection(strConn)
objConn.Open()
objConn.Close()
```

6. Now comment out option 1 and implement option two with the following code to declare and instantiate our connection in a single statement:

```
' Option 2
Dim objConn As OleDbConnection = New OleDbConnection(strConn)
objConn.Open()
objConn.Close()
```

7. Next, comment out option 2 and add option 3. (There is no significant difference between option 2 and 3 except option 3 uses the least code possible.)

```
'Option 3
Dim objConn As New OleDbConnection(strConn)
objConn.Open()
objConn.Close()
```

8. You won't spend any more time on the connection object, but to give you a quick taste of features you may want to look into, add the following code to the `btnGetOleDbSchemaTable` button's click event. Next, double-click the `btnGetOleDbSchemaTable_Click` button and place the following code into it. This will extract data about the add databases, tables, columns, or procedures depending on which option you leave uncommented:

```
' These are only a few options for creating and opening a connection
'object.
Dim strConn As String
strConn = "Provider=SQLOLEDB;Data Source=localhost;Initial " & _
"Catalog=AddressBook;User Id=sa;Pwd=;"
Dim objConn As New OleDbConnection(strConn)
Dim objDataTable As DataTable
Dim objDataSet As DataSet = New DataSet()

objConn.Open()

'Getting Database Schema
objDataTable = objConn.GetOleDbSchemaTable( _
                         'OleDbSchemaGuid.Catalogs, Nothing)
'objDataTable = objConn.GetOleDbSchemaTable( _
                         'OleDbSchemaGuid.Columns, Nothing)
'objDataTable = objConn.GetOleDbSchemaTable( _
                         'OleDbSchemaGuid.Indexes, Nothing)
'objDataTable = objConn.GetOleDbSchemaTable( _
                         'OleDbSchemaGuid.Procedures, Nothing)
'objDataTable = objConn.GetOleDbSchemaTable( _
                         'OleDbSchemaGuid.Tables, Nothing)

objDataSet.Tables.Add(objDataTable)
DataGrid1.DataSource = objDataSet

objConn.Close()
```

9. Now run the application.

SQLConnection

The `SQLConnection` object works very much like the `OleDbConnection` object except that it requires a few minor changes. The namespace for referencing the SQL Connection object is `System.Data.SqlClient`. (When building the connection string, you don't need to specify the provider since the data provider we are using can only work with SQL Server 7 and above.) Your connection string might look something like this:

```
Data Source=localhost;Initial Catalog=AddressBook;User Id=sa;Pwd=;
```

Both the OleDb and SQL data providers can be used for accessing SQL Server 7 and above; however, as mentioned earlier, the SQL-specific provider has more direct access to SQL Server and therefore gives much better performance. If you need to access any other data source, use the OleDb provider or a data provider specific to the desired data source.

Command Object

The command object is used for executing commands against a data source. Like the connection object it comes in two flavors: The `SqlCommand` and `OleDbCommand` objects, which can be accessed through the `System.Data.SqlClient` and `System.Data.OleDb` namespaces respectively. The following object declarations use the fully qualified names of each class, showing their respective locations in the .NET Framework hierarchy:

```
Dim objSqlCommand As System.Data.SqlClient.SqlCommand
Dim objOleDbCommand as System.Data.OleDb.OleDbCommand
```

As with the connection object you can also import the appropriate namespace and use only the class name to declare the object:

```
Imports System.Data.SqlClient.SqlCommand
Public Class Form1
    Dim objSqlCommand as SqlCommand
...
```

The command object can be leveraged to perform different tasks. For example, the `CommandType` property of the command object determines the type of data access command to be performed. You set the `CommandType` property with the `CommandType` enumerator provided by the .NET Framework. Available CommandType enumerations include:

```
CommandType.StoredProcedure
CommandType.TableDirect
CommandType.Text
```

Building a Pass Through Query

Here's an example of how to build and call a pass through query. While this is not how you should build an application in the real world, it is a way to examine the command object and possibly build prototype applications. (We'll discuss this method in more detail as the chapter continues.)

```
' Create a string to hold the connection string then us it
' to instantiate the objConn connection class.
Dim strConn as string
strConn = "Provider=SQLOLEDB;Data Source=localhost;Initial " & _
    "Catalog=AddressBook;User Id=sa;Pwd=;"
Dim objConn As New SqlConnection(strConn)

' Use the connection object to instantiation of the command object.
Dim objCmd As New SqlCommand("SELECT * FROM AddressBook")
objCmd.CommandType = CommandType.Text

' Open the connection.
objConn.Open()

' Run the ExecuteReader method of the command object
objCmd.ExecuteReader(CommandBehavior.CloseConnection)

' Close the connection.
objConn.Close()
```

Notice that the command type used was CommandType.Text. This is an enumerated value used to determine which type of command will be utilized. Each of these CommanType types will be discussed in more detail as well as demonstrated in code:

- **CommandType.StoredProcedure:** Determines that a stored procedure will be executed. The stored procedure name and parameters, if required, must be supplied.

- **CommandType.TableDirect:** Determines that all records of a given table will be returned.

- **CommandType.Text:** Allows the use of pass through like queries to be passed.

You will find this example quite a bit more useful than the previous example because you will be doing much more than simply connecting to a data source. In fact, to retrieve and modify data, all you need to do is to combine the connection and command objects (although you probably don't want to rely on the functionality that is provided by using only these two objects alone). You will also want to leverage the use of the DataReader object to read the data you've retrieved.

NOTE *Don't become completely dependent on limiting the number of ADO.NET classes you master. The DataAdapter and DataSet objects are very powerful and can significantly reduce your* *development time. Learn how to use these objects but remind yourself that just because you can do a thing doesn't mean you should. Learn the appropriate scenarios in which you apply to different data classes. Must of this is covered in the remainer of this chapter.*

To build the pass through query, follow these steps:

1. Create a new Visual Basic Windows Application project named "Command Objects" and apply the following controls and property settings. Use the controls that are listed in Table 9-2 to build the form.

2. Place our imports statement before the Form1 class declaration:

```
Imports System.Data.SqlClient
```

Table 9-2: Control Properties for Command Objects

Control	Property	Value
Label	ID	Label1
	Text	Command Types:
Label	ID	Label2
	Text	Execution Methods:
Button	ID	btnCommandObjects
	Text	Command Objects
Button	ID	btnText
	Text	CommandType.Text
Button	ID	btnTableDirect
	Text	CommandType.TableDirect
Button	ID	btnStoredProcedure
	Text	CommandType.StoredProcedure
Button	ID	btnExecuteNonQuery
	Text	ExecuteNonQuery
Button	ID	btnExecuteReader
	Text	ExecuteReader
Button	ID	btnExecuteScalar
	Text	ExecuteScalar
Button	ID	btnExecuteXMLReader
	Text	ExecuteXMLReader
ComboBox	ID	ComboBox1
	Text	
DataGrid	ID	DataGrid1

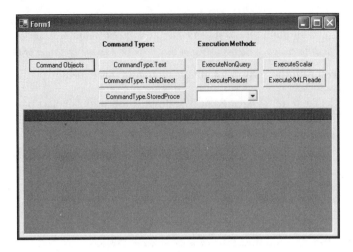

Figure 9-1: Your command object example should look like this.

Command Objects Button

While this doesn't necessarily demonstrate much more than how to properly declare and instantiate the command object, go ahead and place the following code behind the "Command Objects" button:

```
    Dim strConn as string
  strConn = " Data Source=localhost;Initial " & _
    "Catalog=AddressBook;User Id=sa;Pwd=;"
    Dim objConn As New SqlConnection(strConn)

    'Instantiation of the command object.
    Dim objCmd As New SqlCommand("SELECT * FROM AddressBook")
    objCmd.CommandType = CommandType.Text

    objConn.Open()

    objConn.Close()
```

CommandType.Text

The text command type allows you to pass queries through to the data source. This is most often used when performing in-line database calls. Of course, this is not looked upon as a best practice when developing multitiered scalable applications. In fact, this is one of the best ways to eliminate scalability even when you are using compiled code supplied by ASP.NET.

Place the following code behind the "CommandType.Text" button:

```
    Dim strConn as string
strConn = "Data Source=localhost;Initial " & _
    "Catalog=AddressBook;User Id=sa;Pwd=;"
    Dim strSQL As String = "SELECT FName, MName, LName, " & _
                                        "Email FROM AddressBook"

    Dim objConn As New SqlConnection(strConn)
    Dim objCmd As New SqlCommand()
    Dim objDataAdapter As New SqlDataAdapter()
    Dim objDataSet As New DataSet()

    'CommandType.Text
    objCmd.CommandType = CommandType.Text
    objCmd.CommandText = strSQL

    Try
        objDataAdapter.SelectCommand = objCmd
        objDataAdapter.SelectCommand.Connection = objConn
        objConn.Close()
        objDataAdapter.Fill(objDataSet, "AddressBook")

        DataGrid1.SetDataBinding(objDataSet, "AddressBook")

    Catch ex As Exception
        MessageBox.Show(ex.ToString)
    End Try
```

CommandType.TableDirect:

The TableDirect command type pulls all data from a given table. Notice that in this example you are accessing SQL Server with OleDb while the previous examples used the System.Data.SqlClient namespace. This is because the SqlClient classes do not support TableDirect. Rather than importing the appropriate namespace, you are going to explicitly declare your ADO.NET objects by using the fully qualified path of the class. Also, notice that the connection string is a little different. Because you are using OleDb, you must provide the "Provider":

```
    Dim strConn as string
        strConn = "Provider=SQLOLEDB;Data Source=localhost;Initial " & _
    "Catalog=AddressBook;User Id=sa;Pwd=;"
    Dim objConn As New System.Data.OleDb.OleDbConnection(strConn)
    Dim objCmd As New System.Data.OleDb.OleDbCommand()
    Dim objDataAdapter As New System.Data.OleDb.OleDbDataAdapter()
```

(continued on next page)

```
Dim objDataSet As New DataSet()

'CommandType.TableDirect
objCmd.CommandType = CommandType.TableDirect
objCmd.CommandText = "AddressBook"

Try
  objDataAdapter.SelectCommand = objCmd
  objDataAdapter.SelectCommand.Connection = objConn
  objDataAdapter.Fill(objDataSet, "AddressBook")

  DataGrid1.SetDataBinding(objDataSet, "AddressBook")

Catch ex As Exception
  MessageBox.Show(ex.ToString)
End Try
```

CommandType.StoredProcedure

Stored procedures that are provided by SQL Server allow for the most efficient method of data access currently available. Before you can build your stored procedure example, you must have a stored procedure to execute.

Create the stored procedure by following these steps:

1. Open SQL Server Enterprise Manager.
2. Select the AddressBook database and then open Query Analyzer from the Tools menu.
3. Select Open from the file menu, navigate to the "Ch9 Examples" directory on the CD-ROM, select the "ab_GetContactInfo_ssp.sql" file, and press Open.
4. Execute the script by selecting Execute from the Query menu item.

Running the script will drop any stored procedure in the AddressBook database with the same name, then continue to recreate the stored procedure based on the script. The stored procedure will accept one parameter of @FName, allowing you to return all records with whatever first name you specify.

Add the following code to the "btnStoredProcedure" click event. This code will call the "ab_GetContactInfo_ssp.sql" stored procedure passing in the desired first name. Of course, you can create a stored procedure to accept any number of parameters and populate those parameters based on user controls. You simply want to demonstrate how to use the stored procedure itself. Your example will search for any records whose first name is "Tamarah". For you to get a result back, you will need to replace this name with one in your AddressBook database:

```
Dim strConn as string
  strConn = "Data Source=localhost;Initial " & _
"Catalog=AddressBook;User Id=sa;Pwd=;"
Dim objConn As New SqlConnection(strConn)
Dim objCmd As New SqlCommand()
Dim objDataAdapter As New SqlDataAdapter()
Dim objDataSet As New DataSet()
Dim objParamFName As New SqlParameter("@FName", _
SqlDbType.VarChar, 20)
  objParamFName.Direction = ParameterDirection.Input
  objParamFName.Value = "Robert"

  'CommandType.StoredProcedure
  objCmd.CommandType = CommandType.StoredProcedure
  objCmd.CommandText = "ab_GetContactInfo_ssp"
  objCmd.Parameters.Add(objParamFName)

  objCmd.Connection = objConn

Try
  objDataAdapter.SelectCommand = objCmd
  objDataAdapter.Fill(objDataSet, "AddressBook")

  DataGrid1.SetDataBinding(objDataSet, "AddressBook")

Catch ex As Exception
  MessageBox.Show(ex.ToString)
End Try
```

Command Object Execution Methods

As you have discovered, there are a few different command types that can significantly alter what data is returned, if any, and the performance of your data access components. The method of execution that you use is as important as the type of command that you choose. The command object provides four methods for executing commands, each with their own characteristics in terms of the data they return and the type of command they process:

• **ExecuteNonQuery:** This method executes a command while disregarding any potential returned data. This method is used for executing statements such as Insert, Update, and Delete. The number of rows is affected by the executed command returned.

- **ExecuteReader:** This method is used to return read-only or forward-only data records. This can easily be leveraged for populating lists, collections, or list type functions.

- **ExecuteScalar:** This method returns only a single value. All other data that could potentially be returned is ignored. This is helpful when returning a count of records or some calculation returned with a single value.

- **ExecuteXMLReader:** This method returns all data in XML format; however, the data must be requested in XML format for the ExecuteXMLReader method to work (XML AUTO or XML AUTO, ELEMENTS).

You will integrate each of these execution methods into the command objects sample application.

ExecuteNonQuery

You will use the ExecuteNonQuery execution method to insert the first and last names of a contact, "John Smith". After executing this command, click the "CommandType.TableDirect" button to refresh the data grid. You should see the new "John Smith" contact.

Place the following code behind the "ExecuteNonQuery" click event:

```
Dim strConn as string
 strConn = "Data Source=localhost;Initial " & _
"Catalog=AddressBook;User Id=sa;Pwd=;"
 Dim objConn As New SqlConnection(strConn)
Dim strSQL As String = "INSERT AddressBook(FName, LName)" & _
                                    " Values ('John', 'Smith')"


 objConn.Open()

 Dim objCmd As New SqlCommand(strSQL, objConn)
 Dim intResult
 intResult = objCmd.ExecuteNonQuery()


 ' If you want to see the number of rows affected by the
'ExecuteNonQuery execution method simply declare an
   'integer and set this statement equal to the method call
   'intResult = objCmd.ExecuteNonQuery()
```

ExecuteReader

This example will populate a ComboBox control with a DataReader object that you will populate using the ExecuteReader execution method. Place the following code behind the "btnExecuteReader" click event:

```
Dim strConn as string
  strConn = "Data Source=localhost;Initial " & _
"Catalog=AddressBook;User Id=sa;Pwd=;"
Dim strSQL As String = "SELECT FName FROM AddressBook"
Dim objConn As New SqlConnection(strConn)
Dim objCmd As New SqlCommand()

objCmd.CommandType = CommandType.Text
objCmd.CommandText = strSQL
objCmd.Connection = objConn

ComboBox1.Items.Clear()

Try
  objConn.Open()
  Dim objReader As SqlDataReader = _
          objCmd.ExecuteReader(CommandBehavior.CloseConnection)

  Do While objReader.Read
    ComboBox1.Items.Add(objReader(0))
  Loop

Catch ex As Exception
  MessageBox.Show(ex.ToString)
End Try
```

ExecuteScalar

This example will return the number of records that are available in the AddressBook table. Placing the following code in the "btnExecuteScalar" click event will select the number of records in the AddressBook table and display the results on the button itself:

```
Dim strConn as string
  strConn = "Data Source=localhost;Initial " & _
"Catalog=AddressBook;User Id=sa;Pwd=;"
Dim objConn As New SqlConnection(strConn)
Dim strSQL As String = "SELECT COUNT(*) FROM AddressBook"

objConn.Open()
```

(continued on next page)

```
Dim objCmd As New SqlCommand(strSQL, objConn)
Dim intResult
intResult = objCmd.ExecuteScalar

btnExecuteScalar.Text = "ExecuteScalar = " & intResult
```

Click on the "ExecuteNonQuery" button to insert another contact then press the "ExecuteScalar" button again. You will see that the number of records increases by one.

ExecuteXmlReader

This example will execute a query that returns XML data using the "FOR XML AUTO, ELEMENTS" statement. The returned XML data will be returned to a message box. Place the following code behind the "btnExecuteXMLReader" click event:

```
Dim strConn as string
  strConn = "Data Source=localhost;Initial " & _
"Catalog=AddressBook;User Id=sa;Pwd=;"
Dim objConn As New SqlConnection(strConn)
Dim strSQL As String = "SELECT FName, LName, Email" & _
                 " FROM AddressBook FOR XML AUTO, ELEMENTS"

objConn.Open()

Dim objCmd As New SqlCommand(strSQL, objConn)
Dim strResult As String
strResult = objCmd.ExecuteScalar

MessageBox.Show(strResult)
```

DataReader Object

The DataReader object is an ADO.NET object that is designed to retrieve data in a forward-only fashion. The DataReader object is distinguished from the DataSet object in that the DataReader does not actually hold or maintain a record set, but iterates through each record, loading only the current record into memory. When the DataReader moves to the next record, the previous record is removed from memory.

The DataReader object can be declared from one of the following name-spaces depending on the data provider you have chosen:

- System.Data.OleDb
- System.Data.SqlClient
- System.Data.odbc

The DataReader object is instantiated by the ExecuteReader of the Command object:

```
objDataReader = objCmd.ExecuteReader
```

The only objects that are required to access data with the DataReader object are the connection and command objects and, of course, the DataReader object as shown in Figure 9-2.

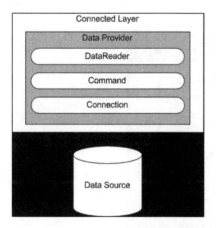

Figure 9-2: The DataReader object within the ADO.NET model.

DataReader Object Example

Our DataReader object example really doesn't do much except demonstrate some basic uses of the DataReader object. It will not have a full-blown user interface. In fact, one of the command buttons sends its output to the Visual Studio .NET Output window:

1. Create a new Visual Basic .NET windows application and name it "DataReader Objects".

2. Place the following imports statement before the Form1 class declaration:

```
Imports System.Data.SQLClient
```

3. Drag-and-drop three command buttons and a single combo box onto the form and set the properties that are listed in Table 9-3.

Table 9-3: Control Properties for DataReader Objects

Control	Property	Value
Button	ID	btnDRInitialize
	Text	DataReader Initialization
Button	ID	btnDRComboBox
	Text	Populate a Combo Box with DR
Button	ID	btnDataType
	Text	Explicitly requesting data and type.
ComboBox	ID	ComboBox1
	Text	

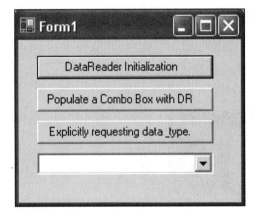

Figure 9-3: The DataReader sample application.

Initializing the DataReader Object

Place the following code into the "btnDRInitialize" click event. This will simply demonstrate how to initialize the DataReader object:

```
Dim strConn as string
   strConn = "Data Source=localhost;Initial " & _
"Catalog=AddressBook;User Id=sa;Pwd=;"
Dim strSQL As String = "SELECT FName FROM AddressBook"
Dim objConn As New SqlConnection(strConn)
Dim objCmd As New SqlCommand()
```

```
objCmd.CommandType = CommandType.Text
objCmd.CommandText = strSQL
objCmd.Connection = objConn

objConn.Open()

Dim objReader As SqlDataReader = _
        objCmd.ExecuteReader(CommandBehavior.CloseConnection)
```

The DataReader object makes use of an open connection and, in fact, cannot operate without it. After the connection is closed, you may access properties and output parameters; however, you cannot access data at all. The DataReader is designed for high-performance but should be used appropriately, otherwise the DataReader can actually hinder performance. If a connection is held open any longer than absolutely necessary, server memory and network resources are wasted and could possibly impact the performance of other applications that share the same network or database resources.

The DataReader is not ideal for all data access scenarios. You do not want to use the DataReader object when accessing a large number of records because the connection will be held open for a long period of time. Also, if additional filtering, sorting, and searching are required, the DataReader should not be used. One reason is that the DataReader reads data as it comes and cannot sort the returning data. Another reason is while filtering can be achieved programmatically and searching can be achieved with multiple data scans, using the DataReader will waste unnecessary server and network resources when other ADO.NET objects, such as the DataSet object, are designed for these scenarios.

While the DataReader object is not ideal for all situations, it is designed for low overhead and high-performance when accessing a relatively small number of records. Populating drop-down boxes or any list, collection, or list control are all ideal situations for using the DataReader. Often an application requires only a row of data, similar to the sample application, AddressBook, where detailed information about a specific contact is displayed. This is also an ideal place to take advantage of the high performing nature of the DataReader object.

Another way to take advantage of the DataReader object is when populating multiple lists. The DataReader has the ability to read multiple result sets from a single database call. To learn more about accessing multiple result sets with the DataReader object, refer to MSDN online. The ability to access multiple result sets is huge because the connection object only needs to be opened once and all metadata for any given page can be stored in a single stored procedure, promoting code organization. A single stored procedure can be related to a given page for application metadata.

Populate ComboBox Example

The following code is an example of how you might use a DataReader to populate a combo box.

Insert the code into the "btnDRComboBox" click event:

```
Dim strConn as string
  strConn = "Data Source=localhost;Initial " & _
"Catalog=AddressBook;User Id=sa;Pwd=;"
Dim strSQL As String = "SELECT FName FROM AddressBook"
  Dim objConn As New SqlConnection(strConn)
Dim objCmd As New SqlCommand()

objCmd.CommandType = CommandType.Text
objCmd.CommandText = strSQL
objCmd.Connection = objConn

ComboBox1.Items.Clear()

Try
  objConn.Open()
  Dim objReader As SqlDataReader = _
           objCmd.ExecuteReader(CommandBehavior.CloseConnection)

  Do While objReader.Read
    ComboBox1.Items.Add(objReader(0))
  Loop

Catch ex As Exception
  MessageBox.Show(ex.ToString)
End Try
```

DataReader Performance Tips

- Don't use the DataReader object for large sets of data.
- Open the connection just before it is needed and close the connection as soon as possible.
- Use multiple result sets whenever possible; for example, when you are populating multiple combo boxes or drop down lists.
- Use the ordinal rather than the string name of a column when retrieving values. The DataReader must call an additional method to locate the correct ordinal of the column if only the column's name is provided.
- The DataReader object allows you to specify the data type of the data you are requesting. This increases performance by reducing unnecessary data conversions by the DataReader.

To demonstrate the use of this feature place the following code into the "btnDataType" click event. The result of the DataReader will be displayed in the Output window. As a quick and dirty example, this example will select the Id, FName, and LName columns and access their data by requesting the data from the DataReader in their native data types. (For more information on OleDb and SQL Server data types, refer to MSDN online.)

```
Dim strConn as string
   strConn = "Data Source=localhost;Initial " & _
"Catalog=AddressBook;User Id=sa;Pwd=;"
Dim strSQL As String = "SELECT id, FName, LName FROM AddressBook"
Dim objConn As New SqlConnection(strConn)
Dim objCmd As New SqlCommand()

objCmd.CommandType = CommandType.Text
objCmd.CommandText = strSQL
objCmd.Connection = objConn

Try
  objConn.Open()
  Dim objReader As SqlDataReader = _
            objCmd.ExecuteReader(CommandBehavior.CloseConnection)

  While objReader.Read()
    Console.WriteLine((objReader.GetInt32(0) & ", " & _
            objReader.GetString(1)) & ", " & objReader.GetString(2))
  End While


Catch ex As Exception
  MessageBox.Show(ex.ToString)
End Try
```

Second Look at the AddressBook Example

Open up your AddressBook sample application. Take a look at the "GetContactDetail" function. Notice that you are using the DataReader. Two methods that will improve the read performance of your contacts detail information is to first request each data item explicitly by its native data type, and second, referencing each item by its ordinal. All of the data types are string so you can use "GetString":

```
For example:
If Not IsDBNull(objReader.Item(1)) Then txtFName.Text = _
 objReader.GetString(1) Else txtFName.Text = ""
```

DataAdapter Object

The DataAdapter object is used to populate the DataSet object with data and can be used to resolve changes to a DataSet back to the database.

The DataSet object, discussed later in this chapter, is essentially a disconnected database object, whose data connectivity is through the DataAdapter. The benefit of disconnecting the DataSet object from the data source becomes clear once you begin to use multiple types of data sources for data maintained and related to within the same DataSet object. This would not be possible if the DataSet object connected to a data source.

DataAdapter Object Initialization

You are going to continue using the SQL Server data provider; however, you may choose to utilize the OleDb data provider. The fully qualified names of the DataAdapter objects are:

```
System.Data.OleDb.OleDbDataAdapter
System.Data.SqlClient.SqlDataAdapter
```

As usual, verify that the appropriate namespace is imported:

```
Imports System.Data.SqlClient
```

The DataAdapter depends on the Command object which, in turn, depends on the Connection object (Figure 9-4).

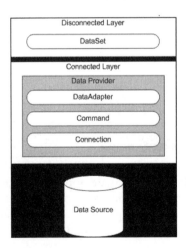

Figure 9-4: The DataAdapter object within the ADO.NET model.

The following code is not a working example of how to use the DataAdapter object; however, the objects demonstrated here are all required in order to use the DataAdapter. This example simply shows how to initialize the DataAdapter using the command object:

```
Dim objConn As New SqlConnection(strConn)
Dim objCmd As New SqlCommand()
Dim objDataAdapter.SelectCommand = objCmd
objCmd.Connection = objConn
objDataAdapter.SelectCommand = objCmd
```

Another way to instantiate the DataAdapter is to instantiate it with no parameters and then set each individual property. The connection and command objects are already created:

```
Dim objDataAdapter As New SqlDataAdapter
objDataAdapter.SelectCommand = objCmd
objDataAdapter.SelectCommand.Connection = objConn
```

Another way to instantiate a DataAdapter object is by providing string data in place of what the connection and command objects would provide:

```
Dim objDataAdapter As New SqlDataAdapter( _
    "SELECT * FROM Addressbook", _
    "Data Source=localhost;Initial Catalog=AddressBook;" & _
    "User Id=sa;Pwd=;"
```

DataAdapter Object Example

All we are going to do with this project is fill a DataSet using the DataAdapter and use the DataSet as the source for a DataGrid:

1. Create a new Visual Basic .NET windows application and name it "DataAdapter Objects".

2. Drag-and-drop one command button and a single DataGrid onto the form and set the properties that are listed in Table 9-4.

Table 9-4: Control Properties for DataAdapter Objects

Control	Property	Value
Button	ID	btnDAExample
	Text	Using the DataAdapter object to populate a DataSet object
DataGrid	ID	DataGrid1

Everything that you need to populate the DataGrid is in the click event of the "btnDAExample" button:

1. Add the imports statement for SQL Server data objects:

```
Imports System.Data.SqlClient
```

2. Place this code behind the "btnDAExample" click event:

```
Dim strConn as string
  strConn = "Data Source=localhost;Initial " & _
"Catalog=AddressBook;User Id=sa;Pwd=;"
Dim objConn As New SqlConnection(strConn)
Dim objCmd As New SqlCommand()
Dim objDataAdapter As New SqlDataAdapter()
Dim objDataSet As New DataSet()

objCmd.CommandType = CommandType.StoredProcedure
objCmd.CommandText = "ab_GetAllContactInfo_ssp"

objCmd.Connection = objConn

Try

    objDataAdapter.SelectCommand = objCmd
    objDataAdapter.Fill(objDataSet, "AddressBook")

    DataGrid1.SetDataBinding(objDataSet, "AddressBook")

Catch ex As Exception
  MessageBox.Show(ex.ToString)
End Try
```

DataAdapter Fill Method

The Fill method of the `DataAdapter` is used to fill a DataSet table with a set of data. The Fill method, however, works in coordination with the SelectCommand property.

From your earlier example, you can see how the DataAdapter fills the "AddressBook" table of the DataSet:

```
objDataAdapter.SelectCommand = objCmd
objDataAdapter.Fill(objDataSet, "AddressBook")
```

In this case, the first parameter holds the name of the DataSet object that is populated and the second parameter is the name of the DataTable object that receives the data. The Fill method is overloaded, so feel free to use the signature that best meets your needs.

The DataAdapter also has the capability to read and write XML data for the DataSet object. You will learn about this in more detail when the DataSet object is discussed in the next section.

Resolving Changes

The DataAdapter object provides facilities for resolving changes back to the data source. These features are not covered here; however, you may want to take a look at the `InsertCommand`, `UpdateCommand`, and `DeleteCommand` properties of the DataAdapter. Approach these features with caution as they do not easily promote scalability and can be misused easily. Remember that as you include additional abstraction and automation, as provided by these features, you also reduce performance and scalability.

DataSet Object

As shown previously in Table 9-4, the DataSet object represents the disconnected layer of ADO.NET. More importantly, it represents data in a relational model. Don't mistake the DataSet for a record set because while a DataSet object is similar to the classic ADO data shape, it more resembles relational data.

The DataSet object holds a collection of objects such as the DataTable, DataColumn, DataRow, and DataRelation objects. When they are combined, an accurate representation of relational data can be created, persisted, and transmitted using the DataSet objects.

There are specific advantages of using a DataSet to store relational data. In situations in which a client application will use data from several database tables, the DataSet object can persist data on the client, reducing the number of network calls required to satisfy the client application's needs. Another important and probably more significant advantage of the DataSet object is the ability to pull data from multiple sources and then relate that data in memory much in the same way a database relates tables. This can be, in many cases, the only way to successfully relate incompatible data sources.

Another advantage is the ability to work with XML. XML data can be used to fill a DataSet object and XML data can be easily extracted from a DataSet. In fact, when a DataSet object is passed between layers or transmitted across the Internet, what is actually transmitted is the XML representation of the DataSet. This promotes cross-platform independence as .NET applications can freely communicate with applications that understand XML.

Quick Look at the AddressBook

The AddressBook application used a DataSet object and `DataTable` to bind to the DataGrid control. In your AddressBook code, these are the objects that are used:

```
Dim objConn As SqlConnection
Dim objCmd As SqlCommand
Dim objDataAdapter As New SqlDataAdapter()
Dim objDataSet As New DataSet()

Dim strSQL As String
Dim strConn As String
```

The objects that are required for using the Fill method to populate DataSet objects are the connection, command, DataAdapter, and DataSet objects (Figure 9-5).

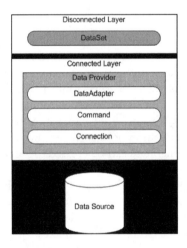

Figure 9-5: The DataSet object within the ADO.NET model.

Once you have declared all of your objects, you can populate your connection and SQL strings and then open the connection:

```
    strSQL = "SELECT id, FName + ' ' + MName + ' ' + LName" & _
" as [Name], NName,"
    strSQL += " Email FROM AddressBook"

    strConn = "server=localhost;uid=sa;pwd=;database=addressbook"

    objConn = New SqlConnection(strConn)
    objConn.Open()
```

Next, you pass the connection object and SQL string to a new Command object:

```
objCmd = New SqlCommand(strSQL, objConn)
```

Notice the next couple lines. Here you are telling the DataAdapter that it is selecting data and passing in our command object. From here, the DataAdapter has everything it needs to populate a DataSet table using the Fill method. The first parameter is the DataSet object and the second parameter is the name of the DataTable object we wish to fill:

```
objDataAdapter.SelectCommand = objCmd
objDataAdapter.Fill(objDataSet, "AddressBook")
```

If you think that was easy, take a look at the last two lines of code. Binding the DataSet objects to a DataGrid control is a two-step process. First, set the DataSet object as the DataGrid source, then use the DataBind method to bind the data:

```
DataGridAddressList.DataSource = objDataSet
DataGridAddressList.DataBind()
```

DataSet Object Example

This example of the DataSet object is a bit more complicated. You will be using objects that are outside the scope of this book. In this example, you will take data from two different data sources, relate them in memory, then display the results, and finally export the resulting relationship as XML:

1. Create a new Visual Basic .NET windows application and name it "DataSet Objects".

2. Drag-and-drop four command Buttons, one DataGrid, and one TextBox onto the form and set the properties that are listed in Table 9-5.

Table 9-5: Control Properties for DataSet Objects

Control	Property	Value
Button	ID	btnBuildDataSetFromExcel
	Text	Build DataSet From Excel
Button	ID	btnDataSetFromSQL
	Text	Build DataSet from SQL Server
Button	ID	btnBuildDataRelationship
	Text	Build Data Relationship
Button	ID	btnExtractXML
	Text	Extract XML from Related Data
DataGrid	ID	DataGrid1
TextBox	ID	TextBox1
	Multiline	True

Your application should look something like Figure 9-6.

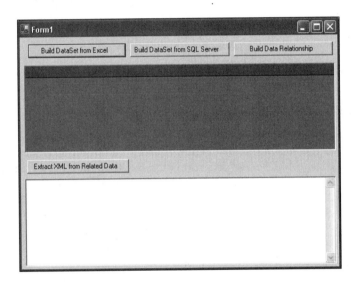

Figure 9-6: The DataSet.

Now you need to build an Excel file. Copy the Excel file from the "Ch9 Examples" directory from the website for this book at http://www.nostarch.com/vsdotnet.htm to anywhere on your hard drive. Open the Excel file and modify it so that the data in the Excel file relates to the data in your AddressBook.

First Column
The first column must be numbered incrementally, beginning with 1.

Second Column

The second column is the important one. You'll need to open up SQL Server Enterprise Manager and view the data of the AddressBook table to determine what value to store in this column. The Excel document will actually hold notes about contacts in your AddressBook. The Id column of the AddressBook table is related to the AddressBook_Id column of the Excel document.

Notice that the AddressBook_Id column has 1 in Column B Cell 2 and also a 1 in Column B Cell 3. Both of these columns relate to the first record in the image of the AddressBook table on the left. Go ahead and look at your data and add notes to your Excel document.

Figure 9-7: The SQL Server Enterprise Manager view of data.

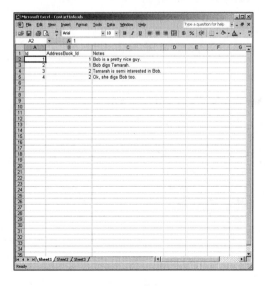

Figure 9-8: The Excel view of data.

Third Column

Go ahead and place your comments in the third column.

Building a DataSet Table from Excel

Place the following code behind the "btnBuildDataSetFromExcel" click event. This will access your Excel document as if it were a database and populate the DataSet. From that point, the client application has no idea where the data came from, only that is exists in a format it understands. You will need to change the path to the Excel document to the path of your Excel document.

```
Dim objConnection As OleDb.OleDbConnection
Dim objCmd As OleDb.OleDbCommand
Dim objDataAdapter As OleDb.OleDbDataAdapter
Dim objDataSet As New DataSet()
Dim strConn As String

strConn = "Provider=Microsoft.Jet.OLEDB.4.0;Data " & _
      "Source=C:\ContactInfo.xls; " & _
      "Extended Properties=Excel 8.0;"

objConnection = New OleDb.OleDbConnection(strConn)
objCmd = New OleDb.OleDbCommand("Select * from [sheet1$]", _
                                         objConnection)

objDataAdapter = New OleDb.OleDbDataAdapter(objCmd)

Try
  objConnection.Open()
  objDataAdapter.Fill(objDataSet, "Notes")
  DataGrid1.SetDataBinding(objDataSet, "Notes")
Catch ex As Exception
  MessageBox.Show(ex.ToString)
End Try
```

Building a DataSet Table from SQL Server

Place the following code behind the "btnDataSetFromSQL" click event:

```
Dim objConn As SqlClient.SqlConnection
Dim objCmd As SqlClient.SqlCommand
Dim objDataAdapter As New SqlClient.SqlDataAdapter()
Dim objDataSet As New DataSet()
Dim strSQL As String
Dim strConn As String
```

```
strSQL = "SELECT id, FName + ' ' + MName + ' ' + " & _
                    "LName as [Name], NName,"
strSQL += " Email FROM AddressBook"

strConn = "server=localhost;uid=sa;pwd=;database=addressbook"

objConn = New System.Data.SqlClient.SqlConnection(strConn)
objConn.Open()

objCmd = New System.Data.SqlClient.SqlCommand(strSQL, objConn)

objDataAdapter.SelectCommand = objCmd
objDataAdapter.Fill(objDataSet, "AddressBook")

DataGrid1.SetDataBinding(objDataSet, "AddressBook")
```

Building the Relationship

Now this is when things become a little more interesting. In this example, you will be calling nearly the same code for populating your DataSet object as was used in the previous two command buttons. Then you'll create two DataColumn objects and finally a DataRelation object to solidify the relationship between the DataTables.

Place the following code behind the "btnBuildDataRelationship" click event:

```
'The DataSet object will be used by both SQL Server and Excel
Dim objDataSet As New DataSet()


'************************************************
'Getting data from the Excel document.
'************************************************
Dim objConnection1 As OleDb.OleDbConnection
Dim objCmd1 As OleDb.OleDbCommand
Dim objDataAdapter1 As OleDb.OleDbDataAdapter
Dim strConn1 As String

strConn1 = "Provider=Microsoft.Jet.OLEDB.4.0;Data " & _
      "Source=C:\ContactInfo.xls; " & _
      "Extended Properties=Excel 8.0;"

objConnection1 = New OleDb.OleDbConnection(strConn1)
objCmd1 = New OleDb.OleDbCommand( _
                        "Select * from [sheet1$]", objConnection1)

objDataAdapter1 = New OleDb.OleDbDataAdapter(objCmd1)
```

(continued on next page)

```
Try
  objConnection1.Open()
  objDataAdapter1.Fill(objDataSet, "Notes")
  objConnection1.Close()
Catch ex As Exception
  MessageBox.Show(ex.ToString)
End Try


'************************************************
'Getting data from SQL Server
'************************************************


Dim objConn2 As System.Data.SqlClient.SqlConnection
Dim objCmd2 As System.Data.SqlClient.SqlCommand
Dim objDataAdapter2 As New System.Data.SqlClient.SqlDataAdapter()
Dim strSQL2 As String
Dim strConn2 As String

strSQL2 = "SELECT CAST(id AS FLOAT) as id, FName +" & _
" ' ' + MName + ' ' + LName as [Name], NName," & _
" Email FROM AddressBook"

strConn2 = "server=localhost;uid=sa;pwd=;database=addressbook"

objConn2 = New System.Data.SqlClient.SqlConnection(strConn2)
objConn2.Open()

objCmd2 = New System.Data.SqlClient.SqlCommand(strSQL2, objConn2)

objDataAdapter2.SelectCommand = objCmd2
objDataAdapter2.Fill(objDataSet, "AddressBook")


'************************************************
'Relating Tables
'************************************************


Dim objDataColumn1Fk As New DataColumn( _
                          "AddressBook_Id")
objDataColumn1Fk = objDataSet.Tables( _
                      "Notes").Columns("AddressBook_Id")

Dim objDataColumn2Pk As New DataColumn("id")
objDataColumn2Pk = objDataSet.Tables("AddressBook").Columns("id")

Try
  Dim col1 As DataColumn
```

```
        Dim objDataRelation As New DataRelation( _
                "Contact Notes", objDataColumn2Pk, objDataColumn1Fk, True)


        objDataSet.Relations.Add(objDataRelation)


    Catch ex As Exception
        MessageBox.Show(ex.ToString)
    End Try
    '**********************************************
    'Populating Grid.
    '**********************************************


    Try
        DataGrid1.DataSource = objDataSet
    Catch ex As Exception
        MessageBox.Show(ex.ToString)
    End Try
```

Extracting XML

Place the following code behind the "**btnExtractXML**" click event:

```
    Dim objDataSet As New DataSet()


    '**********************************************
    'Getting data from the Excel document.
    '**********************************************
    Dim objConnection1 As OleDb.OleDbConnection
    Dim objCmd1 As OleDb.OleDbCommand
    Dim objDataAdapter1 As OleDb.OleDbDataAdapter
    Dim strConn1 As String


    strConn1 = "Provider=Microsoft.Jet.OLEDB.4.0;Data " & _
        "Source=C:\ContactInfo.xls; " & _
        "Extended Properties=Excel 8.0;"


    objConnection1 = New OleDb.OleDbConnection(strConn1)
    objCmd1 = New OleDb.OleDbCommand( _
                    "Select * from [sheet1$]", objConnection1)


    objDataAdapter1 = New OleDb.OleDbDataAdapter(objCmd1)


    Try
        objConnection1.Open()
        objDataAdapter1.Fill(objDataSet, "Notes")
        objConnection1.Close()
```

(continued on next page)

```vb
Catch ex As Exception
   MessageBox.Show(ex.ToString)
End Try


'**************************************************
'Getting data from SQL Server
'**************************************************


Dim objConn2 As System.Data.SqlClient.SqlConnection
Dim objCmd2 As System.Data.SqlClient.SqlCommand
Dim objDataAdapter2 As New System.Data.SqlClient.SqlDataAdapter()
Dim strSQL2 As String
Dim strConn2 As String

strSQL2 = "SELECT CAST(id AS FLOAT) as id, FName +" & _
          " ' ' + MName + ' ' + LName as [Name], NName, "
strSQL2 += " Email FROM AddressBook"

strConn2 = "server=localhost;uid=sa;pwd=;database=addressbook"

objConn2 = New System.Data.SqlClient.SqlConnection(strConn2)
objConn2.Open()

objCmd2 = New System.Data.SqlClient.SqlCommand(strSQL2, objConn2)

objDataAdapter2.SelectCommand = objCmd2
objDataAdapter2.Fill(objDataSet, "AddressBook")


'**************************************************
'Relating Tables
'**************************************************


Dim objDataColumn1Fk As New DataColumn("AddressBook_Id")
objDataColumn1Fk = _
        objDataSet.Tables("Notes").Columns("AddressBook_Id")

Dim objDataColumn2Pk As New DataColumn("id")
objDataColumn2Pk = objDataSet.Tables("AddressBook").Columns("id")

Try
   Dim col1 As DataColumn

   Dim objDataRelation As New DataRelation( _
           "Contact Notes", objDataColumn2Pk, objDataColumn1Fk, True)

   objDataSet.Relations.Add(objDataRelation)
```

```
Catch ex As Exception
  MessageBox.Show(ex.ToString)
End Try
'************************************************
'Populating Grid.
'************************************************

Try
  TextBox1.Text = ""
  TextBox1.Text = objDataSet.GetXml
Catch ex As Exception
  MessageBox.Show(ex.ToString)
End Try
```

Stored Procedures

Stored procedures are SQL Server database objects that store and execute scripts or groups of scripts as batches. The scripting language supported by stored procedures is Transact SQL or T-SQL.

All applications should perform data access exclusively through stored procedures when using SQL Server. Stored procedures are precompiled code. You need to understand this point. You will not find compiled binary files that are compiled stored procedures anywhere on an SQL Server. The fact is that stored procedures are not actually compiled. The query plan, created the first time the stored procedure is run, is stored in memory so that the next time the stored procedure is run, a query plan does not need to be created again. This precompiled query plan greatly increases performance.

You will create stored procedures to replace the data access code in your AddressBook example. The stored procedures that are needed to replace the data access for our AddressBook will be relatively simple as compared to the work they perform in real-life applications. It's not uncommon for a stored procedure to be as large as forty to fifty pages.

Upgrading to Stored Procedures

The first thing you must do before upgrading the AddressBook application to use stored procedures is to create the stored procedures.

Running Stored Procedure Scripts

You will find the following stored procedure scripts in the "Ch9 Examples" directory on the CD-ROM. Open and execute these scripts with SQL Server Query Analyzer:

- ab_GetAddressBookInfo_ssp.sql
- ab_GetContactDetailInfo_ssp.sql
- ab_InsertContact_isp.sql
- ab_UpdateContact_usp.sql
- ab_DeleteContact_dsp.sql

ab_GetAddressBookInfo_ssp

Use the following code to create the new stored procedure:

```
if exists (select * from dbo.sysobjects where id =
object_id(N'[dbo].[ab_GetAddressBookInfo_ssp]') and OBJECTPROPERTY(id,
N'IsProcedure') = 1)
drop procedure [dbo].[ab_GetAddressBookInfo_ssp]
GO
SET QUOTED_IDENTIFIER OFF
GO
SET ANSI_NULLS OFF
GO
CREATE PROCEDURE dbo.ab_GetAddressBookInfo_ssp
 AS
SELECT id, FName + ' ' + MName + ' ' + LName as [Name], NName, Email FROM
AddressBook ORDER BY FName
GO
SET QUOTED_IDENTIFIER OFF
GO
SET ANSI_NULLS ON
GO
```

ab_GetContactDetailInfo_ssp

Use the following code to create the new stored procedure:

```
if exists (select * from dbo.sysobjects where id =
object_id(N'[dbo].[ab_GetContactDetailInfo_ssp]') and OBJECTPROPERTY(id,
N'IsProcedure') = 1)
drop procedure [dbo].[ab_GetContactDetailInfo_ssp]
GO
SET QUOTED_IDENTIFIER OFF
GO
```

```
SET ANSI_NULLS OFF
GO
CREATE PROCEDURE dbo.ab_GetContactDetailInfo_ssp
@intID int
 AS
SELECT * FROM AddressBook WHERE id=@intID
GO
SET QUOTED_IDENTIFIER OFF
GO
SET ANSI_NULLS ON
GO
```

....

ab_InsertContact_isp

Use the following code to create the new stored procedure:

....

```
if exists (select * from dbo.sysobjects where id =
object_id(N'[dbo].[ab_InsertContact_isp]') and OBJECTPROPERTY(id, N'IsProcedure') =
1)
drop procedure [dbo].[ab_InsertContact_isp]
GO
SET QUOTED_IDENTIFIER OFF
GO
SET ANSI_NULLS OFF
GO
CREATE PROCEDURE dbo.ab_InsertContact_isp
@strFName varchar(20),
@strMName varchar(20),
@strLName varchar(20),
@strNName varchar(20),
@strSName varchar(50),
@strAddress varchar(50),
@strCity varchar(50),
@strState varchar(2),
@strZip varchar(10),
@strHomePhone varchar(14),
@strCellPhone varchar(14),
@strEmail varchar(100),
@strComments varchar(8000),
@strChild1 varchar(20),
@strChild2 varchar(20),
@strChild3 varchar(20)
 AS
INSERT AddressBook (FName, MName, LName,
                    NName, SpouseName, Address,
                City, State, Zip, HomePhone,
```

(continued on next page)

```
                    CellPhone, EMail, Comments,
                Child1, Child2, Child3)
        VALUES (@strFName, @strMName,
            @strLName, @strNName,
            @strSName, @strAddress,
            @strCity, @strState, @strZip,
            @strHomePhone, @strCellPhone,
            @strEmail , @strComments,
            @strChild1, @strChild2, @strChild3 )
GO
SET QUOTED_IDENTIFIER OFF
GO
SET ANSI_NULLS ON
GO
```

ab_UpdateContact_usp

Use the following code to create the new stored procedure:

```
if exists (select * from dbo.sysobjects where id =
object_id(N'[dbo].[ab_UpdateContact_usp]') and OBJECTPROPERTY(id, N'IsProcedure') =
1)
drop procedure [dbo].[ab_UpdateContact_usp]
GO
SET QUOTED_IDENTIFIER OFF
GO
SET ANSI_NULLS OFF
GO
CREATE PROCEDURE dbo.ab_UpdateContact_usp
@strFName varchar(20),
@strMName varchar(20) = '',
@strLName varchar(20),
@strNName varchar(20) = '',
@strSName varchar(50) = '',
@strAddress varchar(50) = '',
@strCity varchar(50) = '',
@strState varchar(2) = '',
@strZip varchar(10) = '',
@strHomePhone varchar(14) = '',
@strCellPhone varchar(14) = '',
@strEmail varchar(100) = '',
@strComments varchar(8000) = '',
@strChild1 varchar(20) = '',
@strChild2 varchar(20) = '',
@strChild3 varchar(20) = '',
@intID int
  AS
```

```
UPDATE AddressBook
SET      FName = @strFName,
      MName = @strMName,
      LName = @strLName,
      NName = @strNName,
      SpouseName = @strSName,
      Address = @strAddress,
      City = @strCity,
      State = @strState,
      Zip =@strZip ,
      HomePhone = @strHomePhone,
      CellPhone = @strCellPhone,
      EMail = @strEmail,
      Comments = @strComments,
      Child1 = @strChild1,
      Child2 = @strChild2,
      Child3 = @strChild3
WHERE id = @intID
GO
SET QUOTED_IDENTIFIER OFF
GO
SET ANSI_NULLS ON
GO
```

ab_DeleteContact_dsp

Use the following code to create the new stored procedure:

```
if exists (select * from dbo.sysobjects where id =
object_id(N'[dbo].[ab_DeleteContact_dsp]') and OBJECTPROPERTY(id, N'IsProcedure') =
1)
drop procedure [dbo].[ab_DeleteContact_dsp]
GO
SET QUOTED_IDENTIFIER OFF
GO
SET ANSI_NULLS OFF
GO
CREATE PROCEDURE dbo.ab_DeleteContact_dsp
@intID int
AS
DELETE FROM AddressBook Where id = @intID
GO
SET QUOTED_IDENTIFIER OFF
GO
SET ANSI_NULLS ON
GO
```

Creating the New SP_GetAddressBookInfo Function

```
Private Sub SP_GetAddressBookInfo()

    Dim strConn As String = "Data Source=localhost;Initial " & _
                            "Catalog=AddressBook;User Id=sa;Pwd=;"
    Dim objConn As New SqlConnection(strConn)
    Dim objCmd As New SqlCommand()
    Dim objDataAdapter As New SqlDataAdapter()
    Dim objDataSet As New DataSet()

    'CommandType.StoredProcedure
    objCmd.CommandType = CommandType.StoredProcedure
    objCmd.CommandText = "ab_GetAddressBookInfo_ssp"

    objCmd.Connection = objConn

    objDataAdapter.SelectCommand = objCmd
    objDataAdapter.Fill(objDataSet, "AddressBook")

    DataGridAddressList.DataSource = objDataSet
    DataGridAddressList.DataBind()

End Sub
```

Creating the New SP_GetContactDetailInfo function

```
Private Sub SP_GetContactDetailInfo(ByVal strID As String)

    txtID.Text = strID

    Dim strConn As String = "Data Source=localhost;Initial " & _
                            "Catalog=AddressBook;User Id=sa;Pwd=;"
    Dim objConn As New SqlConnection(strConn)
    Dim objReader As SqlDataReader

    Dim objCmd As New SqlCommand()

    Dim objParamID As New SqlParameter("@intID", SqlDbType.Int)
    objParamID.Direction = ParameterDirection.Input
    objParamID.Value = CInt(strID)
```

```
'CommandType.StoredProcedure
objCmd.CommandType = CommandType.StoredProcedure
objCmd.CommandText = "ab_GetContactDetailInfo_ssp"
objCmd.Parameters.Add(objParamID)

objCmd.Connection = objConn
objCmd.Connection.Open()

objReader = objCmd.ExecuteReader
objReader.Read()

If Not IsDBNull(objReader.Item("id")) _
 Then txtID.Text = objReader.Item("id") Else txtID.Text = ""
If Not IsDBNull(objReader.Item(1)) _
 Then txtFName.Text = objReader.GetString(1) Else txtFName.Text = ""
If Not IsDBNull(objReader.Item("MName")) _
 Then txtMName.Text = objReader.Item("MName") Else txtMName.Text = ""
If Not IsDBNull(objReader.Item("LName")) _
 Then txtLName.Text = objReader.Item("LName") Else txtLName.Text = ""
If Not IsDBNull(objReader.Item("NName")) _
 Then txtNName.Text = objReader.Item("NName") Else txtNName.Text = ""
If Not IsDBNull(objReader.Item("SpouseName")) _
 Then txtSName.Text = objReader.Item("SpouseName") _
Else txtSName.Text = ""
 If Not IsDBNull(objReader.Item("Child1")) _
  Then txtChild1.Text = objReader.Item("Child1") Else txtChild1.Text = ""
 If Not IsDBNull(objReader.Item("Child2")) _
  Then txtChild2.Text = objReader.Item("Child2") Else txtChild2.Text = ""
 If Not IsDBNull(objReader.Item("Child3")) _
  Then txtChild3.Text = objReader.Item("Child3") Else txtChild3.Text = ""
 If Not IsDBNull(objReader.Item("Address")) _
  Then txtAddress.Text = objReader.Item("Address") _
Else txtAddress.Text = ""
 If Not IsDBNull(objReader.Item("City")) _
  Then txtCity.Text = objReader.Item("City") Else txtCity.Text = ""
 If Not IsDBNull(objReader.Item("State")) _
  Then txtState.Text = objReader.Item("State") Else txtState.Text = ""
 If Not IsDBNull(objReader.Item("Zip")) _
  Then txtZip.Text = objReader.Item("Zip") Else txtZip.Text = ""
 If Not IsDBNull(objReader.Item("HomePhone")) _
  Then txtHomePhone.Text = objReader.Item("HomePhone") _
   Else txtHomePhone.Text = ""
 If Not IsDBNull(objReader.Item("CellPhone")) _
  Then txtCellPhone.Text = objReader.Item("CellPhone") _
```

(continued on next page)

```
Else txtCellPhone.Text = ""
    If Not IsDBNull(objReader.Item("Email")) _
     Then txtEmail.Text = objReader.Item("Email") Else txtEmail.Text = ""
    If Not IsDBNull(objReader.Item("Comments")) _
     Then txtComments.Text = objReader.Item("Comments") _
Else txtComments.Text = ""

    objReader.Close()

End Sub
```

Creating the New SP_InsertContact Function

```
Private Sub SP_InsertContact()
    Dim strConn As String = "Data Source=localhost;Initial " & _
                            "Catalog=AddressBook;User Id=sa;Pwd=;"
    Dim objConn As New SqlConnection(strConn)

    Dim objCmd As New SqlCommand()

    'CommandType.StoredProcedure
    objCmd.CommandType = CommandType.StoredProcedure
    objCmd.CommandText = "ab_InsertContact_isp"

    Dim objParamFName As New SqlParameter("@strFName", _
                                    SqlDbType.VarChar, 20)
    objParamFName.Direction = ParameterDirection.Input
    Dim objParamMName As New SqlParameter("@strMName", _
                                    SqlDbType.VarChar, 20)
    objParamMName.Direction = ParameterDirection.Input
    Dim objParamLName As New SqlParameter("@strLName", _
                                    SqlDbType.VarChar, 20)
    objParamLName.Direction = ParameterDirection.Input
    Dim objParamNName As New SqlParameter("@strNName", _
                                    SqlDbType.VarChar, 20)
    objParamNName.Direction = ParameterDirection.Input
    Dim objParamSName As New SqlParameter("@strSName", _
                                    SqlDbType.VarChar, 50)
    objParamSName.Direction = ParameterDirection.Input
    Dim objParamAddress As New SqlParameter("@strAddress", _
                                    SqlDbType.VarChar, 50)
    objParamAddress.Direction = ParameterDirection.Input
    Dim objParamCity As New SqlParameter("@strCity", _
                                    SqlDbType.VarChar, 50)
```

```vbnet
objParamCity.Direction = ParameterDirection.Input
Dim objParamState As New SqlParameter("@strState", _
                                SqlDbType.VarChar, 2)
objParamState.Direction = ParameterDirection.Input
Dim objParamZip As New SqlParameter("@strZip", _
                                SqlDbType.VarChar, 10)
objParamZip.Direction = ParameterDirection.Input
Dim objParamHomePhone As New SqlParameter("@strHomePhone", _
                                SqlDbType.VarChar, 14)
objParamHomePhone.Direction = ParameterDirection.Input
Dim objParamCellPhone As New SqlParameter("@strCellPhone", _
                                SqlDbType.VarChar, 14)
objParamCellPhone.Direction = ParameterDirection.Input
Dim objParamEmail As New SqlParameter("@strEmail", _
                                SqlDbType.VarChar, 100)
objParamEmail.Direction = ParameterDirection.Input
Dim objParamComments As New SqlParameter("@strComments", _
                                SqlDbType.VarChar, 8000)
objParamComments.Direction = ParameterDirection.Input
Dim objParamChild1 As New SqlParameter("@strChild1", _
                                SqlDbType.VarChar, 20)
objParamChild1.Direction = ParameterDirection.Input
Dim objParamChild2 As New SqlParameter("@strChild2", _
                                SqlDbType.VarChar, 20)
objParamChild2.Direction = ParameterDirection.Input
Dim objParamChild3 As New SqlParameter("@strChild3", _
                                SqlDbType.VarChar, 20)
objParamChild3.Direction = ParameterDirection.Input

'Add values
objParamFName.Value = txtFName.Text
objParamMName.Value = txtMName.Text
objParamLName.Value = txtLName.Text
objParamNName.Value = txtNName.Text
objParamSName.Value = txtSName.Text
objParamAddress.Value = txtAddress.Text
objParamCity.Value = txtCity.Text
objParamState.Value = txtState.Text
objParamZip.Value = txtZip.Text
objParamHomePhone.Value = txtHomePhone.Text
objParamCellPhone.Value = txtCellPhone.Text
objParamEmail.Value = txtEmail.Text
objParamComments.Value = txtComments.Text
objParamChild1.Value = txtChild1.Text
objParamChild2.Value = txtChild2.Text
objParamChild3.Value = txtChild3.Text
```

(continued on next page)

```
    'Add parameters to command object
    objCmd.Parameters.Add(objParamFName)
    objCmd.Parameters.Add(objParamMName)
    objCmd.Parameters.Add(objParamLName)
    objCmd.Parameters.Add(objParamNName)
    objCmd.Parameters.Add(objParamSName)
    objCmd.Parameters.Add(objParamAddress)
    objCmd.Parameters.Add(objParamCity)
    objCmd.Parameters.Add(objParamState)
    objCmd.Parameters.Add(objParamZip)
    objCmd.Parameters.Add(objParamHomePhone)
    objCmd.Parameters.Add(objParamCellPhone)
    objCmd.Parameters.Add(objParamEmail)
    objCmd.Parameters.Add(objParamComments)
    objCmd.Parameters.Add(objParamChild1)
    objCmd.Parameters.Add(objParamChild2)
    objCmd.Parameters.Add(objParamChild3)

    objCmd.Connection = objConn
    objCmd.Connection.Open()

    objCmd.ExecuteNonQuery()
End Sub
```

Creating the New SP_UpdateContact Function:

```
Private Sub SP_UpdateContact()
    Dim strConn As String = "Data Source=localhost;Initial " & _
                            "Catalog=AddressBook;User Id=sa;Pwd=;"
    Dim objConn As New SqlConnection(strConn)

    Dim objCmd As New SqlCommand()

    'CommandType.StoredProcedure
    objCmd.CommandType = CommandType.StoredProcedure
    objCmd.CommandText = "ab_UpdateContact_usp"

    Dim objParamID As New SqlParameter("@intID", SqlDbType.Int)
    objParamID.Direction = ParameterDirection.Input
    Dim objParamFName As New SqlParameter("@strFName", _
                                          SqlDbType.VarChar, 20)
    objParamFName.Direction = ParameterDirection.Input
    Dim objParamMName As New SqlParameter("@strMName", _
                                          SqlDbType.VarChar, 20)
```

```
objParamMName.Direction = ParameterDirection.Input
Dim objParamLName As New SqlParameter("@strLName", _
                                      SqlDbType.VarChar, 20)
objParamLName.Direction = ParameterDirection.Input
Dim objParamNName As New SqlParameter("@strNName", _
                                      SqlDbType.VarChar, 20)
objParamNName.Direction = ParameterDirection.Input
Dim objParamSName As New SqlParameter("@strSName", _
                                      SqlDbType.VarChar, 50)
objParamSName.Direction = ParameterDirection.Input
Dim objParamAddress As New SqlParameter("@strAddress", _
                                      SqlDbType.VarChar, 50)
objParamAddress.Direction = ParameterDirection.Input
Dim objParamCity As New SqlParameter("@strCity", _
                                      SqlDbType.VarChar, 50)
objParamCity.Direction = ParameterDirection.Input
Dim objParamState As New SqlParameter("@strState", _
                                      SqlDbType.VarChar, 2)
objParamState.Direction = ParameterDirection.Input
Dim objParamZip As New SqlParameter("@strZip", _
                                      SqlDbType.VarChar, 10)
objParamZip.Direction = ParameterDirection.Input
Dim objParamHomePhone As New SqlParameter("@strHomePhone", _
                                      SqlDbType.VarChar, 14)
objParamHomePhone.Direction = ParameterDirection.Input
Dim objParamCellPhone As New SqlParameter("@strCellPhone", _
                                      SqlDbType.VarChar, 14)
objParamCellPhone.Direction = ParameterDirection.Input
Dim objParamEmail As New SqlParameter("@strEmail", _
                                      SqlDbType.VarChar, 100)
objParamEmail.Direction = ParameterDirection.Input
Dim objParamComments As New SqlParameter("@strComments", _
                                      SqlDbType.VarChar, 8000)
objParamComments.Direction = ParameterDirection.Input
Dim objParamChild1 As New SqlParameter("@strChild1", _
                                      SqlDbType.VarChar, 20)
objParamChild1.Direction = ParameterDirection.Input
Dim objParamChild2 As New SqlParameter("@strChild2", _
                                      SqlDbType.VarChar, 20)
objParamChild2.Direction = ParameterDirection.Input
Dim objParamChild3 As New SqlParameter("@strChild3", _
                                      SqlDbType.VarChar, 20)
objParamChild3.Direction = ParameterDirection.Input
```

(continued on next page)

```vb
'Add values
objParamID.Value = CInt(txtID.Text)
objParamFName.Value = txtFName.Text
objParamMName.Value = txtMName.Text
objParamLName.Value = txtLName.Text
objParamNName.Value = txtNName.Text
objParamSName.Value = txtSName.Text
objParamAddress.Value = txtAddress.Text
objParamCity.Value = txtCity.Text
objParamState.Value = txtState.Text
objParamZip.Value = txtZip.Text
objParamHomePhone.Value = txtHomePhone.Text
objParamCellPhone.Value = txtCellPhone.Text
objParamEmail.Value = txtEmail.Text
objParamComments.Value = txtComments.Text
objParamChild1.Value = txtChild1.Text
objParamChild2.Value = txtChild2.Text
objParamChild3.Value = txtChild3.Text

'Add parameters to command object
objCmd.Parameters.Add(objParamID)
objCmd.Parameters.Add(objParamFName)
objCmd.Parameters.Add(objParamMName)
objCmd.Parameters.Add(objParamLName)
objCmd.Parameters.Add(objParamNName)
objCmd.Parameters.Add(objParamSName)
objCmd.Parameters.Add(objParamAddress)
objCmd.Parameters.Add(objParamCity)
objCmd.Parameters.Add(objParamState)
objCmd.Parameters.Add(objParamZip)
objCmd.Parameters.Add(objParamHomePhone)
objCmd.Parameters.Add(objParamCellPhone)
objCmd.Parameters.Add(objParamEmail)
objCmd.Parameters.Add(objParamComments)
objCmd.Parameters.Add(objParamChild1)
objCmd.Parameters.Add(objParamChild2)
objCmd.Parameters.Add(objParamChild3)

objCmd.Connection = objConn
objCmd.Connection.Open()

objCmd.ExecuteNonQuery()
End Sub
```

Creating the New SP_DeleteContact Function

```
Private Sub SP_DeleteContact()

    Dim strConn As String = "Data Source=localhost;Initial " & _
                                "Catalog=AddressBook;User Id=sa;Pwd=;"
    Dim objConn As New SqlConnection(strConn)

    Dim objCmd As New SqlCommand()

    Dim objParamID As New SqlParameter("@intID", SqlDbType.Int)
    objParamID.Direction = ParameterDirection.Input
    objParamID.Value = CInt(txtID.Text)

    'CommandType.StoredProcedure
    objCmd.CommandType = CommandType.StoredProcedure
    objCmd.CommandText = "ab_DeleteContact_dsp"
    objCmd.Parameters.Add(objParamID)

    objCmd.Connection = objConn
    objCmd.Connection.Open()

    objCmd.ExecuteNonQuery()

End Sub
```

Replacing Function Calls

You are now almost done. Your last task is to replace your previous function calls with your new stored procedure functions.

PopulateAddressBook

Replace the "PopulateAddressBook" function with the SP_GetAddressBookInfo. You will find this functionality in the following functions:

- Page_Load
- ChangeGridPage
- lbtnDelete_Click
- lbtnEnter_Click

Your code will look like this:

```
'PopulateAddressBook()
'Using a Stored Procedure
SP_GetAddressBookInfo()
```

GetContactDetail

Replace the "GetContactDetail" function with the SP_GetContactDetailInfo. You will find this functionality in the following functions:

```
DataGridAddressList_SelectedIndexChanged
```

You code will look like this:

```
'GetContactDetail(strID)
'Using a stored procedure.
SP_GetContactDetailInfo(strID)
```

InsertRecord

Replace the "InsertRecord" function with the SP_InsertContact. You will find this functionality in the following functions:

```
lbtnEnter_Click
```

You code will look like this:

```
'If lblMode.Text = "New" Then InsertRecord()
'Using Stored Procedure
If lblMode.Text = "New" Then SP_InsertContact()
```

UpdateRecord

Replace the "UpdateRecord" function with the SP_UpdateContact. You will find this functionality in the following functions:

```
lbtnEnter_Click
```

You code will look like this:

```
'If lblMode.Text = "Edit" Then UpdateRecord()
'Using Stored Procedure
If lblMode.Text = "Edit" Then SP_UpdateContact()
```

DeleteRecord

Replace the "DeleteRecord" function with the SP_DeleteContact. You will find this functionality in the following functions:

```
lbtnDelete_Click
```

You code will look like this:

```
'DeleteRecord()
'Using Stored Procedure
SP_DeleteContact()
```

Running the AddressBook Application

Go ahead and run the AddressBook sample application. Chances are you will have a few typos and you might need to debug the application to find them. Once you have everything working correctly, you will find that each function you run may take a little longer the first time. This is because the query plan is being built the first time you run each stored procedure. Once everything has been run at least once, you will notice a considerable performance gain. Obviously, the performance gain will be much more noticeable on a larger application, but you should notice a difference even at this level. Something else you will notice is that you can now enter any type of symbol you wish into your application, such as a single or double quote. When building queries dynamically within the application, these symbols can cause exceptions and additional coding to compensate.

Using Stored Procedures and XML

In this section, you will perform four tasks that use SQL Server 2000 stored procedures and XML. First, you will upgrade your AddressBook application with two new stored procedures to replace your Insert and Update functions. These new stored procedures will accept a single parameter of string. Next, you will demonstrate the ability to perform multiple inserts by taking advantage of XML. Finally, you will export your entire AddressBook to XML. Once the XML document has been extracted, you may further enhance the AddressBook application by emailing, saving to disk, or searching the exported XML document.

Insert and Update

Go ahead and replace your new stored procedures for Insert and Update. You will find the following stored procedure scripts in the "Ch9 Examples\XML" directory on the CD-ROM. Open and execute these scripts with SQL Server Query Analyzer:

- dbo.ab_InsertContactXML_isp.sql
- dbo.ab_UpdateContactXML_usp.sql

ab_InsertContactXML_isp

```
if exists (select * from dbo.sysobjects where id =
object_id(N'[dbo].[ab_InsertContactXML_isp]') and OBJECTPROPERTY(id, N'IsProcedure')
= 1)
drop procedure [dbo].[ab_InsertContactXML_isp]
GO
SET QUOTED_IDENTIFIER OFF
GO
SET ANSI_NULLS ON
GO
CREATE PROCEDURE dbo.ab_InsertContactXML_isp
@xmldoc   text
AS
DECLARE @idoc INT
    --Create an internal representation of the XML document.
    EXEC sp_xml_preparedocument @idoc OUTPUT, @xmldoc
    INSERT INTO AddressBook (FName, MName, LName,
                    NName, SpouseName, Address,
                City, State, Zip, HomePhone,
                    CellPhone, EMail, Comments,
                Child1, Child2, Child3)
    SELECT FName, MName, LName, NName, SName, Addr,
        City, State, Zip, Home, Cell, EMail, Comments,
        Child1, Child2, Child3
    FROM OPENXML (@idoc, 'AddressBook/Contact', 2) WITH
        (FName      Varchar(20)    'FName',
        MName       Varchar(20)    'MName',
        LName       Varchar(20)    'LName',
        NName       Varchar(20)    'NName',
        SName       Varchar(50)    'SpouseName',
        Addr        Varchar(50)    'Address',
        City        Varchar(50)    'City',
        State       Varchar(2)     'State',
        Zip         Varchar(10)    'Zip',
        Home        varchar(14)    'HomePhone',
        Cell        varchar(14)    'CellPhone',
        EMail       varchar(100)   'EMail',
        Comments    varchar(8000)  'Comments',
        Child1      Varchar(20)    'Child1',
        Child2      Varchar(20)    'Child2',
        Child3      Varchar(20)    'Child3')
    -- remove the XML document from memory
    EXEC sp_xml_removedocument @idoc
GO
SET QUOTED_IDENTIFIER OFF
```

```
GO
SET ANSI_NULLS ON
GO
```

ab_UpdateContactXML_usp

```
if exists (select * from dbo.sysobjects where id =
object_id(N'[dbo].[ab_UpdateContactXML_usp]') and OBJECTPROPERTY(id, N'IsProcedure')
= 1)
drop procedure [dbo].[ab_UpdateContactXML_usp]
GO
SET QUOTED_IDENTIFIER OFF
GO
SET ANSI_NULLS ON
GO
CREATE PROCEDURE dbo.ab_UpdateContactXML_usp
@xmldoc varchar(2000)
AS
DECLARE @idoc INT
    --Create an internal representation of the XML document.
    EXEC sp_xml_preparedocument @idoc OUTPUT, @xmldoc
    UPDATE AddressBook
    SET     FName = XMLUpdate.FName,
        MName = XMLUpdate.MName,
        LName = XMLUpdate.LName,
        NName = XMLUpdate.NName,
        SpouseName = XMLUpdate.SName,
        Address = XMLUpdate.Addr,
        City = XMLUpdate.City,
        State = XMLUpdate.State,
        Zip =XMLUpdate.Zip ,
        HomePhone = XMLUpdate.Home,
        CellPhone = XMLUpdate.Cell,
        EMail = XMLUpdate.Email,
        Comments = XMLUpdate.Comments,
        Child1 = XMLUpdate.Child1,
        Child2 = XMLUpdate.Child2,
        Child3 = XMLUpdate.Child3
    FROM OPENXML (@idoc, 'AddressBook/Contact', 2) WITH
        (ContactID   int        'id',
        FName     Varchar(20)     'FName',
        MName     Varchar(20)     'MName',
        LName     Varchar(20)     'LName',
        NName     Varchar(20)     'NName',
```

(continued on next page)

```
        SName       Varchar(50)      'SpouseName',
        Addr        Varchar(50)      'Address',
        City        Varchar(50)      'City',
        State       Varchar(2)       'State',
        Zip         Varchar(10)      'Zip',
        Home        varchar(14)      'HomePhone',
        Cell        varchar(14)      'CellPhone',
        EMail       varchar(100)     'EMail',
        Comments    varchar(8000)    'Comments',
        Child1      Varchar(20)      'Child1',
        Child2      Varchar(20)      'Child2',
        Child3      Varchar(20)      'Child3')XMLUpdate, AddressBook
    WHERE AddressBook.id = XMLUpdate.ContactID
    -- remove the XML document from memory
    EXEC sp_xml_removedocument @idoc
GO
SET QUOTED_IDENTIFIER OFF
GO
SET ANSI_NULLS ON
GO
```

SP_InsertContact

Replace the "SP_InsertContact" function with the SP_InsertContactXML. You will find this functionality in the following functions:

lbtnEnter_Click

You code will now look like this:

```
    'If lblMode.Text = "New" Then InsertRecord()
    'Using Stored Procedure
    'If lblMode.Text = "New" Then SP_InsertContact()
    'Using a Stored Procedure with XML
    If lblMode.Text = "New" Then SP_InsertContactXML()
```

SP_UpdateContact

Replace the "SP_UpdateContact" function with the SP_UpdateContactXML. You will find this functionality in the following functions:

lbtnEnter_Click

Your code will now look like this:

```
'If lblMode.Text = "Edit" Then UpdateRecord()
'Using Stored Procedure
'If lblMode.Text = "Edit" Then SP_UpdateContact()
'Using a Stored Procedure with XML
If lblMode.Text = "Edit" Then SP_UpdateContactXML()
```

Updating the AddressBook Functions

Now that you've created the stored procedures, go ahead and open up the
AddressBook sample application.

Creating the New SP_InsertContactXML Function

```
Private Sub SP_InsertContactXML()

    Dim strConn As String = "Data Source=localhost;Initial " & _
                            "Catalog=AddressBook;User Id=sa;Pwd=;"
    Dim objConn As New SqlConnection(strConn)
    Dim objCmd As New SqlCommand()
    Dim StringBuilderXML As New StringBuilder()

    'Build XML string
    StringBuilderXML.Append("<AddressBook>")
    StringBuilderXML.Append("<Contact>")
    StringBuilderXML.Append("<FName>" & txtFName.Text & "</FName>")
    StringBuilderXML.Append("<MName>" & txtMName.Text & "</MName>")
    StringBuilderXML.Append("<LName>" & txtLName.Text & "</LName>")
    StringBuilderXML.Append("<NName>" & txtNName.Text & "</NName>")
    StringBuilderXML.Append("<SpouseName>" & txtSName.Text & _
                                            "</SpouseName>")
    StringBuilderXML.Append("<Address>" & txtAddress.Text & "</Address>")
    StringBuilderXML.Append("<City>" & txtCity.Text & "</City>")
    StringBuilderXML.Append("<State>" & txtState.Text & "</State>")
    StringBuilderXML.Append("<Zip>" & txtZip.Text & "</Zip>")
    StringBuilderXML.Append("<HomePhone>" & txtHomePhone.Text & _
                                            "</HomePhone>")
    StringBuilderXML.Append("<CellPhone>" & txtCellPhone.Text & _
                                            "</CellPhone>")
    StringBuilderXML.Append("<EMail>" & txtEmail.Text & "</EMail>")
    StringBuilderXML.Append("<Comments>" & txtComments.Text & _
                                            "</Comments>")
```

(continued on next page)

```
StringBuilderXML.Append("<Child1>" & txtChild1.Text & "</Child1>")
StringBuilderXML.Append("<Child2>" & txtChild2.Text & "</Child2>")
StringBuilderXML.Append("<Child3>" & txtChild3.Text & "</Child3>")
StringBuilderXML.Append("</Contact>")
StringBuilderXML.Append("</AddressBook>")

Dim objParamID As New SqlParameter("@xmldoc", SqlDbType.Text)
objParamID.Direction = ParameterDirection.Input
objParamID.Value = StringBuilderXML.tostring

'CommandType.StoredProcedure
objCmd.CommandType = CommandType.StoredProcedure
objCmd.CommandText = "ab_InsertContactXML_isp"
objCmd.Parameters.Add(objParamID)

objCmd.Connection = objConn
objCmd.Connection.Open()

objCmd.ExecuteNonQuery()

End Sub
```

Creating the New SP_UpdateContactXML Function

```
Private Sub SP_UpdateContactXML()

    Dim strConn As String = "Data Source=localhost;Initial " & _
                            "Catalog=AddressBook;User Id=sa;Pwd=;"
    Dim objConn As New SqlConnection(strConn)
    Dim objCmd As New SqlCommand()
    Dim StringBuilderXML As New System.Text.StringBuilder()

    'Build XML string
    StringBuilderXML.Append("<AddressBook>")
    StringBuilderXML.Append("<Contact>")
    StringBuilderXML.Append("<id>" & txtID.Text & "</id>")
    StringBuilderXML.Append("<FName>" & txtFName.Text & "</FName>")
    StringBuilderXML.Append("<MName>" & txtMName.Text & "</MName>")
    StringBuilderXML.Append("<LName>" & txtLName.Text & "</LName>")
    StringBuilderXML.Append("<NName>" & txtNName.Text & "</NName>")
    StringBuilderXML.Append("<SpouseName>" & txtSName.Text & _
                                            "</SpouseName>")
    StringBuilderXML.Append("<Address>" & txtAddress.Text & "</Address>")
    StringBuilderXML.Append("<City>" & txtCity.Text & "</City>")
    StringBuilderXML.Append("<State>" & txtState.Text & "</State>")
```

```
StringBuilderXML.Append("<Zip>" & txtZip.Text & "</Zip>")
StringBuilderXML.Append("<HomePhone>" & txtHomePhone.Text & _
                                          "</HomePhone>")
StringBuilderXML.Append("<CellPhone>" & txtCellPhone.Text & _
                                          "</CellPhone>")
StringBuilderXML.Append("<EMail>" & txtEmail.Text & "</EMail>")
StringBuilderXML.Append("<Comments>" & txtComments.Text & _
                                          "</Comments>")
StringBuilderXML.Append("<Child1>" & txtChild1.Text & "</Child1>")
StringBuilderXML.Append("<Child2>" & txtChild2.Text & "</Child2>")
StringBuilderXML.Append("<Child3>" & txtChild3.Text & "</Child3>")
StringBuilderXML.Append("</Contact>")
StringBuilderXML.Append("</AddressBook>")

Dim objParamID As New SqlParameter("@xmldoc", SqlDbType.Text)
objParamID.Direction = ParameterDirection.Input
objParamID.Value = StringBuilderXML.ToString

'CommandType.StoredProcedure
objCmd.CommandType = CommandType.StoredProcedure
objCmd.CommandText = "ab_UpdateContactXML_usp"
objCmd.Parameters.Add(objParamID)

objCmd.Connection = objConn
objCmd.Connection.Open()

objCmd.ExecuteNonQuery()

End Sub
```

XML Batch Insert Example

What's attractive about using XML with stored procedures is the ability to perform multiple inserts and updates. Previously, you had to call an insert procedure once for each insert you wanted to perform. When passing in an XML document holding multiple records, SQL Server stored procedures can perform all the inserts and updates in a single call. Actually, the stored procedure treats the XML document like a collection of data when extracting data, then applies the change. Making a single call to the database when it performs multiple inserts or updates greatly reduces overhead and increases both scalability and performance. To create the application, follow these steps:

1. Create a new Visual Basic .NET windows application and name it "XMLBatchInsert".

2. Drag-and-drop one Command Button, one Label, and one TextBox onto the form and set the properties that are listed in Table 9-6.

Table 9-6: Control Properties for XMLBatchInsert

Control	Property	Value
Button	ID	btnXMLBatchInsert
	Text	Perform XML batch insert.
Label	ID	Label1
	Text	Path to XML Document:
TextBox	ID	TextBox1
	Text	D:\ Ch9 Examples\XML\Contacts.xml

Import Namespaces

Use the following import statements:

```
Imports System
Imports System.IO
```

btnXMLBatchInsert_Click

```
'Read XML from a file.
    Dim strXMLFile As String
    strXMLFile = TextBox1.Text

    Dim objXMLStringBuilder As New System.Text.StringBuilder()

    Dim objStreamReader As StreamReader = File.OpenText(strXMLFile)
    Dim strXMLString As String
    strXMLString = objStreamReader.ReadLine()
    While Not strXMLString Is Nothing
      objXMLStringBuilder.Append(strXMLString)
      strXMLString = objStreamReader.ReadLine()
    End While

    'Perform XML Insert.
        Dim strConn As String = "Data Source=localhost;Initial " & _
                                "Catalog=AddressBook;User Id=sa;Pwd=;"

    Dim objConn As New System.Data.SqlClient.SqlConnection(strConn)
    Dim objCmd As New System.Data.SqlClient.SqlCommand()

    Dim objParamID As New System.Data.SqlClient.SqlParameter("@xmldoc", _
SqlDbType.Text)
    objParamID.Direction = ParameterDirection.Input
    objParamID.Value = objXMLStringBuilder.ToString
```

```
'CommandType.StoredProcedure
objCmd.CommandType = CommandType.StoredProcedure
objCmd.CommandText = "ab_InsertContactXML_isp"
objCmd.Parameters.Add(objParamID)

objCmd.Connection = objConn
objCmd.Connection.Open()

objCmd.ExecuteNonQuery()
```

The Imported XML File

The file you are using from which to import is a basic XML formatted file.

```
<?xml version="1.0" encoding="utf-8" ?>
<AddressBook>
    <Contact>
        <FName>David</FName>
        <MName>E.</MName>
        <LName>Pledger</LName>
        <NName>Dave</NName>
        <SpouseName></SpouseName>
        <Address>556 XML Lane</Address>
        <City>Dayton</City>
        <State>OH</State>
        <Zip>55555</Zip>
        <HomePhone>555-555-5556</HomePhone>
        <CellPhone>555-555-5556</CellPhone>
        <EMail>Pledger@MyEmail.com</EMail>
        <Comments>Dave owns Strategic Data Systems, Inc.</Comments>
        <Child1>girl1</Child1>
        <Child2>girl2</Child2>
        <Child3></Child3>
    </Contact>
    <Contact>
        <FName>William</FName>
        <MName>B</MName>
        <LName>O'Reilly</LName>
        <NName>Bill</NName>
        <SpouseName>Mrs. O'Reilly</SpouseName>
        <Address>555 No Spin Zone</Address>
        <City>New York</City>
        <State>NY</State>
        <Zip>33333</Zip>
        <HomePhone>555-555-5555</HomePhone>
```

(continued on next page)

```
            <CellPhone>555-555-5555</CellPhone>
            <EMail>Oreilly@FoxNews.com</EMail>
            <Comments>Bill works for Foxnews.</Comments>
            <Child1>kid1</Child1>
            <Child2>kid2</Child2>
            <Child3>kid3</Child3>
        </Contact>
        <Contact>
            <FName>William</FName>
            <MName>H</MName>
            <LName>Bennethum</LName>
            <NName>Bill</NName>
            <SpouseName></SpouseName>
            <Address>555 No Spin Zone</Address>
            <City>Cincinnati</City>
            <State>OH</State>
            <Zip>45555</Zip>
            <HomePhone>555-555-5555</HomePhone>
            <CellPhone>555-555-5555</CellPhone>
            <EMail>Bill@myMail.com</EMail>
            <Comments>Bill's Company</Comments>
            <Child1>Robert</Child1>
            <Child2>William</Child2>
            <Child3></Child3>
        </Contact>
</AddressBook>
```

Running the Application

Go ahead and run the application. Make sure the path that references the Contact.xml document is correct. After you have run this application, you can verify that the new records have been inserted by running the AddressBook application.

Summary

ADO.NET offers a variety of data access methods to address different scenarios. As you learned, there really is an appropriate way to use certain techniques. The way in which you implement data access technologies directly relates to an application's ability to both perform and scale. You also learned that additional performance gains can be obtained by working with other technologies optimized for data access, such as SQL Server stored procedures. The use of stored procedures cannot be emphasized enough. Finally, by leveraging the use of XML with stored procedures improves both performance and scalability when dealing with multiple inserts or updates.

10

WEB SERVICES

Since the inception of the network and, more recently, the Internet, attempts have been made to allow programs to extend their functionality across machine boundaries. Several successful attempts have encompassed much of the distributed world, including Java RMI, CORBA, and DCOM, but they have tended to be both platform and language dependent.

A web service is a remotely accessible method in which data is stored in XML and transmitted over HTTP. In English, that means a web service method is accessible by clients while communicate using TCP/IP and understand XML. This includes nearly every programming platform available. The application service provider builds the web services and makes it available to client applications known as consumers.

In this chapter, you'll learn about the industry accepted technologies that make cross-platform interoperability possible, and the underlying concept of web services.

Web Service Technologies

Web services are delivered using a combination of technologies. While Visual Studio .NET shields you from much of the complexities of these technologies, you should have a basic understanding of what these technologies are and how they work. If you work with web services for any length of time you will need to be able to modify some of the supporting files manually, just as a web developer might modify HTML pages after they are generated. So, let's have a quick look at the basics of each underlying technology.

XML

XML is designed for ease of implementation and for interoperability with both SGML and HTML. XML (Extensible Markup Language) is a self-describing language that is stored and transmitted as a string. The ability to transmit XML as a string is significant because all programming languages and platforms understand how to handle a string, making XML ideal for passing between disparate systems. Figure 10-1 shows an example of how contact information might be stored in XML format. The plain English tags of XML (for example, `<contact>`, `</contact>`) make XML readable and easy to learn and understand.

```
<contacts>
    <contact>
        <name>Tamarah Dunaway</name>
        <phone>555-555-5555</phone>
        <email>td@myEmail.com</email>
    </contact>
    <contact>
        <name>David Hill</name>
        <phone>555-555-5555</phone>
        <email>dh@myEmail.com</email>
    </contact>
    <contact>
        <name>Sharon Hill</name>
        <phone>555-555-5555</phone>
        <email>sh@myEmail.com</email>
    </contact>
    <contact>
        <name>Zac Hill</name>
        <phone>555-555-5555</phone>
        <email>zh@myEmail.com</email>
    </contact>
    <contact>
        <name>Lindzee Hill</name>
        <phone>555-555-5555</phone>
        <email>lh@myEmail.com</email>
    </contact>
</contacts>
```

Figure 10-1: Contact information stored in XML format.

XML Schema

XML Schemas define the data schema of the data stored in the XML document and is a handy tool for further defining the data structure, data types, and constraints for XML documents. The data schema can be used by applications that understand XML to enforce data specific business rules such as data types.

This extended data definition (XML Schema) can reflect the underlying database, such as data types and rules, in an effort to validate the data before transmitting it. This will save both time and effort for developers because all data validation is defined in a single location as well as reduces unnecessary round trips for data that doesn't transmit properly the first time due to data violations. As a result, an XML Schema is often referred to as a contract between exchanging partners because it defines what is (and is not) valid data.

XSLT

XSLT (eXtensible Stylesheet Language Transformations) is a language used to transform XML data into other XML data formats. For instance, two different companies store customer information but store different information for each customer. Transforming XML documents extends the usability of your XML document for other systems and devices by transforming XML data into a format that other systems use. XML documents can also be formatted, using XSLT, for display purposes.

HTTP

HTTP (HyperText Transfer Protocol) is an IP protocol used for transition. HTTP is the data transfer mechanism of SOAP, as well as Microsoft's web services, although web services are not strictly defined as using HTTP as its sole form of transport. Other forms of transfer are available for web services, such as .NET Remoting; however, this is beyond the scope of this book. For additional information on SOAP and .NET Remoting, refer to "Applied SOAP: Implementing .NET XML Web Services" or MSDN online.

WSDL

WSDL (Web Service Definition Language) defines the interface and behavior of web services. WSDL allows remote developers to communicate with web services without necessarily contacting the developer of the web service. WSDL effectively decouples the web service consumer's developer from the web service's developer. Visual Studio .NET creates the WSDL for each Web Service.

UDDI

UDDI (Universal Description, discovery, and Integration) is like a DNS server for web services. A DNS server stores a list of domain names and associated IP addresses; when a request is made to the DNS server for the IP address of a specific domain name, the DNS server resolves the name to an IP address, and the client can connect directly to the desired domain.

The UDDI aids in the discovery of businesses that provide Web Services. Businesses use UDDI to publish Web Services so that consumers can find and consume the Web Services.

Eliminating Batch Processing Paradigms

For example, how many times have you suggested that a system might provide a better service to the customer if it were real-time, only to have a developer tell you that it can't be real-time because it is based on a batch process of file transfers between disparate systems, followed by nightly processing of those files. While it is not necessarily true that the system cannot be modified to support real-time transactions, the batch process tends to be the hammer or the only tool available. Web services allow us to get rid of old batch processing paradigms and begin working toward more transactional based, real-time solutions.

Ability to Charge for Web Services

Another advantage of web services is the ability to charge for services rendered by your web service. If your web service provides a proprietary function that other applications wish to use, you can charge back to the customer a monthly service or even a transactional fee. Charge back options are truly endless and limited only by the imagination.

Web Service Hubs

Web services can also be combined to form hubs for other services offering greater flexbility in the way information is distributed. For example, as shown in Figure 10-2, one financial company might act as a hub for other financial services: The web services client would call each web service (such as Taxes, Loans, etc.), or talk only to the hub (the Financial Hub), while the hub communicates with the appropriate service on the client's behalf.

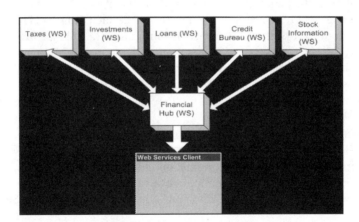

Figure 10-2: Diagram of a web services hub model.

Creating a Simple Web Service

Let's create a simple web service to demonstrate several common tasks that must be performed on all new web services.

1. Create a new project using the "ASP.NET Web Service" application template under the "Visual Basic Projects" project types.

2. When creating the new project, change the web service name by replacing the location with the desired service name "FullName", as shown in Figure 10-3, which includes the namespace of the new web service.

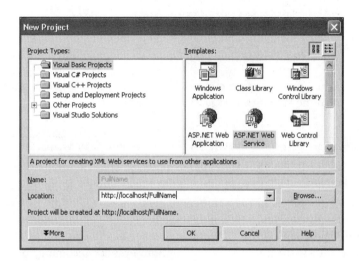

Figure 10-3: Creating a new web service.

3. Rename the "Service1.asmx" file, which is automatically added to the project, to "NameService.asmx".

4. Open the code window of the "NameService.asmx" file and replace the default class name with "FullName".

```
Public Class FullName
    Inherits System.Web.Services.WebService
```

5. Now, import the System.Text namespace at the very top of the code window for the NameService.asmx file.

```
Imports System.Text
```

6. Create a new web method with the following code that uses the `StringBuilder` class. (You imported the `System.Text` namespace so you could access the class more easily. If you hadn't imported it you could have accessed the class with its fully qualified namespace, `System.Text.StringBuilder`.)

```
<WebMethod()> Public Function FullName(ByVal strFName As String, _
                                       ByVal strLName As String) As String
    Dim objStringBuilder As StringBuilder
    objStringBuilder.Append(strFName)
    objStringBuilder.Append(" ")
    objStringBuilder.Append(strLName)
    Return objStringBuilder.ToString
End Function
```

7. Add a description to our new web service as an attribute of the FullName with the web method's class declaration statement:

```
<WebService(Description:="This web service returns a full name.", _
            Namespace:="http://tempuri.org/")> _
Public Class FullName
```

Compiling the Web Service

You can test the new web service without even a consuming application. To do so, press F5 to run the web method. The web service will first compile and then display a web page pointing to the "NameService.asmx" web service, as shown in Figure 10-4. The URL, http://localhost/FullName/NameService.asmx, contains the fully qualified namespace of the web service. As you can see in the figure, the browser window displays the name of the web service class, FullName, as well as a description of the class: "This web service returns a full name."

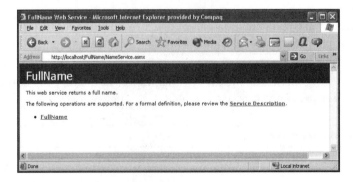

Figure 10-4: The web page displayed when running a web service from within the Visual Studio .NET IDE.

Finally, you'll see the warning displayed in Figure 10-5. When creating a new web service a temporary namespace is supplied by default; this warning reminds you that you need to replace the default.

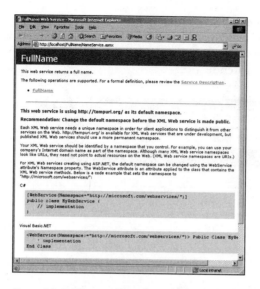

Figure 10-5: This warning tells you that you need to change the namespace of the web service.

To replace this temporary namespace, return to the code window and replace "http://tempuri.org/" with "http://localhost/FullName/". Once you have a server on the Internet, replace "localhost" with your server's real host name. Run the web service again and you'll see that the warning is gone.

Viewing the WSDL

To see the WSDL for the web service, select "Service Description". You should see the screen shown in Figure 10-6.

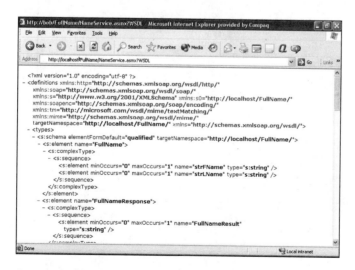

Figure 10-6: The WSDL for the FullName web service.

Testing the Web Service

Now that you've compiled the web service and examined its WDSL, you should test it:

1. Press the browser's Back button to return to our web service page then click the "FullName" hyperlink. You should see the test page shown in Figure 10-7. The test page, automatically generated by Visual Studio .NET, is the consumer of our web service.

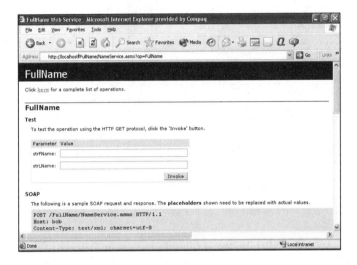

Figure 10-7: The web service's test screen.

2. Now enter a first and last name in the text boxes and then click Invoke. The result is an HTTP 500 – Internal server error, as shown in Figure 10-8.

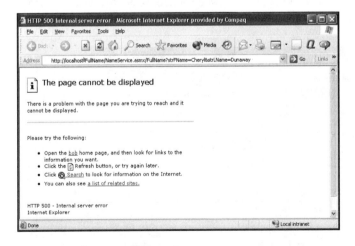

Figure 10-8: The HTTP 500 Internal server error.

Oops! Looks like you've got a bug. The page can't be displayed.

Debugging our Web Service

Like many error messages this one tells you nearly nothing about what has gone disastrously wrong, so you'll have to debug things:

1. Close the browser and return to the web service code page. Because the error message provides little information concerning the violation, you'll place a breakpoint on the declaration line of the "FullName" web method, which will trigger once the breakpoint is reached.

2. Run the web service again and then enter a first and last name. Click Invoke. The break point will trigger, as shown in Figure 10-9, stopping execution, and allowing you to step through the code.

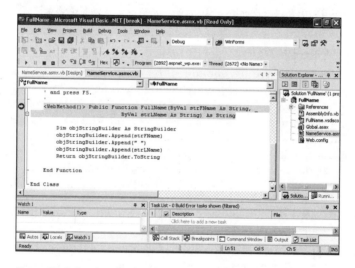

Figure 10-9: Displays the break point that is triggered.

3. Step into the code by pressing F11. You'll notice that while you declared "objStringBuilder" as a StringBuilder object, you never actually created the object in memory before referencing it. To correct this, replace the objStringBuilder declaration line with the following declaration and instantiation line.

```
Dim objStringBuilder As New StringBuilder
```

4. Remove the breakpoint and run the web service again. This time it should execute successfully, as shown in Figure 10-10.

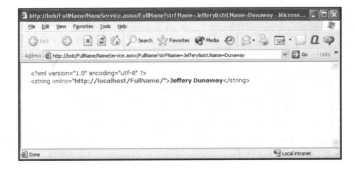

Figure 10-10: The result of a successful execution of your web service.

Consuming the Web Service

Now that you've created and tested the web service, your job may be complete. However, in many cases, you are creating web services for consumption by your own applications. For instance, you may want to expose functionality to a Windows Form application that resides outside the company network. (Historically, form-based applications could not communicate through a firewall because all but port 80 were often blocked. Because web services operate on port 80, this manner of distributed computing is made possible.)

The following sample application will consume the new web service:

1. Create a new Visual Basic "Windows Application" and name it "WinFullName."

2. Drag-and-drop the controls that are listed in Table 10-1 onto the Windows Form. (The end result should look similar to Figure 10-11.)

Table 10-1: Windows Form Controls

Control	Property	Value
TextBox	Name	txtFName
	Text	""
TextBox	Name	txtLName
	Text	""
Label	Name	lblResult
	Text	""
Button	Name	btnSubmit
	Text	"Submit"

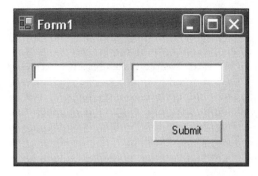

Figure 10-11: The consuming application.

Adding a Web Reference to Access the Service

Before you can access the web service you must reference it from the consuming application. To do so, follow these steps:

1. Right-click on the "WinFullName" project and select "Add Web Reference".

2. Enter the URL of the web service in the "Address" text box and press enter. A screen should appear similar to Figure 10-12. Press "Add Reference."

3. Right-click on "localhost" under Web References and rename it to

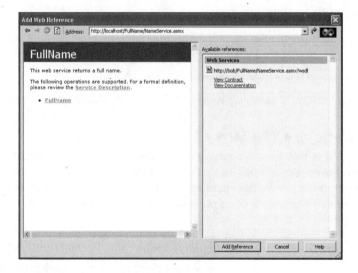

Figure 10-12: The "Add Web Reference" dialog box.

"WSFullName". (This allows you to couple the code loosely in the client with the web service. If you ever choose another web service provider for your client, all you need to do is change the reference.)

4. Place the following code behind the "Submit" button. This code will

consume the web service and then display the results.

```
Private Sub btnSubmit_Click(ByVal sender As System.Object, _
            ByVal e As System.EventArgs) Handles btnSubmit.Click

    Dim objWSFullName As New WSFullName.FullName()
    lblResult.Text = objWSFullName.FullName(txtFName.Text, _
                                                txtLName.Text)
End Sub
```

5. Now test the application by inputting a first and last name. Click Submit. If all goes well, your Windows Form should look like Figure 10-13. The Web Service concatenated the first and last names and returned the full name for display in the consuming client application.

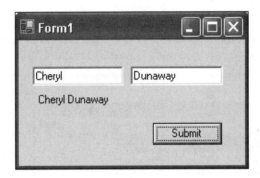

Figure 10-13: The consuming Windows Form.

Debugging a Web Service from the Client

As you've just seen, it's easy to debug a web service with Visual Studio .NET, but you have yet to debug the web service from the new client. The ability to debug a web service from the client application can be useful as the web service developer may not always be in possession of the client code. To do so, follow these steps:

1. Load both projects in separate instances of Visual Studio .NET.

2. Place breakpoints in the web service project and run it (ignoring the test web page).

3. Now run the WinFullName application and click the Submit button. The web service project will break into debug mode; you may perform any debugging task you wish.

Summary

Web services are a new and powerful addition to your development tool set, allowing you to build applications with other developers and to build their consuming applications independently. Thanks to technologies such as WSDL, you can couple both developers and applications.

The cross-platform characteristics of web services means a new paradigm must exist for building and delivering distributed applications. This new paradigm extends the Windows DNA application architecture and mode to include components of platforms other than Microsoft specific platforms. As the .NET paradigm shift continues and the Windows DNA model adjusts to the new technology, you will discover and learn new models or alterations of models for delivering N-tier distributed applications.

This chapter has demonstrated each aspect of web service development. Despite the simplicity of each example, the processes of creation, publication, consumption, and testing are the same.

11

COM INTEROP

As software applications have extended from client server to N-tier architectures, the need for componentization has increased. Microsoft introduced the Component Object Model (COM) as a binary compatible component model that allowed for further modularity and language independence for languages that understand and support binary compatibility. Unfortunately, binary compatibility does not guarantee all languages will support the same data types.

Assembly Development

.NET assemblies support a Type Safe standard which requires all .NET languages to support the same data types, effectively addressing the pitfalls of binary compatibility. All assemblies are consumable by all other assemblies or .NET languages. All data types are understood because .NET languages subscribe to and enforce the Common Type System provided by the .NET Framework; the cross-platform framework that .NET languages subscribe to.

COM Interoperability

COM interoperability allows COM and assemblies to work seamlessly with each other. This interoperability is critical for wide acceptance and the adoption of the .NET platform. Interoperability allows classic COM components to consume assemblies and also allows assemblies to load and use classic COM components. While there is a cost associated with interoperability, there are gains in productivity, migration, and integration.

Building the Assembly

To demonstrate the ability of classic COM to interoperate with assemblies, you'll build an assembly, then a .NET consuming application to test the component, and finally a classic COM consuming application to demonstrate COM interoperability. To begin, follow these steps:

1. Create a new Visual Basic .NET Class Library project named "Math".

2. Rename the "Class1.vb" file to "clsMath.vb".

3. Rename the "Public Class Class1" to "Public Class clsMath" in the code file.

4. Create a public function named "SUM" by applying the following code:

```
Public Class clsMath

    Public Function SUM(ByVal intA As Integer, ByVal intB As Integer) As Integer
        Return intA + intB
    End Function

End Class
```

5. Build the project by selecting Build Solution from the Build menu. Before attempting to consume the assembly by classic COM, test it using a native Windows Form assembly.

6. Add a new Visual Basic .NET Windows Form project named "MathTestClient" by selecting New then Project from the menu.

7. Drag the following controls onto the Windows Form and set the properties that are listed in Table 11-1.

Table 11-1: Control Properties for MathTestClient

Control	Property	Value
Form	Name	Form1
	Text	"MathTestClient"
	Size	300, 164
	StartPosition	CenterScreen
TextBox	Name	txtA
	Location	28, 20
	Text	""
TextBox	Name	txtB
	Location	160, 20
	Text	""
Label	Name	Label1
	Text	+
	Font	Microsoft Sans Serif, 12pt
	Location	136, 20
	Size	16, 20
Button	Name	btnCalculate
	Location	28, 52
	Size	100, 24
	Text	Calculate
Label	Name	lblResult
	Location	160, 52
	Size	100, 20

8. Set the MathTestClient project as the StartUp Project.

9. Right-click on the Reference folder of the MathTestClient and select Add Reference.

10. Select the Projects tab, double-click on the Math project, and select OK. This will add the assembly reference to your test client.

11. Place the following code behind the Calculate button:

```
If IsNumeric(txtA.Text) And IsNumeric(txtB.Text) Then
   Dim objMath As New Math.clsMath()
   lblResult.Text = objMath.SUM(txtA.Text, txtB.Text)
objMath = Nothing
Else
   MessageBox.Show("You must provide a number in each box")
End If
```

12. Run the application to verify that the Math class is working correctly and can be consumed by the .NET test client (Figure 11-1).

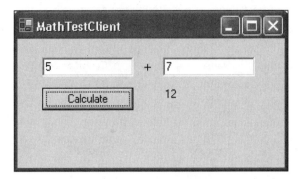

Figure 11-1: The .NET Consuming client application.

Building the COM Component

To continue the demonstration of COM interoperability, you'll create binary compatible COM Components that will later be consumed by your assembly. The example that you'll build here will be exactly like the .NET assembly and consumer, except that it will be built using classic COM.

To begin, create a new Visual Basic 6 project:

1. Open Visual Basic 6 by selecting Start • Programs • Microsoft Visual Studio 6.0 • Microsoft Visual Basic 6.0.

2. Select ActiveX DLL and press Open, as shown in Figure 11-2.

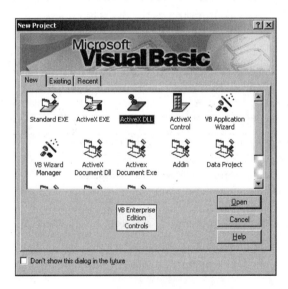

Figure 11-2: Visual Basic 6's new project template selection dialog box.

3. Select Project1 and change the name property to classicCOMMath.

4. Rename the Class1 ClassModule to clsMath.

5. Click the save icon. You will be prompted for the location where you wish to save your new Visual Basic 6 project and the clsMath class.

NOTE *Because Visual Basic 6 supports only one class per ClassModule file, you do not see a class declaration as you might expect. As far as Visual Basic 6 is concerned, a class declaration would be redundant.*

6. Place the following code in the code window of the clsMath ClassModule:

```
Public Function SUM(ByVal intA As Integer, ByVal intB As Integer) As Long
  SUM = intA + intB
End Function
```

NOTE *To return the SUM value, you set the function name, in your case SUM, equal to the value that you wish to return. This is different than the code used to return the function's value with your assembly. The Return keyword enables the return of function values in .NET.*

7. Select Make classicCOMMath.dll from the File menu.

Visual Basic 6 supports Binary, Project, and No Compatibility options. If the classicCOMMath project is configured for project or no compatibility, any client referencing the classicCOMMath component will be outdated because the project and no compatibility options create new GUIDs for the class and components on each compile. Binary compatibility requires that the developer be notified if binary compatibility will be broken during the next build, giving the developer the option to decline the build. Before a project can be binary compatible, there must be an initial component DLL with which to compare binary compatibility with. As such, binary compatibility cannot be configured until the project has been compiled at least one time. Step 7 of this example has compiled your project into the classicCOMMath.dll component. Now you can set the compatibility level to Binary Compatibility:

1. Select classicCOMMath Properties from the Project menu.

2. Select the Component tab (Figure 11-3).

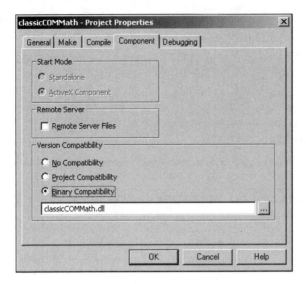

Figure 11-3: The Component tab of the Project Properties dialog box.

3. Select Binary Compatibility and press OK.

4. Select Make classicCOMMath.dll from the File menu.

5. Select OK and click Yes to replace the previously compiled component.

As you did with the assembly, you'll build a classic COM consumer for your new classic COM Component. Once you're satisfied that the component works properly you can consume it with a .NET consumer:

1. Select Add Project from the File menu item.

2. Select Standard EXE (Figure 11-4) and press Open.

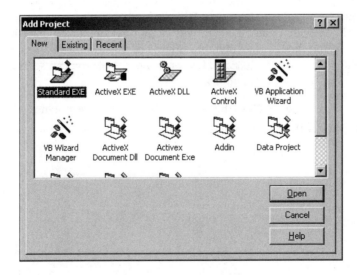

Figure 11-4: The standard EXE template project for Visual Basic 6.

3. Select the Project1 project and set the Name to "classicMathTestClient".

4. Click the Save button to save the new project and the project group.

NOTE *The project group is similar to Visual Studio .NET's Solution.*

5. Double-click on Form1.

6. Drag the following controls onto the Form1 form and set the properties that are listed in Table 11-2.

Table 11-2: Control Properties for classicMathTestClient

Control	Property	Value
Form	Name	Form1
	Height	2100
	Width	4215
	StartPosition	3 – Windows Default
	Caption	MathTestClient
TextBox	Name	txtA
	Top	240
	Left	480
	Width	1215
	Height	285
	Text	""
TextBox	Name	txtB
	Top	240
	Left	2280
	Width	1215
	Height	285
	Text	""
Label	Name	Label1
	Top	240
	Left	1920
	Width	135
	Height	255
	Caption	+

(continued on next page)

Table 11-2: Control Properties for classicMathTestClient (continued)

Control	Property	Value
Button	Name	cmdCalculate
	Top	720
	Left	480
	Width	1215
	Height	375
	Caption	Calculate
Label	Name	lblResult
	Top	840
	Left	2280
	Width	1215
	Height	255
	Caption	""

7. Right-click on the `classicMathTestClient` and select Set as Startup.

8. Select References from the Project menu item.

9. Select the check box by `classicCOMMath` (Figure 11-5) and click OK.

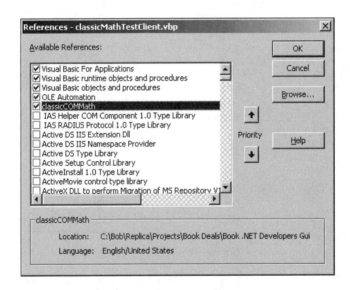

Figure 11-5: The References dialog box of Visual Basic 6.

10. Place the following code behind the cmdCalculate button:

```
Private Sub cmdCalculate_Click()
    If IsNumeric(txtA.Text) And IsNumeric(txtB.Text) Then
      Dim objMath As New classicCOMMath.clsMath
      lblResult.Caption = objMath.Sum(txtA.Text, txtB.Text)
      Set objMath = Nothing
    Else
      MsgBox ("You must provide a number in each box")
    End If
End Sub
```

Notice that there are a few changes in the code here when compared with the client code in the .NET consuming client application. When setting the display value of the lblResult, you use the Caption property. .NET uses the Text property as the display property for all controls, which makes development just a little easier. To make objMath equal to nothing, you use the Set command in Visual Basic 6 while .NET no longer uses the Set keyword. Finally, the MessageBox.Show command has been changed to MsgBox.

11. Run the project by selecting Start from the Run menu.

NOTE *Once you are satisfied that the application works, save your changes then shut down the development environment.*

Now that you have a .NET assembly and .NET consumer, and a classic COM component and consumer, you are ready to learn about COM Interoperation.

Consuming Classic COM with .NET

From this point, your job is pretty easy. You've built the classic COM component and the .NET consuming client; now all you need to do is change your references and change the component's name. (Technically, the assembly's name has nothing to do with COM Interoperability; however, to avoid confusion you named your assembly and classic COM component differently.)

Follow these steps to consume the classic COM component with your .NET consumer client application:

1. Open the "Math" Visual Studio .NET solution.

2. For now, just ignore the Math project and expand the References of the MathTestClient project.

3. Right-click on Math and select Remove.

4. Right-click on References and select Add References.

5. Select the COM tab.

NOTE *When you select the COM tab, it may take several seconds to query the Windows Registry to build a collection of available COM components.*

6. Scroll to `classicCOMMath` (Figure 11-6) and double-click it.

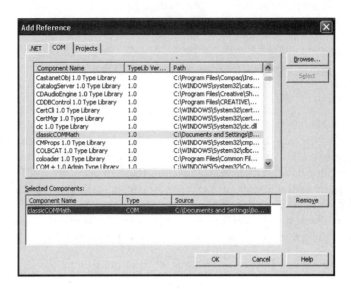

Figure 11-6: The COM tab of the Add Reference dialog box in Visual Studio .NET.

7. Press OK.

8. Bring up the code window for the Form1 class.

9. The only piece of code you will need to change is the component's name. Replace

```
Dim objMath As New Math.clsMath()
```

with

```
Dim objMath As New classicCOMMath.clsMath()
```

10. Run and test the .NET consuming client application.

Exposing Assemblies to Classic COM

Now expose your assembly so classic COM can consume it.

All components within a .NET project are found within the same directory, thus eliminating the need to register its location with the operating system. Classic COM, on the other hand, depends solely on the operating system to expose both its location and interface. When a classic COM component searches for another component, it does so through the Windows Registry.

To make your Math assembly easier to work with, we'll give it a strong name to uniquely identify it. A strong name is required to uniquely identify a component in the GAC (Global Assembly Cache), where the assembly must reside to be accessible by classic COM.

You also need to "export" your assembly's type library, which allows classic COM components to understand how to use the assembly. However, since your component doesn't really have a type library, you'll generate one based on the assembly manifest. (For the purposes of this discussion, consider the type library exported, especially since the utility used to generate it is tlbexp.exe.)

sn.exe (Strong Name Tool)

Use the sn.exe utility to create a strong name consisting of a public/private key pair. To create a public/private key pair file, follow these steps:

1. Open the Visual Studio .NET Command Prompt by selecting Start • Programs • Microsoft Visual Studio .NET • Visual Studio .NET Tools • Visual Studio .NET Command Prompt.

2. Navigate, using the command line, to the Math project's root directory, then enter the following at the command line:

```
sn -k keypair.snk
```

The file created is not specifically intended for any specific file until you have told your project that this is the key file to use.

Figure 11-7 displays a list of features that are available with the sn.exe utility. Some of the more notable ones appear in bold.

```
Microsoft (R) .NET Framework Strong Name Utility  Version 1.0.3705.0
Copyright (C) Microsoft Corporation 1998-2001. All rights reserved.


Usage: SN [-q(uiet)] <option> [<parameters>]
Options:
 -c [<csp>]
    Set/reset the name of the CSP to use for MSCORSN operations.
 -d <container>
    Delete key container named <container>.
 -D <assembly1> <assembly2>
    Verify <assembly1> and <assembly2> differ only by signature.
 -e <assembly> <outfile>
    Extract public key from <assembly> into <outfile>.
 -i <infile> <container>
    Install key pair from <infile> into a key container named <container>.
 -k <outfile>
    Generate a new key pair and write it into <outfile>.
 -m [y|n]
    Enable (y), disable (n) or check (no parameter) whether key containers
    are machine specific (rather than user specific).
 -o <infile> [<outfile>]
    Convert public key in <infile> to text file <outfile> with comma separated
    list of decimal byte values.
    If <outfile> is omitted, text is copied to clipboard instead.
 -p <infile> <outfile>
    Extract public key from key pair in <infile> and export to <outfile>.
 -pc <container> <outfile>
    Extract public key from key pair in <container> and export to <outfile>.
 -q
    Quiet mode. This option must be first on the command line and will suppress
    any output other than error messages.
 -R <assembly> <infile>
    Re-sign signed or partially signed assembly with the key pair in <infile>.
 -Rc <assembly> <container>
    Re-sign signed or partially signed assembly with the key pair in the key
    container named <container>.
 -t[p] <infile>
    Display token for public key in <infile> (together with the public key
    itself if -tp is used).
 -T[p] <assembly>
    Display token for public key of <assembly> (together with the public key
    itself if -Tp is used).
 -v[f] <assembly>
    Verify <assembly> for strong name signature self consistency. If -vf is
    specified, force verification even if disabled in the registry.
```

(continued on next page)

```
-Vl
   List current settings for strong name verification on this machine.
-Vr <assembly> [<userlist>]
   Register <assembly> for verification skipping (with an optional, comma
   separated list of usernames for which this will take effect). <assembly>
   can be specified as * to indicate all assemblies or *,<public key token> to
   indicate that all assemblies with the given public key token. Public key
   tokens should be specified as a string of hex digits.
-Vu <assembly>
   Unregister <assembly> for verification skipping. The same rules for
   <assembly> naming are followed as for -Vr.
-Vx
   Remove all verification skipping entries.
-?
-h
   Displays this help text.
```

Figure 11-7: Strong Name Utility (SN) options.

tlbexp.exe (Type Library Exporter)

Before you can expose assemblies to classic COM, you must export a type
library. You'll use the tlbexp.exe utility to generate or export a type library that
binary compatible classic COM understands. To do so, enter the following command at the Visual Studio .NET command to generate a type library with the
name of Math.tlb:

```
tlbexp Math.dll
```

Figure 11-8 displays a list of features that are available with the tlbexp.exe
utility with the more notable ones appearing in bold.

```
Syntax: TlbExp AssemblyName [Options]
Options:
   /out:FileName        File name of type library to be produced
   /nologo              Prevents TlbExp from displaying logo
   /silent              Prevents TlbExp from displaying success message
   /verbose             Displays extra information
   /names:FileName      A file in which each line specifies the
                        captialization of a name in the type library.
   /? or /help          Display this usage message
```

Figure 11-8: Type Library Converter (TlbExp) options.

regasm.exe (Assembly Registration Tool)

You may also use the regasm.exe utility to both generate a type library and register your assemblies with COM. The following command will create a type library and register the Math.dll with the operating system:

```
regasm /tlb:Math.tlb Math.dll
```

Figure 11-9 displays a list of features that are available with the `regasm.exe` utility. Some of the more notable features appear in bold.

```
Syntax: RegAsm AssemblyPath [Options]
Options:
    /unregister          Unregister types
    /tlb[:FileName]      Export the assembly to the specified type library
                         and register it
    /regfile[:FileName]  Generate a reg file with the specified name
                         instead of registering the types. This option
                         cannot be used with the /u or /tlb options
    /codebase            Set the code base in the registry
    /registered          Only refer to already registered type libraries
    /nologo              Prevents RegAsm from displaying logo
    /silent              Silent mode. Prevents displaying of success messages
    /verbose             Displays extra information
    /? or /help          Display this usage message
```

Figure 11-9: Assembly Registration Utility (RegAsm) options.

galutil.exe (Global Assembly Cache Tool)

No matter how you designate a strong name and generate a type library, there is no getting around the galutil.exe. Use gacutil.exe to add all assemblies to the GAC (Global Assembly Cache) so that classic COM can know what the component is:

```
gacutil /i Math.dll
```

Figure 11-10 displays a list of features that are available with the gacutil.exe utility. The more notable ones appear in bold.

```
Usage: Gacutil <option> [<parameters>]
 Options:
  /i
    Installs an assembly to the global assembly cache.  Include the
    name of the file containing the manifest as a parameter.
    Example:  /i myDll.dll
  /if
    Installs an assembly to the global assembly cache and forces
    overwrite if assembly already exists in cache.  Include the
    name of the file containing the manifest as a parameter.
    Example:  /if myDll.dll
  /ir
    Installs an assembly to the global assembly cache with traced
    reference. Include the name of file containing manifest,
    reference scheme, ID and description as parameters
    Example:  /ir myDll.dll FILEPATH c:\apps\myapp.exe MyApp
  /u[ngen]
    Uninstalls an assembly. Include the name of the assembly to
    remove as a parameter. If ngen is specified, the assembly is
    removed from the cache of ngen'd files, otherwise the assembly
    is removed from the global assembly cache
    Examples:.
      /ungen myDll
      /u myDll,Version=1.1.0.0,Culture=en,PublicKeyToken=874e23ab874e23ab
  /ur
    Uninstalls an assembly reference. Include the name of the
    assembly, type of reference, ID and data as parameters.
    Example:  /ur
myDll,Version=1.1.0.0,Culture=en,PublicKeyToken=874e23ab874e23ab
                    FILEPATH c:\apps\myapp.exe MyApp
  /uf
    Forces uninstall of an assembly by removing all install references
    Include the full name of the assembly to remove as a parameter..
    Assembly will be removed unless referenced by Windows Installer.
    Example:  /uf
myDll,Version=1.1.0.0,Culture=en,PublicKeyToken=874e23ab874e23ab
  /l
    Lists the contents of the global assembly cache. Allows optional
    assembly name parameter to list matching assemblies only
  /lr
    Lists the contents of the global assembly cache with traced
    reference information. Allows optional assembly name parameter
    to list matching assemblies only
  /cdl
    Deletes the contents of the download cache
```

(continued on next page)

```
/ldl
  Lists the contents of the downloaded files cache
/nologo
  Suppresses display of the logo banner
/silent
  Suppresses display of all output
/?
  Displays this help screen
```

Figure 11-10: Global Assembly Cache Utility (Gacutil) options.

Consuming .NET with classic COM

Now you'll expose your `Math.dll` to classic COM and configure the classic COM consuming application to use it:

1. Open the Visual Studio .NET Command Prompt.
2. Navigate to the Math project's root directory. (Not the `\bin` directory)
3. Use the Strong Name Tool to generate a public/private key pair.

```
sn -k keypair.snk
```

4. Open the .NET Math Solution.
5. Ignore the `MathTestClient` project for now and focus on the Math project.
6. Open the code window for the `AssemblyInfo.vb` file.
7. Insert the following attribute that tells the compiler to use the keypair.snk file that you just created as the public/private key pair file for strong naming the assembly:

```
'Tells the compiler what file to use when assigning a
'strong name to this component.
<Assembly: AssemblyKeyFile("keypair.snk")>
```

NOTE *If you created the KeyPair.snk file using the SN utility while the Math Solution is open, the project will not build. You will need to shut down the project and reload it.*

8. Save your changes and select Rebuild Solution from the Build menu.
9. Now you need to register your assembly in the Global Assembly Cache (GAC) using the Global Assembly Cache Tool (gacutil.exe). First navigate to the Math project's bin directory (cd bin) and type the following command:

```
gacutil /i Math.dll
```

10. After running the `regasm` utility to register your assembly with COM Services, the assembly can be used for late binding. As late binding is often undesirable for performance reasons, you'll use early binding. Use the Type Library Exporter to generate a type library that classic COM objects understand. After running the `tlbexp` utility, your client applications can access the assembly using early binding:

```
tlbexp Math.dll
```

11. Next, you register your assembly with COM Services:

```
regasm Math.dll
```

12. Close down the assembly project as there is nothing left to do here. Open the Visual Basic 6 project named "`classicMathTestClient`".
13. Select References from the Project menu item.
14. Deselect the check box from `classicCOMMath`.
15. Scroll down until you find a component named `Math`.

NOTE *If for some reason you are unable to find the* `Math` *reference, you can navigate directly to the* `Math.tlb` *file using the Browse button.*

16. Select the check box and press OK.
17. Change the declaration like from this

```
Dim objMath As New classicCOMMath.clsMath
```

to

```
Dim objMath As New Math.clsMath
```

18. Select Run and test the application.

Summary

In this chapter, you learned about the significance of COM Interop. You explored COM Interop by creating classic COM components to be consumed by a .NET Windows Form and creating a .NET assembly to be consumed by a Visual Basic 6 Form application. The next step will be to add Enterprise Services as described in Chapter 12, "Enterprise Services."

12

ENTERPRISE SERVICES

Enterprise applications often require enterprise level services. COM+ provided these services for classic COM and the .NET Framework allows access to these COM+ services through the Enterprise Services namespace. These services range from transactional support for a two-phase commit to object pooling.

Throughout this chapter you will add Enterprise Services to the Wedding List sample application. First, you will take a closer look at COM+ and its related services.

What is COM+?

COM+ is not COM (Component Object Model) but rather a set of services that are provided to COM Components. Because COM+ 1.0 was developed before .NET, it does not natively understand assemblies.

A Brief History of COM+

Component technologies have developed significantly over the last decade. Microsoft first introduced componentized code in components described as providing a service called OLE (Object Linking and Embedding) that quickly became COM. For awhile everything seemed to be COM until the technology matured and Microsoft marketing renamed COM to ActiveX. Then, of course, everything became ActiveX but we all know this is still the same old COM, so for the remainder of this chapter we will refer to binary compatible components as COM.

COM continued unchanged until CORBA introduced its RPC (Remote Procedure Call) capabilities. RPC is the ability to make calls to remote methods. Microsoft answered CORBA with DCOM (Distributed Component Object Model). While DCOM's plumbing is complex, you can think of it as COM's ability to instantiate, use, and unload a COM object across process and machine boundaries. In effect, the COM object does not know the actual location of the remote computer. The local COM component talks to a proxy as if the proxy is the desired remote object while the proxy handles security and networking required to communicate with the remote computers stub which acts on the behalf of the remote COM Component.

Figure 12-1 shows a conceptual view of a client (left) communicating with a remote object (right). The proxy working on behalf of the client actually resides within the same machine as the client reducing the client's requirement to know about anything beyond it's machine boundaries. The proxy uses the Window Registry to determine the physical machine name of the machine containing the remote method.

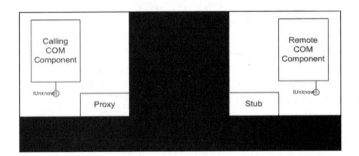

Figure 12-1: This is a simple DCOM scenario.

The stub, as shown in figure 12-1, communicates with the desired remote component. The use of the proxy and stub effectively abstracts the complexity of component location, network protocol development, and security, allowing the component developer to focus more on interface-based programming.

As slick as the DCOM model sounds, one does not need to look too far to discover its shortcomings. One disturbing realization is the time required to load and unload remote components. Often, this time is more than the time required to perform the business process. As you might imagine, without additional effort, a straightforward DCOM solution is not scalable.

Transaction processing, connection pooling, object pooling, and object life time are all developed by the DCOM programmer. Sure, this is fun the first time until you realize that every DCOM solution requires the same type of plumbing.

A DCOM controller (shown in Figure 12-2) is commonly used to address these issues. As shown in the diagram, all remote clients access the same instance of a DCOM object which abstracts the use of all other business objects. The DCOM controller manages the number of components loaded and their life time, thus allowing the same object to be used by multiple clients before unloading the object. This allows the component to perform more business work and to spend less time loading and unloading objects.

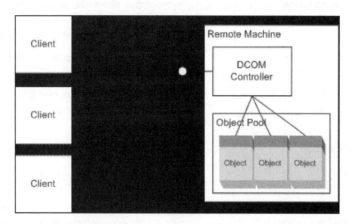

Figure 12-2: DCOM Controller solution.

Microsoft recognized that for developers to be more productive, they must spend more time developing business solutions and less time developing infrastructure. Their solution was MTS (Microsoft Transaction Services).

MTS and COM+

MTS has matured and, with a few additional features, evolved into COM+. While the name Microsoft Transaction Server implies that MTS is all about transactions, MTS actually does much more than that. As such, Microsoft renamed MTS to COM+ to alleviate some of the confusion; however, that name implies that COM+ is somehow an upgrade or new version of COM, when in fact COM+ merely provides services to COM.

Because MTS is now outdated, the remainder of this chapter will focus on COM+.

COM+ Applications

COM+ applications are not applications in the traditional sense in that they do not contain a user interface. COM+ applications are actually containers of components that form an application, and the COM and .NET assembly DLLs serve as the business logic portion of the application.

COM+ provides a number of services to components that once required a great deal of programming and testing from developers. Now with a simple configuration, these services can be integrated into any application library. Table 12-1 provides a list of COM+/Enterprise Services.

Table 12-1: COM+/Enterprise Services.

Service	Function
Application Pooling	Allows COM+ applications to support pooling to promote recoverability and scalability.
Application Recycling	When application errors exceed a predefined tolerance, the Application Recycling feature of COM+ will fix the application by shutting down and reloading the offending process.
Compensating Resource Manager (CRM)	Allows for the integration of application resources using Microsoft's Distributed Transaction Coordinator (MS DTS).
COM+ Events	Often referred to as Loosely Coupled Events, COM+ Events offers components a disconnected event model utilizing a publisher and subscriber model.
Concurrency	Determines the type of threading a COM+ application will subscribe to.
Context	All application components receive a context by which COM+ uniquely identifies component instances.
Just-In-Time Activation (JITA)	Just-In-Time Activation promotes scalability through efficient resource utilization. Components are not loaded until absolutely necessary and based on predefined configurations deactivates components.
Object Pooling	Components are configured to allow objects to be pooled. This component service is available to all components. The Min and Max number of components can be configured as well as how long components can remain loaded. Object Pooling reduces time wasted loading and unloading objects.
Queued Components	Allows components to be configured for messaging by abstracting the complexity of MSMQ (Microsoft Message Queue).
Security	COM+ institutes Role-Based security, thereby alleviating every application from having to build its own security solution. Role-Based security utilizes integrated security available to the underlying operating system.
Shared Property Manager (SPM)	Allows application state to be shared between COM+ application components.
Transaction processing	Allows for components to participate in transactions within the same data source as well as across multiple data sources with the use of the Compensating Resource Manager (CRM).

Creating a COM+ Application

To create a new COM+ application, follow these steps. (You will make configuration changes at the COM+ application level that will apply to all contained components.)

1. Run the Component Services application by selecting Start • Programs • Administrative Tool • Component Services.

2. Expand Computers, MyComputer, and finally, COM+ Applications, as shown in Figure 12-3. (You will see that some COM+ Applications already exist.)

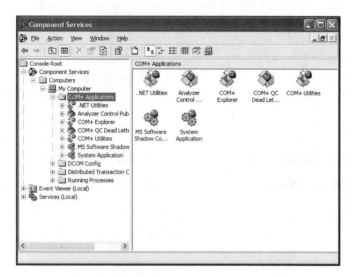

Figure 12-3: Component Services Manager.

3. Click on COM+ Applications to give the folder focus, then right-click COM+ Applications and select New then Application. You should see the COM Application installation wizard shown in Figuire 12-4.

Figure 12-4: COM Application Installation Wizard.

4. Click Next. At this point, you have the option of installing a prebuilt application or a new empty application, as shown in Figure 12-5.

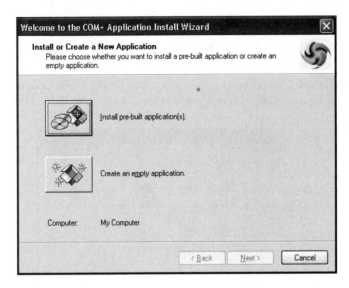

Figure 12-5: Dialog box with options of prebuilt or new application.

5. Select Create Empty Application.
6. Enter the new application name "Math," and leave the Activation Type set to Server Application, as shown in Figure 12-6. This ensures that the components will load into their own application space rather than the client's (as they do when components are contained in a Library Application).

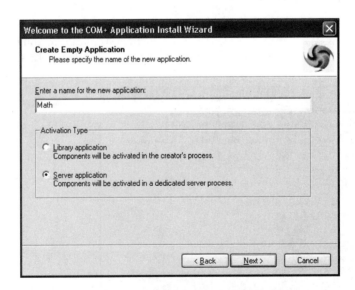

Figure 12-6: Dialog box with options of prebuilt or new application.

7. Click Next and you should see the "Set Application Identity" wizard page, in which you can configure the credentials that are used by components contained in this application. Leave this option set to Interactive user for now as debugging will be simpler; but be aware that your application's components will only be granted access rights when someone with sufficient rights is logged on locally.

8. Click Next and then click Finish.

Congratulations! You now have an application that does nothing. (Not to worry, we will soon remedy this.)

Building Serviced Components

Assemblies receiving services from COM+ are considered Serviced Components. The .NET Framework allows assemblies to receive services from COM+ through classes available in the System.EnterpriseServices namespace. (Attributes are used to implement specific COM+ Services as we'll see in the Enterprise Services example application.)

Components that receive services are called Serviced Components. For a component to become a Serviced Component it must first inherit the ServicedComponents class available within the System.EnterpriseServices namespace as shown below:

```
Imports System.EnterpriseServices
Public Class MyClass
        Inherits ServicedComponents
    ...
```

To demonstrate Enterprise Services you'll build a wedding list application. While the wedding list itself is incidental, it serves as a good model for demonstrating several component services and shows you how to build an entire application.

Initially, the WeddingList will contain a client application built using Windows Forms, with the only access to functionality through a series of layers. These layers effectively abstract the implementation of business rules and data access away from the client. Once we've built our basic application, we'll use Web Services to add a Façade layer so that our application can extend beyond the local network and across the Internet.

The initial WeddingList application model will look like Figure 12-7. As you can see, the client can access the Business Level layer directly but has no direct access to the Data Access layer. This is a simple, yet effective model, as the client programmer does not have to deal with the complexity of data access and most of the data access code that would have normally been duplicated several times is made generic enough to satisfy the needs the entire application.

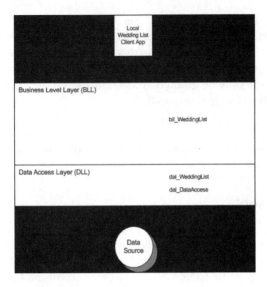

Figure 12-7: The initial logical Wedding List application model.

As you extend the WeddingList application to the Internet we will introduce a slightly different but not insignificant application layer. The Façade layer,
implemented by Web Services, as shown Figure 12-8, allows extensibility, and
makes it easy to implement and support the application. The Façade layer does
little more than pass our requests to the Business Level Layer. What is significant about the Façade layer is allows the Wedding List application components
to be available across the Internet through the use of Web Services as described
in Chapter 10, "Web Services."

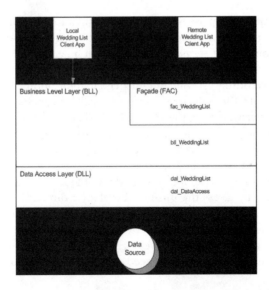

Figure 12-8: The logical WeddingList application model extending across the Internet.

The WeddingList application

While WeddingList may not require a full-blown enterprise architecture, you'll give it one to show you how to implement an enterprise application. In the end, you'll have not only a working application but also a model and a code library that you can use when building future applications.

The Windows Form

To build the WeddingList, follow these steps:

1. Create a new Visual Basic .NET project using the Windows Form template and name the project "WindowsFormWeddingList".

2. Use the controls and properties listed in Table 12-2 to build the user interface.

Table 12-2: Controls, Properties, and Their Related Values for the WeddingList Application

Type	Property	Value
Form	Name	Form1
	Size	568, 396
	Text	Our Wedding List
	Start Position	Center Screen
Label	Name	Label1
	Font	Arial, 12pt, style = Bold
	Location	188, 4
	Size	156, 24
	Text	Our Wedding List
Button	Name	btnPrintList
	Location	92, 32
	Text	Print List
Button	Name	btnRefresh
	Location	12, 32
	Text	Refresh
ListBox	Name	ListBoxWeddingList
	Location	8, 60
	Size	336, 228
	Font	Courier New 8.25
	Item Height	14

(continued on next page)

Type	Property	Value
Label	Name	lblNumberInvited
	ForeColor	MidnightBlue
	Location	8, 308
	Size	48, 23
	Text	#
	TextAlign	TopRight
Label	Name	Label2
	Location	64, 308
	Size	76, 23
	Text	invited
Label	Name	lblNumberConfirmed
	ForeColor	MidnightBlue
	Location	148, 308
	Size	48, 23
	Text	#
	TextAlign	TopRight
Label	Name	Label4
	Location	204, 308
	Size	76, 23
	Text	confirmed
Label	Name	Label3
	Location	356, 60
	Size	48, 23
	Text	Party:
	TextAlign	TopRight
Label	Name	Label5
	Location	356, 80
	Size	48, 23
	Text	Guests:
	TextAlign	TopRight

(continued on next page)

Table 12-2: Controls, Properties, and Their Related Values for the WeddingList Application (continued)

Type	Property	Value
TextBox	Name	txtParty
	BorderStyle	Fixed Single
	Location	404, 56
	Size	132, 20
TextBox	Name	txtGuests
	BorderStyle	Fixed Single
	Location	404, 80
	Size	28, 20
GroupBox	Name	GroupBox1
	Location	352, 104
	Size	200, 112
	Text	Guest of
Radio (Drag this control onto the GroupBox1 control)	Name	RadioBride
	Location	16, 20
	Size	176, 24
	Text	Bride
Radio (Drag this control onto the GroupBox1 control)	Name	RadioGroom
	Location	16, 48
	Size	176, 24
	Text	Groom
Radio (Drag this control onto the GroupBox1 control)	Name	RadioShared
	Location	16, 76
	Size	176, 24
	Text	Shared
GroupBox	Name	GroupBox2
	Location	352, 220
	Size	200, 112
	Text	Status
Radio (Drag this control onto the GroupBox1 control)	Name	RadioConfirmed
	Location	16, 20
	Size	176, 24
	Text	Confirmed

(continued on next page)

Table 12-2: Controls, Properties, and Their Related Values for the WeddingList Application (continued)

Type	Property	Value
Radio (Drag this control onto the GroupBox1 control)	Name	RadioUnconfirmed
	Location	16, 48
	Size	176, 24
	Text	Unconfirmed
Radio (Drag this control onto the GroupBox1 control)	Name	RadioDeclined
	Location	16, 76
	Size	176, 24
	Text	Declined
Button	Name	btnClear
	Enabled	False
	Location	340, 336
	Size	68, 23
	Text	Clear
Button	Name	btnAdd
	Enabled	False
	Location	412, 336
	Size	68, 23
	Text	Add New
Button	Name	btnModify
	Enabled	False
	Location	484, 336
	Size	68, 23
	Text	Modify
Button	Name	btnDelete
	Enabled	False
	Location	12, 340
	Size	72, 23
	Text	Delete
ErrorProvider	Name	ErrorProviderParty

Adding Application Behavior

To build the behavior aspects of the Wedding List application, follow these steps:

1. Open the code window for Form1 and add a new region after the Form1 class declaration.

```
Public Class Form1
   Inherits System.Windows.Forms.Form
      #Region " Application Behavior "

      #End Region
```

2. Build the ClearControls procedure by placing the following code in the Application Behavior region:

```
    Private Sub ClearControls()
    'Clears all text fields and disables selected button controls.
    txtParty.Text = ""
    txtGuests.Text = ""
    RadioBride.Checked = False
    RadioGroom.Checked = False
    RadioShared.Checked = False
    RadioConfirmed.Checked = False
    RadioUnconfirmed.Checked = False
    RadioDeclined.Checked = False
    btnDelete.Enabled = False
    btnClear.Enabled = False
    btnModify.Enabled = False
    btnAdd.Enabled = False
End Sub
```

3. Add the code that's listed in Table 12-3 behind the button controls.

Table 12-3: Code for Button Controls

Button Control	Code
btnClear (click event)	```'Clears controls
ClearControls()```
btnDelete (click event)	```'TODO: Remove selected items from database.
'TODO: Run a refresh sub procedure.
'Clears controls
ClearControls()```
btnAdd (click event)	```'TODO: Add the new record to the database.
'TODO: Run a refresh sub procedure.
'Clears controls
ClearControls()```
btnModify (click event)	```'TODO: Modifies the selected record.
'TODO: Run a refresh sub procedure.
'Clears controls
ClearControls()```
btnRefresh (click event)	```'TODO: Run a refresh sub procedure.
'Clears controls
ClearControls()```

4. Place the following code behind the double-click event of the ListBoxWeddingList control:

```
'TODO: Pull data based on selected item and place into
'edit the controls.

'Clears controls
   ClearControls()
   btnModify.Enabled = True
   btnClear.Enabled = True
btnDelete.Enabled = True
```

5. Place this code behind the keypress event of the txtParty control:

```
'Checking to see if a modification is already occurring.
If btnModify.Enabled = False Then
  btnAdd.Enabled = True
  btnClear.Enabled = True
End If
```

Creating the Database

In Chapter 9, "Retrieving Data," you performed the database tasks using Enterprise Manager. While many developers will continue using Enterprise Manager their first choice, you will build the database for this example using Visual Studio .NET. (The exercise will show how Visual Studio .NET database tools work.)

To create the database, follow these steps:

1. Using Server Explorer, expand Servers then your machine's name. Expand SQL Servers, and finally your SQL Server.
2. Right-click on your SQL Server's name and select New Database.
3. Enter WeddingList as the New Database Name.
4. Select either Integrated Security or SQL Server Authentication. This is used to supply rights to create the new database.

NOTE *If you are unsure, select SQL Server authentication using the user id sa and its related password (for testing purposes only). You can also create a new SQL Server user id and password (the safer option).*

5. Expand the new database, right-click on Tables, and select New Table.
6. Add the following column information to the new table (Table 12-4):

Table 12-4: Column Information

Column Name	Data Type	Length	Allow Nulls
ID	int	4	Deselect checkbox
Change the Identity attribute of the ID column in the matrix below to "yes".			
Party	varchar	23	Deselect checkbox
Guests	int	4	Deselect checkbox
Change the Default Value attribute of the Guests column to "1".			
GuestOf	char	1	Deselect checkbox
Change the Default Value of the GuestOf column to "'S'".			
Status	char	1	Deselect checkbox
Change the Default Value of the Status column to "'U'".			
CreateDate	datetime	8	Deselect checkbox
Change the Default Value of the CreateDate column to "GetDate()".			
ModifyDate	datetime	8	Leave checkbox selected

7. Click the Save icon.
8. Enter "PartyList" as the table's name.

You will notice that the interface (Figure 12-9) is not much different than the Enterprise Manager interface that you used in previous chapters.

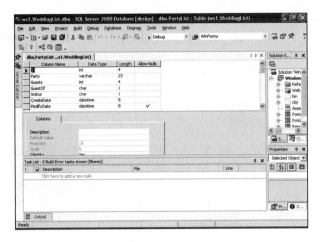

Figure 12-9: End result of building the PartyList table schema.

Adding Test Data

Before you can test the sample application, you need test data. Follow the steps below to add test data:

1. Expand the Tables icon and double click the PartyList table icon.
2. Add the values in Table 12-5 for testing purposes. When finished, your screen should look like Figure 12-10.

Table 12-5: Values of Test Data

ID	Party	Guests	GuestOf	Status	Create	Modify
	Mike Browning	5	G	C		
	David Hill	4	B	C		
	Jeff Dunaway	3	G	C		
	William Bennethum	2	G	C		
	Dale Campfield	4	G	U		
	Annette Retter	3	S	U		
	Lee Brown	2	S	U		
	David Pledger	2	S	U		
	Keith Stafford	2	S	U		
	Bill Potter	2	S	U		
	Kenn Schribner	2	S	U		
	Rob Schneidler	2	G	U		
	Bob Yexely	2	G	U		
	Steve Austin	2	G	U		
	Don Smith	2	G	U		

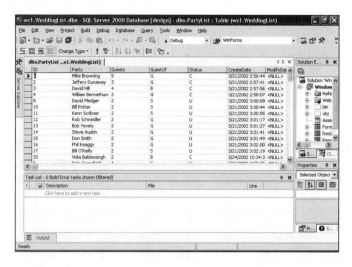

Figure 12-10: Results of entering data.

Creating the Supporting Stored Procedures

You'll implement data access through SQL Server stored procedures to improve performance and to add XML support. You'll pass all of the stored procedure parameters in a single XML string. This will allow the application to process multiple data requests significantly faster because a single call can now perform the same work that once required multiple database calls. Also, your dependency on interface compatibility in the component layers is significantly reduced when adding and removing columns and parameters.

You will build the following stored procedures:

- wl_AddParty_isp
- wl_DeleteParty_dsp
- wl_GetConfirmed_ssp
- wl_GetInvited_ssp
- wl_GetPartyList_ssp
- wl_GetPartyListDetail_ssp
- wl_UpdateParty_usp

The naming convention that is used for the stored procedures is a prefix that represents the application "wl" for WeddingList, followed by the action it performs, and then the type of data access as represented by ssp (Select stored procedure), isp (Insert stored procedure), usp (Update stored procedure), and dsp (Delete stored procedure).

If you are dealing with a larger application with dozens, hundreds, or even thousands of stored procedures, consider placing that application area before the action. For instance, if you were to build a select stored procedure for Sales, you might use the stored procedure name, wl_SalesGetPartyList_ssp. Using this naming convention will allow the stored procedures to sort by application and then application section, making it much easier to work with stored procedures in a medium to large application.

The wl_GetPartyList_ssp Stored Procedure

The first task of the sample application is to display a party list. The following stored procedure accepts no parameters because you simply want all items in the list. You will notice that the returned data is preformatted before the client application receives it. The added formatting allows the data to be displayed cleanly:

1. Right-click on the Stored Procedures icon under the WeddingList database in the Server Explorer.

2. Select New Stored Procedure.

3. Replace everything in the New Stored Procedure window with the following T-SQL (Transact SQL) code:

```
CREATE PROCEDURE dbo.wl_GetPartyList_ssp
AS
-- Returns all Parties with an ID and data for display in
-- a list control.
SELECT ID, CASE WHEN Party IS NULL THEN SPACE(22)
ELSE REPLACE(REPLACE(REPLACE(LEFT(Party + SPACE(23), 23), '\', '\\'), '(', '\('), ')', '\)') END
+ SPACE (1)
+ CASE WHEN Guests IS NULL THEN SPACE(0)
ELSE REPLACE(REPLACE(REPLACE(LEFT(Guests + SPACE(1), 1), '\', '\\'), '(', '\('), ')', '\)') END
+ SPACE (1)
+ CASE WHEN GuestOf IS NULL THEN SPACE(5)
WHEN GuestOf = 'S' THEN 'Shared'
WHEN GuestOf = 'G' THEN 'Groom '
WHEN GuestOf = 'B' THEN 'Bride '
ELSE REPLACE(REPLACE(REPLACE(LEFT(GuestOf + SPACE(6), 6), '\', '\\'), '(', '\('), ')', '\)') END
+ SPACE (1)
+ CASE WHEN Status IS NULL THEN SPACE(10)
WHEN Status = 'C' THEN 'Confirmed '
WHEN Status = 'U' THEN 'Unconfirmed'
WHEN Status = 'D' Then 'Declined   '
ELSE REPLACE(REPLACE(REPLACE(LEFT(Status + SPACE(11), 11), '\', '\\'), '(', '\('), ')', '\)') END
AS PartyList
FROM PartyList
ORDER BY Party
Return
```

4. Click Save. You will not be prompted for the stored procedure name as it is already provided as part of the CREATE PROCEDURE statement.

Notice that after saving the stored procedure that the CREATE PROCEDURE statement has been change to ALTER PROCEDURE.

5. To test the stored procedure, right-click in the stored procedure window and select Run Stored Procedure. (You may also run any stored procedure in the stored procedure list by right-clicking the specific stored procedure and selecting Run Stored Procedure.) The results of the stored procedure will be displayed in the Output Window, as shown in Figure 12-11.

If the stored procedure requires parameters, they are requested before the output is displayed.

```
Running dbo."wl_GetPartyList_ssp".

ID          PartyList
----------  -----------------------------------------------------------
6           Annette Retter       2 Shared Confirmed
17          Bill O'Reilly        2 Shared Unconfirmed
10          Bill Potter          2 Shared Unconfirmed
13          Bob Yexely           2 Groom  Unconfirmed
5           Dale Campfield       4 Groom  Unconfirmed
3           David Hill           4 Bride  Confirmed
8           David Pledger        2 Shared Unconfirmed
15          Don Smith            2 Groom  Unconfirmed
2           Jeffery Dunaway      3 Groom  Confirmed
11          Kenn Scribner        2 Shared Unconfirmed
7           Lee Brown            2 Shared Unconfirmed
1           Mike Browning        5 Groom  Confirmed
16          Phil Keaggy          2 Groom  Unconfirmed
12          Rob Schneidler       2 Groom  Unconfirmed
14          Steve Austin         2 Groom  Unconfirmed
33          Vidia Baldeosingh    2 Bride  Confirmed
4           William Bennethum    2 Groom  Confirmed
No more results.
(17 row(s) returned)
@RETURN_VALUE = 0
Finished running dbo."wl_GetPartyList_ssp".
```

Figure 12-11: Expected results of running the stored procedure.

The wl_GetPartyListDetail_ssp **Stored Procedure**

When a party list item is selected, the wl_GetPartyListDetail_ssp returns the detail of the party item, allowing for a closer inspection and updating of the selected item.

1. Right-click on the Stored Procedures icon and select New Stored Procedure.

2. Replace all the code in the New Stored Procedure code window with the following code:

```
CREATE PROCEDURE dbo.wl_GetPartyListDetail_ssp
@xmldoc NTEXT
AS
DECLARE @idoc INT
--Create an internal representation of the XML document.
EXEC sp_xml_preparedocument @idoc OUTPUT, @xmldoc

SELECT PartyList.ID, PartyList.Party, PartyList.Guests, PartyList.GuestOf,
PartyList.Status
FROM OPENXML (@idoc, 'Parties/Party', 2) with
                (id int 'ID')XMLSelect, PartyList
WHERE PartyList.ID = XMLSelect.ID
-- remove the XML document from memory
EXEC sp_xml_removedocument @idoc
/*
The advantage of using XML in a stored procedure that you only
plan on passing a sinlge parameter, as we plan on using this
stored procedure, is the flexability to pass in multiple Pary IDs
to return detail information about multiple parties. For instance,
you may wish you allow the user to select multiple items in a listbox
and return the details for all.
<Parties>
    <Party>
        <ID>1</ID>
    </Party>
    <Party>
        <ID>2</ID>
    </Party>
</Parties>
*/
```

3. Click Save.

4. Test the new stored procedure as you did the previous stored procedure (Figure12-12).

5. Supply the Value to be passed to the stored procedure and press OK (Figure 12-13).

Because you are passing XML strings to the stored procedures, you will need to supply the values in the form of a XML string. Each stored procedure has an example of this XML string commented out at the end of the T-SQL script, such as <Parties><Party><ID>5</ID></Party></Parties>.

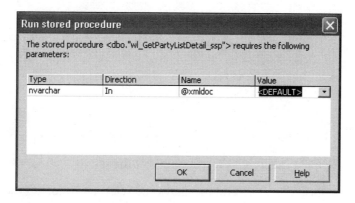

Figure 12-12: Prompting for stored procedure parameters.

```
Running dbo."wl_GetPartyListDetail_ssp" ( @xmldoc =
<Parties><Party><ID>5</ID></Party></Parties> ).

ID          Party                   Guests      GuestOf Status
----------- ----------------------- ----------- ------- ------
5           Dale Campfield          4           G       U
No more results.
(1 row(s) returned)
@RETURN_VALUE = 0
Finished running dbo."wl_GetPartyListDetail_ssp".
```

Figure 12-13: Expected results of running the stored procedure with the XML string.

The wl_AddParty_isp

Earlier, you learned some of the advantages of using XML to pass parameters between application layers. Doing so reduces interface dependence. Another advantage of using XML is the ability to place multiple sets of data within the same XML string.

Your application will only pass one party as XML to the wl_AddParty_isp. However, because the stored procedure will process a XML string, you can process a bulk of inserts in a single database call. (The design of the previous stored procedure wasn't covered because it only accepted a single parameter; however, this stored procedure and XML string format is a little more complex and deserves your attention.)

First, you need to identify the XML document that the stored procedure will process. (Keep in mind that the stored procedure is case sensitive when dealing with XML.) You'll build the stored procedure to accept XML documents that follow this format:

```
<Parties>
    <Party>
        <PartyName></PartyName>
        <Guests></Guests>
        <GuestOf></GuestOf>
        <Status></Status>
    </Party>
</Parties>
```

To build the stored procedure, follow these steps:

1. Right-click on Stored Procedures and select New Stored Procedure.
2. Replace all the code in the New Stored Procedure code window with the following T-SQL code:

```
CREATE PROCEDURE dbo.wl_AddParty_isp
@xmldoc Ntext
AS
DECLARE @idoc INT

--Create an internal representation of the XML document.
EXEC sp_xml_preparedocument @idoc OUTPUT, @xmldoc

INSERT PartyList (Party, Guests, GuestOf, Status)

SELECT Party, CASE WHEN Guests = '' THEN 1  ELSE Guests END ,
           CASE WHEN GuestOf = '' THEN 'S' ELSE GuestOf END,
           CASE WHEN Status = '' THEN 'U' ELSE Status END
       FROM OPENXML (@idoc, 'Parties/Party', 2) WITH
               (Party        Varchar(23)      'PartyName',
                Guests       Int              'Guests',
                GuestOf      Char(1)          'GuestOf',
                Status       Char(1)          'Status')

-- remove the XML document from memory
EXEC sp_xml_removedocument @idoc
/*

<Parties>
    <Party>
```

```
            <PartyName></PartyName>
            <Guests></Guests>
            <GuestOf></GuestOf>
            <Status></Status>
        </Party>
</Parties>
*/
```

....

3. Click Save.

At times, Visual Studio .NET seems to be unable to save the stored procedure to SQL Server. This doesn't always mean that there is actually anything wrong with your stored procedure. If you run into this problem, use SQL Server Enterprise Manager to create the stored procedure.

The wl_UpdateParty_usp Stored Procedure

The wl_UpdateParty_usp stored procedure updates the detailed party information. Build the wl_UpdateParty_usp stored procedure using the following T-SQL:

....

```
CREATE PROCEDURE dbo.wl_UpdateParty_usp
@xmldoc NTEXT
AS
DECLARE @idoc INT
--Create an internal representation of the XML document.
EXEC sp_xml_preparedocument @idoc OUTPUT, @xmldoc

UPDATE PartyList

SET     Party = XMLUpdate.PartyName,
            Guests = CASE WHEN XMLUpdate.Guests = '' THEN 1
        ELSE XMLUpdate.Guests END,
            GuestOf = CASE WHEN XMLUpdate.GuestOf = '' THEN 'S'
        ELSE XMLUpdate.GuestOf END ,
            Status = CASE WHEN XMLUpdate.Status = '' THEN 'U'
ELSE XMLUpdate.Status END

FROM OPENXML (@idoc, 'Parties/Party', 2) WITH
            (PartyID    int            'ID',
            PartyName  Varchar(20)    'PartyName',
            Guests     Varchar(20)    'Guests',
            GuestOf    Varchar(20)    'GuestOf',
            Status     Varchar(20)    'Status',
            SName      Varchar(50)    'SpouseName')XMLUpdate, PartyList
```

(continued on next page)

```
WHERE PartyList.id = XMLUpdate.PartyID
-- remove the XML document from memory
EXEC sp_xml_removedocument @idoc
/*
<Parties>
    <Party>
        <ID></ID>
        <PartyName></PartyName>
        <Guests></Guests>
        <GuestOf></GuestOf>
        <Status></Status>
    </Party>
</Parties>
*/
```

The wl_DeleteParty_dsp Stored Procedure

The wl_DeleteParty_dsp stored procedure receives an XML document that contains one or more party ids. After it receives them, the stored procedure will iterate through the list of ids and remove them from the database. Build the wl_DeleteParty_dsp stored procedure using the following T-SQL:

```
CREATE PROCEDURE dbo.wl_DeleteParty_dsp
@xmldoc NTEXT
AS
DECLARE @idoc INT
--Create an internal representation of the XML document.
EXEC sp_xml_preparedocument @idoc OUTPUT, @xmldoc

DELETE PartyList
FROM OPENXML (@idoc, 'Parties/Party', 2) WITH
        (PartyID  int  'ID')XMLDelete, PartyList
WHERE PartyList.id = XMLDelete.PartyID
-- remove the XML document from memory
EXEC sp_xml_removedocument @idoc

/*

<Parties>
    <Party>
        <ID></ID>
    </Party>
</Parties>
*/
```

The wl_GetInvited_ssp Stored Procedure

Build the wl_GetInvited_ssp stored procedure using the following T-SQL:

```
CREATE PROCEDURE dbo.wl_GetInvited_ssp
 AS
SELECT SUM(Guests) FROM Partylist
```

The wl_GetComfirmed_ssp Stored Procedure

The wl_GetComfirmed_ssp stored procedure is a simple stored procedure that does not accept parameters and returns all confirmed parties as indicated by a status of "C". Build the wl_GetInvited_ssp stored procedure using the following T-SQL:

```
CREATE PROCEDURE dbo.wl_GetConfirmed_ssp
 AS
SELECT SUM(Guests) FROM Partylist WHERE Status = 'C'
```

The Middle-Tier Components

Now you are ready to build the middle-tier components that will serve intially as class libraries to the Windows Form client application. You'll test the components with the client to ensure that everything is working according to design, after which you'll implement Serviced Component attributes and deploy to a COM+ application. Finally, you'll implement web services to expose the application to other platforms (although you'll first need to modify the client to perform its function through your newly created web services).

The dal_DataAccess component

You will be implementing all data access through XML and stored procedures. There are two reasons for this:

*   Passing all parameters as a single XML string reduces interface dependence so when adding columns to a table or passing additional parameters, there is no need to be concerned with class interfaces. No matter how many parameters are to be passed, as long as they are passed in the XML string, the XML string will occupy only a single parameter of the interface.
*   Using a XML string to hold parameters brings increased flexibility and a significant increase in performance. When inserting, updating, and deleting multiple records, you would, in the past, have to make multiple calls to the database. Passing all inserts, updates, or deletes in a single XML string allows for multiple data updates in a single database call because a single XML string can hold multiple sets of records that can be processed by SQL Server. When considering that, connecting to a data source and running a stored procedure often takes longer than the intended data request or modification.

Go ahead and create the dal_DataAccess component by following these steps:

1. Create a new Visual Basic .NET project using the Class Library template and name the project WeddingList.

2. Rename the Class1.vb file to dal_DataAccess.vb.

3. Open the code window for the dal_DataAccess.vb and rename the Class1 class to dal_DataAccess.

NOTE *While you can place more than one class into each file, your code will tend to be more organized if you use a separate file for each new class.*

4. Import the appropriate namespace for SQL Server:

```
Imports System.Data.SQLClient
```

5. Add the following code to the dal_DataAccess class:

```
Public Sub XML_ModifyDataSource(ByVal strSP As String, _
                                ByVal strXML As String)

'Generic procedure that accept a SP name and XML string.
  Dim strConn As String = _
  "Data Source=localhost;Initial Catalog=WeddingList" & _
                          ";User Id=sa;Pwd=;"

        Dim objConn As New SqlConnection(strConn)
        Dim objCmd As New SqlCommand()

        Dim objParamID As New SqlParameter("@xmldoc", SqlDbType.NText)
        objParamID.Direction = ParameterDirection.Input
        objParamID.Value = strXML

        objCmd.CommandType = CommandType.StoredProcedure
        objCmd.CommandText = strSP
        objCmd.Parameters.Add(objParamID)

        objCmd.Connection = objConn
        objCmd.Connection.Open()

        objCmd.ExecuteNonQuery()

        objCmd.Connection.Close()

        End Sub
```

```
            Public Function XML_GetDataSet(ByVal strSP As String, _
ByVal strDataTable As String, _
                                    Optional ByVal strXML As String = "") _
                                                        As DataSet


        'Generic procedure for returning a DataSet
    Dim strConn As String = _
    "Data Source=localhost;Initial Catalog=WeddingList" & _
                        ";User Id=sa;Pwd=;"


        Dim objConn As New SqlConnection(strConn)
        Dim objCmd As New SqlCommand()
        Dim objDataAdapter As New SqlDataAdapter()
        Dim objDataSet As New DataSet()

        'Notice that the parameter is of type "NText". This should be
        'much larger than anything you may need to use thereby not
        'limiting the size of the XML document that can be passed.
        If strXML <> "" Then
            Dim objParamID As New SqlParameter("@xmldoc", SqlDbType.NText)
            objParamID.Direction = ParameterDirection.Input
            objParamID.Value = strXML
            objCmd.Parameters.Add(objParamID)
        End If

        objCmd.CommandType = CommandType.StoredProcedure
        objCmd.CommandText = strSP

        objCmd.Connection = objConn
        objCmd.Connection.Open()

        objDataAdapter.SelectCommand = objCmd
        objDataAdapter.Fill(objDataSet, strDataTable)

        objCmd.Connection.Close()

        Return objDataSet

    End Function
```

NOTE *The* XML_ModifyDataSource *function accepts the stored procedure name and the XML document, describing the data to be modified. Normally, you would return success or failure information of a transaction. You would also expect to pass in the connection string to make your code more general and usable by other applications. To save time, you will implement the method as a sub-procedure, returning nothing, and hard code the connection string.*

The dal_WeddingList class

The dal_WeddingList class is the only class that communicates with the dal_DataAccess class directly. The dal_WeddingList class abstracts all data access knowledge from upstream components thereby abstracting all data access knowledge. To build it, follow these steps:

1. Add a new class file to your project named dal_WeddingList.

2. Import the SQL Server client namespace:

```
Imports System.Data.SqlClient
```

3. Add the following methods to the new dal_WeddingList class:

```
Public Function GetPartyList() As DataSet
    'Call generic code to run sp passing the sp
    'name and connection string.
    'This method will return a DataSet.
    Dim objDataAccess As New WeddingList.dal_DataAccess()
    Dim objDataSet As New DataSet()
    objDataSet = objDataAccess.XML_GetDataSet("wl_GetPartyList_ssp", _
                                        "PartyListForListBox")
    Return objDataSet
End Function


Public Function GetInvited() As DataSet
    Dim objDataAccess As New WeddingList.dal_DataAccess()
    Dim objDataSet As New DataSet()
    objDataSet = objDataAccess.XML_GetDataSet("wl_GetInvited_ssp", "Invited")
    Return objDataSet
End Function


Public Function GetConfirmed() As DataSet
    Dim objDataAccess As New WeddingList.dal_DataAccess()
    Dim objDataSet As New DataSet()
    objDataSet = objDataAccess.XML_GetDataSet("wl_GetConfirmed_ssp", _
                                        "Confirmed")
    Return objDataSet
End Function


Public Function GetPartyListDetail(ByVal strXML As String) As DataSet
    'Call generic code to run sp passing the sp name and connection string.
    'This method will return a DataSet.
    Dim objDataAccess As New WeddingList.dal_DataAccess()
    Dim objDataSet As New DataSet()
    objDataSet = objDataAccess.XML_GetDataSet("wl_GetPartyListDetail_ssp", _
                                        "PartyListDetail", strXML)
```

```
        Return objDataSet
End Function

Public Sub AddParty(ByVal strXML As String)
    'Call generic code to run sp passing the sp name and connection string.
    Dim objDataAccess As New WeddingList.dal_DataAccess()
    objDataAccess.XML_ModifyDataSource("wl_AddParty_isp", strXML)
End Sub

Public Sub UpdateParty(ByVal strXML As String)
    'Call generic code to run sp passing the sp name and connection string.
    Dim objDataAccess As New WeddingList.dal_DataAccess()
    objDataAccess.XML_ModifyDataSource("wl_UpdateParty_usp", strXML)
End Sub

Public Sub DeleteParty(ByVal strXML As String)
    'Call generic code to run sp passing the sp name and connection string.
    Dim objDataAccess As New WeddingList.dal_DataAccess()
    objDataAccess.XML_ModifyDataSource("wl_DeleteParty_dsp", strXML)
End Sub
```

The bll_WeddingList class

The bll_WeddingList class is the layer that clients of the same platform access;
the layer also provides all business logic. You will not perform any business logic
here because it does not promote the demonstration of service components.
However, when you are building your own application, this is where you would
add your business logic. You will need the assistance of .NET XML classes that
the .NET Framework provides to implement business logic here.

To build this class, follow these steps:

1. Add a new class library file named bll_WeddingList to the project.

2. Add the following code including the import:

```
Public Function GetPartyList() As DataSet

    ' In addition to getting the PartyList we are returning two
    ' other DataTables for Invited and Confirmed guests. This is an
    ' effort to reduce the number of client calls by packing
    ' 3 calls in the form of DataTables into a single DataSet.

    ' This implementation performs the following actions:
    ' 1. Set a temp DataSet equal to the returned DataSet
    ' 2. Making a reference to the returned DataTable
    ' 3. Remove the returned DataTable from the returned DataSet
```

(continued on next page)

```
' 4. Add the referenced DataTable to the DataSet to be
'    returned to the client.

Dim objDataSet As New DataSet()
Dim objTempDS As New DataSet()
Dim objDataTable As New DataTable()
Dim obj_daa_WeddingList As New WeddingList.dal_WeddingList()

objTempDS = obj_daa_WeddingList.GetPartyList
objDataTable = objTempDS.Tables(0)
objTempDS.Tables.Remove(objDataTable)
objDataSet.Tables.Add(objDataTable)

objTempDS = obj_daa_WeddingList.GetInvited
objDataTable = objTempDS.Tables(0)
objTempDS.Tables.Remove(objDataTable)
objDataSet.Tables.Add(objDataTable)

objTempDS = obj_daa_WeddingList.GetConfirmed
objDataTable = objTempDS.Tables(0)
objTempDS.Tables.Remove(objDataTable)
objDataSet.Tables.Add(objDataTable)

' This implementation will also work; however, it copies
' the DataTable returned in the DataSet to our DataTable.
' This means that not only is the data copies but for a
' brief time the DataTable exists in memory twice. As my
' friend, Vince, pointed out, this solution works but is not
' not necessary so I opted to use the solution shown above.

'objDataTable = obj_daa_WeddingList.GetPartyList.Tables(0).Copy
'objDataSet.Tables.Add(objDataTable)
'objDataTable = obj_daa_WeddingList.GetInvited.Tables(0).Copy
'objDataSet.Tables.Add(objDataTable)
'objDataTable = obj_daa_WeddingList.GetConfirmed.Tables(0).Copy
'objDataSet.Tables.Add(objDataTable)
Return objDataSet
End Function

Public Function GetPartyListDetail(ByVal strXML As String) As DataSet
    Dim obj_daa_WeddingList As New WeddingList.dal_WeddingList()
    Dim objDataSet As DataSet
    objDataSet = obj_daa_WeddingList.GetPartyListDetail(strXML)
    Return objDataSet
End Function
```

```
Public Sub AddParty(ByVal strXML As String)
    Dim obj_daa_WeddingList As New WeddingList.dal_WeddingList()
        obj_daa_WeddingList.AddParty(strXML)
End Sub

Public Sub UpdateParty(ByVal strXML As String)
    Dim obj_daa_WeddingList As New WeddingList.dal_WeddingList()
        obj_daa_WeddingList.UpdateParty(strXML)
End Sub

Public Sub DeleteParty(ByVal strXML As String)
    Dim obj_daa_WeddingList As New WeddingList.dal_WeddingList()
        obj_daa_WeddingList.DeleteParty(strXML)
End Sub
```

3. Open the `AssemblyInfo.vb` files code window and modify the assembly attributes. (Most of this code will be automatically generated by the Visual Studio .NET IDE.) Make sure you go through each line and verify that each attribute is represented and properly configured in your `AssemblyInfo.vb` file. Specifically, verify that the `AssemblyVersion` attribute is 1.0.0.1. Correctly configuring these attributes aids in the identification of your assembly. The Guid in your assembly will be generated by the Visual Studio .NET IDE and does not need to match the Guid value in the following code.

NOTE *It seems that the Visual Studio .NET IDE configures the* `AssemblyVersion` *attribute so that it automatically increments with each compile, forcing you to recompile your clients. You might question why Microsoft has done it this way, but please make it your first step to change the* `AssemblyVersion` *to the desired version when you're building assemblies.*

```
Imports System.Reflection
Imports System.Runtime.InteropServices

' General Information about an assembly is controlled through the following
' set of attributes. Change these attribute values to modify the information
' associated with an assembly.

' Review the values of the assembly attributes

<Assembly: AssemblyTitle("WeddingList")>
<Assembly: AssemblyDescription("The Wedding List Sample Application.")>
<Assembly: AssemblyCompany("The Book of Visual Studio .NET")>
<Assembly: AssemblyProduct("WeddingList")>
<Assembly: AssemblyCopyright("")>
<Assembly: AssemblyTrademark("")>
<Assembly: CLSCompliant(True)>
```

(continued on next page)

```
'The following GUID is for the ID of the typelib if this project is exposed to COM
<Assembly: Guid("738266B8-541A-4B9F-ABD3-91677DE07F84")>

' Version information for an assembly consists of the following four values:
'
'    Major Version
'    Minor Version
'    Build Number
'    Revision
'
' You can specify all the values or you can default the Build and Revision Numbers
' by using the '*' as shown below:
<Assembly: AssemblyVersion("1.0.0.1")>
```

Adding the WeddingList Objects to the GAC (Global Assembly Cache)

Unlike classic COM, assemblies do not register their location or interfaces. This impacts how you reference assemblies in two significant ways. First, all of an application's components do not need to be registered with any system. All metadata concerning a component's interface are stored within the component and the metadata's location is not important because it exists within the calling application.

Second, if you want your component to be made available to other applications it must be added to the GAC (Global Assembly Cache). In this example, you do. There are three ways to do so. One is GUI-based and the other two are implemented using the command line. However, before you can use either option, you must make sure that the component is unique to the machine because it will be exposed to all applications of the machine once it is added to the GAC. To uniquely identify a component, give it a strong name:

1. Run the Visual Studio .NET Command Prompt by selecting Start • Programs • Microsoft Visual Studio .NET • Visual Studio .NET Tools and finally Visual Studio .NET Command Prompt.

2. Navigate to you projects directory and type the following command:

```
sn -k KeyPair.snk
Exit
```

This creates a public/private key pair that will be used by the Visual Studio .NET IDE to give your component a strong name. Also, note that you created our KeyPair.snk file in the projects directory. This is because the Visual Basic compiler looks in the project directory by default. C#, on the other hand, looks for the same file in the bin directory or where ever the assembly is created.

3. Open up the AssemblyInfo.vb files code window and add the following Assembly attribute.

```
<Assembly: AssemblyKeyFile("KeyPair.snk")>
```

NOTE *The strong name public/private key pair is case-sensitive so keep that in mind when adding the assembly name to the* AssemblyKeyFile *attribute.*

4. Compile the project. At this point we are ready to add our components to the GAC.

NOTE *For some reason there are times when the compiler doesn't see the* KeyPair.snk *file. When this occurs, shutting down the project and reloading it seems to alleviate this problem. (Hopefully, a fix will be included in an upcoming service pack.) The problem seems to occur when the* KeyPair.snk *file, which can have any name you desire, is created while the project is open.*

Option 1: Using the .NET Framework Configuration Tool

You will use the .NET Framework Configuration console to add the assembly to the Global Assembly Cache:

1. Open the .NET Framework Configuration Tool by selecting Start • Programs • Administrative Tools • Microsoft .NET Framework Configuration. You should see the .NET Framework Configuration screen that appears in Figure 12-14.

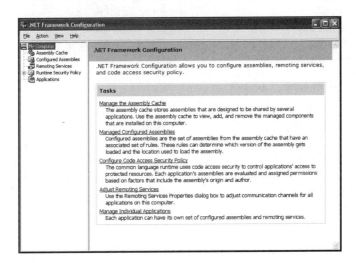

Figure 12-14: The .NET Framework Configuration console.

2. Select Assembly Cache (Figure 12-15). Select View List of Assemblies in the Assembly Cache to view all assemblies in the GAC.

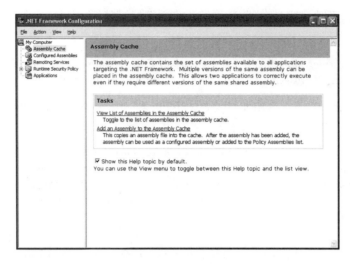

Figure 12-15: The Assembly Cache tasks page.

3. Right-click on the Assembly Cache icon and select Add.
4. Navigate to the WeddingList.dll file in the Bin directory of the project and select Open.

NOTE *If you have not given your component a strong name, you will immediately receive an error indicating that your assembly cannot be added because it does not have a strong name. Makes sense doesn't it? This is a common mistake. It occurs when you forget to add to the AssemblyKeyFile attribute after you've generated the KeyPair.snk file and then compile the project.*

5. Press OK.

Option 2: Using the gacutil.exe utility

Adding an assembly to the GAC using the gacutil.exe command is the same as using the Microsoft .NET Framework Configuration Tool in terms of creating a strong name and adding the attribute clause to the projects AssemblyInfo.vb. To add an assembly, open a command prompt and replace the use of the Microsoft .NET Framework Configuration Tool with the following:

```
gacutil /i WeddingList.dll
```

You may need to use `gacutil.exe` to remove the `WeddingList.dll` from the GAC before you can add it.

To remove the assembly, right-click it and select remove from the Microsoft .NET Framework Configuration Tool or type

```
gacutil /u WeddingList.dll
```

at the command prompt.

Attaching the Client to the Assembly

To make our Windows Form project aware of the components we've built, follow these steps:

1. Open the WindowsFormWeddingList solution.
2. Right-click on References in the Solution Explorer window and select Add Reference.
3. Select the Browse button and navigate to the `WeddingList.dll` file and press Open then OK.

Now you have a reference to the assembly. For now, these components will be loaded in-process and not in COM+. Once you are satisfied that everything is functioning properly, you will move the assembly into COM+ where the components will run out-of-process.

Adding Functionality to the Client

References to our newly created assembly are great, but without functionality in the client to make use of the references, they are of no use. In this section, you will add functionality that will dictate the client's behavior as well as make use of the referenced assembly:

1. Open the code window for Form1 and add the following insert statements.

```
Imports System.Data.SqlClient
Imports System.Text
Imports System.EnterpriseServices
Imports System.Net
```

The `RefreshLish()` method will be used whenever data is modified or the Refresh button is pressed. This method refreshes the `ListBoxWeddingList` control, populates the number of invited guests, and tells us the number of confirmed guests.

2. Add the following code to the Form1 Class:

```
Private Sub RefreshList()
    'ListBoxWeddingList
    Dim obj_bll_WeddingList As New WeddingList.fac_WeddingList()
    Dim objDataSet As New DataSet()
    Dim objDataTable As New DataTable()
    Try
        objDataSet = obj_bll_WeddingList.GetPartyList
    Catch e As Exception
        MessageBox.Show(e.ToString)
        Exit Sub
    End Try
    objDataTable = objDataSet.Tables("PartyListForListBox")

    ListBoxWeddingList.DataSource = objDataTable
    ListBoxWeddingList.DisplayMember = "PartyList"
    ListBoxWeddingList.ValueMember = "ID"

    lblNumberInvited.Text = objDataSet.Tables("Invited").Rows(0).Item(0)
    lblNumberConfirmed.Text = objDataSet.Tables("Confirmed").Rows(0).Item(0)

End Sub
```

3. Add a call to this method in the following procedures:

```
Form1_Load
btnDelete_Click
btnAdd_Click
btnModify_Click
btnRefresh_Click
```

NOTE *These methods may not be readily available. Simply double-click each corresponding button within the form to get the click event procedures. For instance, to gain access to the Form1_Load event procedure, double-click on the Form1 form in the form designer. Place the following code within each of the above mentioned event procedures:*

```
    'Run refresh sub procedure.
    RefreshList()
```

Retrieving Detailed Information

The ListBoxWeddingList_DoubleClick method, not yet created, gets the Id of the selected item, then populates our forms controls so that the detailed information about the party can be viewed and modified. Also, the appropriate buttons are enabled and disabled.

If you double-click on the ListBoxWeddingList control, you will generate the wrong procedure. To correct this, in the Form1 code window use the upper-left drop box to select ListBoxWeddingList, then select DoubleClick from the drop box on the right:

Insert the following code into the newly generated ListBoxWeddingList_DoubleClick event:

```
'Clears controls
ClearControls()

btnModify.Enabled = True
btnClear.Enabled = True
btnDelete.Enabled = True
'Pull data for selected item and place in edit controls.
Dim obj_bll_WeddingList As New WeddingList.fac_WeddingList()
Dim objDataSet As DataSet
Dim objSB As New StringBuilder()

objSB.Append("<Parties><Party><ID>")
objSB.Append(ListBoxWeddingList.SelectedValue)
objSB.Append("</ID></Party></Parties>")

objDataSet = obj_bll_WeddingList.GetPartyListDetail(objSB.ToString)
'Set values of controls
CurrentPartyID = objDataSet.Tables("PartyListDetail").Rows(0).Item("ID")
txtParty.Text = objDataSet.Tables("PartyListDetail").Rows(0).Item("Party")
txtGuests.Text = objDataSet.Tables("PartyListDetail").Rows(0).Item("Guests")

Select Case objDataSet.Tables("PartyListDetail").Rows(0).Item("GuestOf")
    Case "B"
        RadioBride.Checked = True
    Case "G"
        RadioGroom.Checked = True
    Case "S"
        RadioShared.Checked = True
End Select

Select Case objDataSet.Tables("PartyListDetail").Rows(0).Item("Status")
    Case "C"
        RadioConfirmed.Checked = True
    Case "U"
```

```
            RadioUnconfirmed.Checked = True
        Case "D"
            RadioDeclined.Checked = True
End Select
```

Notice that this procedure first builds an XML string using the StringBuilder class, then passes that class to the GetPartyListDetail function. Because all the stored procedures accept an XML string as the parameter, all the functions will build an XML string before calling the associated method.

Validation_Party

The only requirement we will enforce, at the presentation level, is a required Party Name. As a demonstration of the ErrorProvider, you will enforce a rule that states the Party Name must be provided. The ErrorProvider named ErrorProviderParty is the object that is used in this example. The following steps will walk you through adding client side validation code:

1. Place the following code within the Form1 class to create both your validation procedure and Validation Region to aid in the organization of your code:

```
#Region " Validation "

Private Function Validate_Party() As Boolean

    If txtParty.Text = "" Then
        ErrorProviderParty.SetError(txtParty, "Please provide a Party Name.")
        Return True
    Else
        ' Clear the error.
        ErrorProviderParty.SetError(txtParty, "")
    End If
End Function

#End Region
```

2. Add error provider code to the RefreshList() method.

```
    ' Clear the error.
ErrorProviderParty.SetError(txtParty, "")
```

3. Add the following code to the btnClear_Click event.

```
      ' Clear the error.
   ErrorProviderParty.SetError(txtParty, "")
```

4. Add the following code to the first line of the btnModify_Click event.

```
If Validate_Party() Then Exit Sub
```

5. Add the following code to the first line of the btnAdd_Click event.

```
If Validate_Party() Then Exit Sub
```

txtParty_KeyPress

Place the following code in the KeyPress event of the txtParty control to enable the add button as a new party is entered:

```
      'Checking to see if a modification is already occuring.
      If btnModify.Enabled = False Then
          btnAdd.Enabled = True
          btnClear.Enabled = True
   End If
```

btnModify_Click

When all is said and done your XML will look like this:

```
<Parties>
    <Party>
        <ID>17</ID>
        <PartyName> Bill O'Reilly</PartyName>
        <Guests>3</Guests>
        <GuestOf>G</GuestOf>
        <Status>C</Status>
    </Party>
</Parties>
```

The btnModify click event validates the party name, packs all parameters into an XML document, and calls the UpdateParty method of the WeddingList.bll_WeddingList class. To create it, add the following code to the btnModify_Click event:

```
If Validate_Party() Then Exit Sub

'Modifies the selected record
Dim obj_bll_WeddingList As New WeddingList.fac_WeddingList()
Dim objSB As New StringBuilder()

objSB.Append("<Parties><Party>")
objSB.Append("<ID>" & CurrentPartyID & "</ID>")
objSB.Append("<PartyName>" & txtParty.Text & "</PartyName>")
objSB.Append("<Guests>" & txtGuests.Text & "</Guests>")

objSB.Append("<GuestOf>")
If RadioBride.Checked Then objSB.Append("B")
If RadioGroom.Checked Then objSB.Append("G")
If RadioShared.Checked Then objSB.Append("S")
objSB.Append("</GuestOf>")

objSB.Append("<Status>")
If RadioConfirmed.Checked Then objSB.Append("C")
If RadioUnconfirmed.Checked Then objSB.Append("U")
If RadioDeclined.Checked Then objSB.Append("D")
objSB.Append("</Status>")

objSB.Append("</Party></Parties>")

obj_bll_WeddingList.UpdateParty(objSB.ToString)

'Clears controls
ClearControls()

'Run refresh sub procedure.
RefreshList()
```

btnAdd_Click

The Add click event works very similar to btnModify_Click procedure by first building an XML document that represents the new Party and then passing that XML as a string parameter to the Data Access Layer:

```
If Validate_Party() Then Exit Sub

'Add the new record to the database
Dim obj_bll_WeddingList As New WeddingList.fac_WeddingList()
Dim objSB As New StringBuilder()

objSB.Append("<Parties><Party>")
objSB.Append("<PartyName>" & txtParty.Text & "</PartyName>")
objSB.Append("<Guests>" & txtGuests.Text & "</Guests>")

objSB.Append("<GuestOf>")
If RadioBride.Checked Then objSB.Append("B")
If RadioGroom.Checked Then objSB.Append("G")
If RadioShared.Checked Then objSB.Append("S")
objSB.Append("</GuestOf>")

objSB.Append("<Status>")
If RadioConfirmed.Checked Then objSB.Append("C")
If RadioUnconfirmed.Checked Then objSB.Append("U")
If RadioDeclined.Checked Then objSB.Append("D")
objSB.Append("</Status>")

objSB.Append("</Party></Parties>")

obj_bll_WeddingList.AddParty(objSB.ToString)

'Clears controls
ClearControls()

'Run refresh sub procedure.
RefreshList()
```

btnDelete_Click

This procedure works very similar to the two previous procedures except there is no need for validation:

```
'Remove selected items from database.
Dim obj_bll_WeddingList As New WeddingList.fac_WeddingList()
Dim objSB As New StringBuilder()

objSB.Append("<Parties><Party>")
objSB.Append("<ID>" & CurrentPartyID & "</ID>")
objSB.Append("</Party></Parties>")

obj_bll_WeddingList.DeleteParty(objSB.ToString)

'Run refresh sub procedure.
RefreshList()
'Clears controls
ClearControls()
```

Why Use XML?

As you learned earlier, you are using XML to pass all the parameters, thereby reducing the assemblies' interface dependence on parameters. You could take this another step and pass the stored procedure name, making data access even more generic; however, this would make access more SQL Server dependent. As things stand right now, to change database platforms, all you need to do is modify the DAL (Data Access Layer) layer.

Another advantage of using XML is that it allows you to batch process without creating a new procedure. For instance, you could easily allow multiselect of the list box and then pass the selected IDs in an XML string to the Delete stored procedure. The Delete stored procedure would process each item in the XML string until all selected items are deleted. The ability to process multiple records in a single database call significantly increases performance and scalability.

Code Review

All of the code in the following section is provided to give you a full view of what your code should look like. It's important that your current code work properly before you add the components to COM+. Test your application to ensure that it is working properly. Use the following code segments to help troubleshoot any problems you may encounter:

```vb
'Imports of required namespaces.
Imports System.Data.SqlClient
Imports System.Text
Imports System.EnterpriseServices
Imports System.Net

Public Class Form1
  Inherits System.Windows.Forms.Form
#Region " Application Behavior "

  'Behavior methods.
  Dim CurrentPartyID As Integer

  Private Sub Form1_Load(ByVal sender As System.Object, ByVal e ...
    RefreshList()

  End Sub

  'This is the method used to refresh the Party List.
  Private Sub RefreshList()

    'ListBoxWeddingList
    Dim obj_bll_WeddingList As New WeddingList.fac_WeddingList()
    Dim objDataSet As New DataSet()
    Dim objDataTable As New DataTable()

    Try
      objDataSet = obj_bll_WeddingList.GetPartyList
    Catch e As Exception
      MessageBox.Show(e.ToString)
      Exit Sub
    End Try

    objDataTable = objDataSet.Tables("PartyListForListBox")

    ListBoxWeddingList.DataSource = objDataTable
    ListBoxWeddingList.DisplayMember = "PartyList"
    ListBoxWeddingList.ValueMember = "ID"
```

(continued on next page)

```
            lblNumberInvited.Text = objDataSet.Tables("Invited").Rows(0).Item(0)
            lblNumberConfirmed.Text = _
objDataSet.Tables("Confirmed").Rows(0).Item(0)

            ' Clear the error.
            ErrorProviderParty.SetError(txtParty, "")

    End Sub

    Private Sub ClearControls()
        'Clears all text fields and disables selected button controls.
        txtParty.Text = ""
        txtGuests.Text = ""
        RadioBride.Checked = False
        RadioGroom.Checked = False
        RadioShared.Checked = False
        RadioConfirmed.Checked = False
        RadioUnconfirmed.Checked = False
        RadioDeclined.Checked = False
        btnDelete.Enabled = False
        btnClear.Enabled = False
        btnModify.Enabled = False
        btnAdd.Enabled = False

    End Sub

    Private Sub btnClear_Click(ByVal sender As System.Object, ByVal ...
    'Clears controls
        ClearControls()
        ' Clear the error.
        ErrorProviderParty.SetError(txtParty, "")

    End Sub

    Private Sub btnDelete_Click(ByVal sender As System.Object, ByVal ...

        'Remove selected items from database.
        Dim obj_bll_WeddingList As New WeddingList.fac_WeddingList()
        Dim objSB As New StringBuilder()

        objSB.Append("<Parties><Party>")
        objSB.Append("<ID>" & CurrentPartyID & "</ID>")
        objSB.Append("</Party></Parties>")

        obj_bll_WeddingList.DeleteParty(objSB.ToString)
```

```vb
'Run refresh sub procedure.
RefreshList()
'Clears controls
ClearControls()

End Sub

Private Sub btnAdd_Click(ByVal sender As System.Object, ByVal e ...

    If Validate_Party() Then Exit Sub

    'Add the new record to the database
    Dim obj_bll_WeddingList As New WeddingList.fac_WeddingList()
    Dim objSB As New StringBuilder()

    objSB.Append("<Parties><Party>")
    objSB.Append("<PartyName>" & txtParty.Text & "</PartyName>")
    objSB.Append("<Guests>" & txtGuests.Text & "</Guests>")

    objSB.Append("<GuestOf>")
    If RadioBride.Checked Then objSB.Append("B")
    If RadioGroom.Checked Then objSB.Append("G")
    If RadioShared.Checked Then objSB.Append("S")
    objSB.Append("</GuestOf>")

    objSB.Append("<Status>")
    If RadioConfirmed.Checked Then objSB.Append("C")
    If RadioUnconfirmed.Checked Then objSB.Append("U")
    If RadioDeclined.Checked Then objSB.Append("D")
    objSB.Append("</Status>")

    objSB.Append("</Party></Parties>")

    obj_bll_WeddingList.AddParty(objSB.ToString)

    'Clears controls
    ClearControls()

    'Run refresh sub procedure.
    RefreshList()

End Sub

Private Sub btnModify_Click(ByVal sender As System.Object, ByVal e ...

    If Validate_Party() Then Exit Sub
```

(continued on next page)

```
'Modifies the selected record
Dim obj_bll_WeddingList As New WeddingList.fac_WeddingList()
Dim objSB As New StringBuilder()

objSB.Append("<Parties><Party>")
objSB.Append("<ID>" & CurrentPartyID & "</ID>")
objSB.Append("<PartyName>" & txtParty.Text & "</PartyName>")
objSB.Append("<Guests>" & txtGuests.Text & "</Guests>")

objSB.Append("<GuestOf>")
If RadioBride.Checked Then objSB.Append("B")
If RadioGroom.Checked Then objSB.Append("G")
If RadioShared.Checked Then objSB.Append("S")
objSB.Append("</GuestOf>")

objSB.Append("<Status>")
If RadioConfirmed.Checked Then objSB.Append("C")
If RadioUnconfirmed.Checked Then objSB.Append("U")
If RadioDeclined.Checked Then objSB.Append("D")
objSB.Append("</Status>")

objSB.Append("</Party></Parties>")

obj_bll_WeddingList.UpdateParty(objSB.ToString)

'Clears controls
ClearControls()

'Run refresh sub procedure.
RefreshList()

End Sub

Private Sub btnRefresh_Click(ByVal sender As System.Object, ByVal e ...

'Refresh the list with sorted data from the database
RefreshList()

'Clears controls
ClearControls()

End Sub

Private Sub txtParty_KeyPress(ByVal sender As Object, ByVal e ...
```

```
        'Checking to see if a modification is already occuring.
        If btnModify.Enabled = False Then
          btnAdd.Enabled = True
          btnClear.Enabled = True
        End If

    End Sub

    Private Sub ListBoxWeddingList_DoubleClick(ByVal sender As Object, ...

        'Clears controls
        ClearControls()
        btnModify.Enabled = True
        btnClear.Enabled = True
        btnDelete.Enabled = True

        'Pull data for selected item and place in edit controls.
        Dim obj_bll_WeddingList As New WeddingList.fac_WeddingList()
        Dim objDataSet As DataSet
        Dim objSB As New StringBuilder()

        objSB.Append("<Parties><Party><ID>")
        objSB.Append(ListBoxWeddingList.SelectedValue)
        objSB.Append("</ID></Party></Parties>")

        objDataSet = obj_bll_WeddingList.GetPartyListDetail(objSB.ToString)

        'Set values of controls
        CurrentPartyID = _
objDataSet.Tables("PartyListDetail").Rows(0).Item("ID")
        txtParty.Text = _
objDataSet.Tables("PartyListDetail").Rows(0).Item("Party")
        txtGuests.Text = _
objDataSet.Tables("PartyListDetail").Rows(0).Item("Guests")

      Select Case objDataSet.Tables("PartyListDetail").Rows(0).Item("GuestOf")
        Case "B"
          RadioBride.Checked = True
        Case "G"
          RadioGroom.Checked = True
        Case "S"
          RadioShared.Checked = True
      End Select

      Select Case objDataSet.Tables("PartyListDetail").Rows(0).Item("Status")
        Case "C"
```

(continued on next page)

```
              RadioConfirmed.Checked = True
          Case "U"
              RadioUnconfirmed.Checked = True
          Case "D"
              RadioDeclined.Checked = True
      End Select

    End Sub

#End Region

#Region " Validation "

  Private Function Validate_Party() As Boolean

    If txtParty.Text = "" Then
        ErrorProviderParty.SetError(txtParty, _
"Please provide a Party Name.")
        Return True
    Else
        ' Clear the error.
        ErrorProviderParty.SetError(txtParty, "")
    End If
  End Function

#End Region
End Class
```

Enterprise Development

Often, development of an enterprise application requires careful consideration of resource usage and distribution of processing. The following sections carefully evaluate options that are available through the .NET Framework.

Connection Pooling

When using ADO.NET, a connection pool is automatically generated in an effort to reuse database connections that have already been created. Connection pooling may not seem significant until you realize the enormous resources that are required simply to create a database connection. You tend to forget this because you are developing the client (WeddingList.dll, in this case) on the same machine as the one on which your database resides. When developing locally like this, you eliminate the need and overhead of network calls and authentication that will be made in a production environment.

It is not uncommon for the time and effort it takes to create a database connection to far exceed the time required to perform our database transaction.

This is where connection pooling comes in. With connection pooling implemented, a newly created connection is returned to a connection pool when the client releases it. This allows the next client to use the connection without having to wait for a new connection, thereby greatly improving the client's performance by reducing the overhead.

Connection pools are based on the connection string. The connection string serves as a signature where new connection pools are created or existing pools are used. When a connection string matches the connection string of an existing connection pool, an available connection is released to the requesting client. If the new connection string does not match the connection string or signature of any pool, a new connection pool is created. Therefore, multiple connection pools are likely to exist within the same application.

But just because connection pooling is automatic doesn't mean that your job is done. You still need to set the minimum and maximum number of connections in a connection pool.

Unfortunately, there is no simple way to determine your minimum and maximum connection pool settings because every application is different. For example, if the work your application performs in any single transaction is far less than the time required to create a new connection, you should create a few connections in your connection pool, and lower the maximum connection pool setting so that your requests will not become quoted. (In this case, a queued request will perform more quickly than if the request was forced to first created its own connection.)

For example, say you have a small application (around 100 users) with a lot of chatty-type transactions, whose actual database work is short and sweet. In this case, you may want to implement a connection pool minimum of 5 and a max of 8 to 10.

Furthermore, most applications will have more than one type of transaction, and many will have both long and short running ones. This is where the use of multiple connection pools can become handy.

The minimum and maximum connection pool size are a part of your connection string. When a different minimum or maximum are specified in the connection, the string no longer matches the current connection pools and a new pool is created. If you produce too many connections, you may be defeating the purpose of reusing existing connections. It's completely up to you as the developer to determine the number of connection pools you create. Keep in mind that:

- If part of your application performs long running transactions you should be more concerned with avoiding queuing than with creating new connections. In a case like this, choose a minimum based on the number of concurrent transactions of this transaction type and a maximum that will be large enough to accommodate most transactions without causing queuing.

- For short running transactions, avoid creating new connections. In this case, use a higher minimum value and a smaller maximum because, as mentioned earlier, queuing in this scenario is much faster than waiting for a new connection to be created.

When considering the WeddingList example, you can assume that the XML_ModifyDataSource method performs very quickly because you only modify a single piece of data and return no data. As such, you will set the minimum connection to 1 and maximum to 3. Consequently, if many requests come in at one time, they will be satisfied more quickly when connections are pooled (unless the number of requests is exaggerated).

The XML_GetDataSet Connection Pools

The XML_GetDataSet method will take slightly longer as data is returned. The performance difference is nearly immeasurable, but for the sake of argument, you can assume that this is true. The return time is expected to grow as data increases. Because the return time is only slightly longer, you will have nearly the same minimum and maximum connection parameters. In a larger application, you may not want to discriminate between data access methods whose response times are this close. You'll create two connection pools for this example, one connection pool that supports the retrieval of data and another connection pool that modifies the data:

1. Open the WeddingList project.

2. Open the code window for dal_DataAccess.vb.

3. Replace the connection string of the XML_ModifyDataSource method with the following:

```
Dim strConn As String = _
"Data Source=localhost;Initial Catalog=WeddingList" & _
        ";User Id=sa;Pwd=Enterprise;" & _
"Pooling=true;Min Pool Size=1;Max Pool Size=3"
```

4. Replace the connection string of the XML_GetDataSet method with the following:

```
Dim strConn As String = _
"Data Source=localhost;Initial Catalog=WeddingList" & _
        ";User Id=sa;Pwd=Enterprise;" & _
"Pooling=true;Min Pool Size=2;Max Pool Size=5"
```

Adding Enterprise Service References

Before you can add your assembly to COM+ in order to take advantage of Enterprise Services, you need to do a little preparation work. To use COM+ services, you must reference the EnterpriseServices.dll. To do so, follow these steps:

1. Open the WeddingList project.
2. Right-click on References and select Add Reference.
3. Under the .NET tab scroll until you reach System.EnterpriseServices.
4. Select System.EnterpriseServices and press select then OK.

Adding Namespaces

To make your job just a little easier you'll import a few namespaces. Import the following namespaces to the bll_WeddingList, dal_WeddingList, and dal_DataAccess classes;

```
Imports System.Data.SqlClient
'COM+ Imports
Imports System.EnterpriseServices
Imports System.Runtime.CompilerServices
Imports System.Reflection
```

Inheriting the Serviced Component Class

To take advantage of ContextUtil, you need to inherit the ServicedComponent class. To do so, place the ServicedComponent inheritance statement after the declaration of the bll_WeddingList, dal_WeddingList, and dal_DataAccess classes. For example:

```
Public Class bll_WeddingList
    Inherits ServicedComponent
```

Adding Assembly Attributes

The AssemblyInfo.vb file in the WeddingList project holds metadata about your projects classes. Until now you have provided values for the AssemblyTitle, AssemblyDescription, AssemblyCompany, and AssemblyProduct. Before you can add Enterprise Services Assembly attributes, you must import the EnterrpiseServices namespace. Then you will add assembly attributes that will configure the newly created COM+ application:

1. Open the code window of the AssemblyInfo.vb file of the WeddingList project.

2. Add the new import:

```
Imports System.EnterpriseServices
```

3. Add the following code below the current attributes:

```
'COM+ Application Name
<Assembly: ApplicationName("WeddingList")>
'COM+ Activation Type (In this case Server which is out-of-process)
<Assembly: ApplicationActivation(ActivationOption.Server)>
```

NOTE *This is the last thing you need to do for your assembly to take advantage of COM+ Services. By now the entire file should look like this:*

```
Imports System.Reflection
Imports System.Runtime.InteropServices
Imports System.EnterpriseServices

' General Information about an assembly is controlled through the following
' set of attributes. Change these attribute values to modify the information
' associated with an assembly.

' Review the values of the assembly attributes

<Assembly: AssemblyTitle("WeddingList")>
<Assembly: AssemblyDescription("The Wedding List Sample Application.")>
<Assembly: AssemblyCompany("The Book of Visual Studio .NET")>
<Assembly: AssemblyProduct("WeddingList")>
<Assembly: AssemblyCopyright("")>
<Assembly: AssemblyTrademark("")>
<Assembly: CLSCompliant(True)>

' Strong Name public/private key pair.
<Assembly: AssemblyKeyFile("KeyPair.snk")>
' COM+ Application Name
<Assembly: ApplicationName("WeddingList")>
' COM+ Activation Type (In this case Server which is out-of-process)
<Assembly: ApplicationActivation(ActivationOption.Server)>
' The following GUID is for the ID of the typelib if this project is exposed to COM
<Assembly: Guid("738266B8-541A-4B9F-ABD3-91677DE07F84")>
' Version information for an assembly consists of the following four values:
```

```
'
'    Major Version
'    Minor Version
'    Build Number
'    Revision
'
' You can specify all the values or you can default the Build and Revision Numbers
' by using the '*' as shown below:
<Assembly: AssemblyVersion("1.0.0.1")>
```

Creating the COM+ Application and Registering our Assembly

Now that you have inherited the ServicedComponent, imported the
System.EnterpriseServices, System.Runtime.CompilerServices, and
System.Reflection namespaces, and added the appropriate assembly information, you are ready to add your assembly to COM+. Of course, before you do
this you must create the COM+ application.

You'll use the regsvcs.exe executable to export your assembly's type library,
add your assembly to an existing COM+ application, and (as determined by the
/c switch), create the COM+ application. To register your assembly with an existing COM+ application, use the following command:

```
regsvcs WeddingList.dll
```

To create the COM+ application and registration of your assembly with that
COM+ application, use the following command:

```
regsvcs /c WeddingList.dll
```

To create a new COM+ application and register your WeddingList assembly
in the new COM+ application, follow these steps:

1. Compile the WeddingList project by selecting Rebuild Solution from the
    Build menu.
2. Open the Visual Studio .NET Command Prompt.
3. Navigate to the location of your WeddingList.dll.
4. At the command line, type

```
regsvcs /c WeddingList.dll
```

Viewing the COM+ Application

Now that you've created the COM+ application, you can view the results using the Component Services Manager:

1. Select Start • Programs • Administrative Tools • Component Services.
2. Expand MyComputer • COM+ Applications • WeddingList and Components.

   Here is where you will view your component's statistics.

Modifying the Client

The WindowsFormWeddingList client application called our WeddingList.dll as an in-process assembly. For the client to access the WeddingList.dll assembly, now configured for Enterprise Services, you must make some minor modifications:

1. Add a reference to the EnterpiseServices DLL by right-clicking References, then Add Reference, and choosing the assembly named System.Enterprise.

NOTE *You must also have a reference to the* WeddingList.dll *file, but this should have already been done.*

2. Add the System.EnterpriseServices import statement to the Form1 class:

```
Imports System.EnterpriseServices
```

Object Pooling

Object pooling is very similar to connection pooling in that it addresses the time it takes to perform infrastructure work (object creation and destruction) rather than business processing. These processes are very time consuming and, like connection pooling, service components and the application that use them.

.NET assemblies don't actually provide object pooling, but configuring assemblies for pooling tells COM+ to provide object pooling as a service to our assembly. Consequently, your assembly, loaded and receiving services from COM+, is considered a serviced component.

You indicate to COM+ that your assemblies require services through attributes. To implement object pooling at the class level, apply the following attributes to each class of the WeddingList project:

```
<ObjectPooling(MinPoolsize:=3, MaxPoolsize:=6)>
```

Next, modify the class declaration for the bll_WeddingList, dal_WeddingList, and dal_DataAccess classes with the following object pooling attributes:

bll_WeddingList

```
<ObjectPooling(MinPoolsize:=2, MaxPoolSize:=5)> _
Public Class bll_WeddingList
  Inherits ServicedComponent
```

dal_WeddingList

```
<ObjectPooling(MinPoolsize:=3, MaxPoolSize:=15)> _
Public Class dal_WeddingList
  Inherits ServicedComponent
```

dal_DataAccess

```
<ObjectPooling(MinPoolsize:=2, MaxPoolSize:=6)> _
Public Class dal_DataAccess
  Inherits ServicedComponent
```

Event Tracking

If you compile the assembly and run the WindowsForm client application, the assemblies are pooled. Then, when you open up Component Services found under Administrative Tools, you will find your COM+ application named WeddingList.

Expand the WeddingList application and select the Components folder (Figure 12-16); your serviced components are in the right-hand panel. Above the panel are a series of buttons that offer different views of the components. If you select the button at the far left, you will see tracking information on the serviced components. This is where you can view the statistics of serviced components after you have implemented event tracking.

Event tracking is implemented automatically for classic COM components, but not for .NET Serviced Components. Event tracking displays statistical information about your assemblies, such as the number of pooled and active assemblies, as well as the time (in milliseconds) it takes for an assembly to perform a task.

NOTE *Tracking information is not always necessary and uses extra CPU processing. If you don't feel a need to track the number of pulled objects or you don't want to spend the time that the tasks are taking to complete, do not use event tracking.*

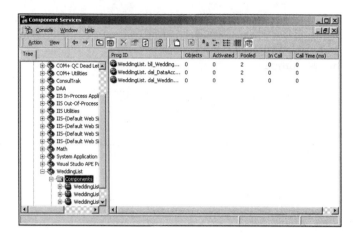

Figure 12-16: Component Services manager.

Implementing Event Tracking

To implement Event Tracking, modify the class declaration for the bll_WeddingList, dal_WeddingList, and dal_DataAccess classes with the following Event Tracking attributes:

bll_WeddingList

```
<ObjectPooling(MinPoolsize:=2, MaxPoolSize:=5), _
EventTrackingEnabled(True)> _
Public Class bll_WeddingList
   Inherits ServicedComponent
```

dal_WeddingList

```
<ObjectPooling(MinPoolsize:=3, MaxPoolSize:=15), _
EventTrackingEnabled(True)> _
Public Class dal_WeddingList
   Inherits ServicedComponent
```

dal_DataAccess

```
<ObjectPooling(MinPoolsize:=2, MaxPoolSize:=6), _
EventTrackingEnabled(True)> _
Public Class dal_DataAccess
   Inherits ServicedComponent
```

Just-In-Time Activation (JITA)

Just-In-Time Activation tells COM+ to load the context of components, but not to activate them until the component's functionality is required. Once the client application is finished, the component and all of its resources are released, leaving only the object's context in memory.

You do not need to include JITA when using COM+ Transactional support because JITA is required for Automatic Transactions. Because JITA does not need to be included with Automatic Transactions, Synchronization (which allows only a single client to access an object at one time) is automatically configured as required when JITA is implemented.

JITA components are activated when the client executes one of the class's methods; however, the client must tell COM+ when it is safe to deactivate the component and return it back to the pool. This is done using the ContextUtil object and the DeactivateOnReturn method.

Your next step is to add the required attributes for implementing JITA. Modify the class declaration for the bll_WeddingList, dal_WeddingList, and dal_DataAccess classes with the following JITA attributes:

bll_WeddingList

```
<JustInTimeActivation(True), _
ObjectPooling(MinPoolsize:=2, MaxPoolSize:=5), _
EventTrackingEnabled(True)> _
Public Class bll_WeddingList
  Inherits ServicedComponent
```

dal_WeddingList

```
<JustInTimeActivation(True), _
ObjectPooling(MinPoolsize:=3, MaxPoolSize:=15), _
EventTrackingEnabled(True)> _
Public Class dal_WeddingList
  Inherits ServicedComponent
```

dal_DataAccess

```
<JustInTimeActivation(True), _
ObjectPooling(MinPoolsize:=2, MaxPoolSize:=6), _
EventTrackingEnabled(True)> _
Public Class dal_DataAccess
  Inherits ServicedComponent
```

Also, to tell COM+ that it is safe to deactivate your assembly, place the following line of code within each method and before the return statement:

```
ContextUtil.DeactivateOnReturn = True
```

Transactional Support

It's as easy to configure serviced components for transactional support as it is to configure COM+ services. Furthermore, you can use attributes to configure the transaction level that you need to support your business process needs.

With the ContextUtil object, your component can tell COM+ that a transaction should be committed or aborted. After adding transactional support to the AddParty, UpdateParty, and DeleteParty methods of the bll_WeddingList class, the component should look something like this:

```
<AutoComplete()> _
Public Sub AddParty(ByVal strXML As String)
  Dim obj_daa_WeddingList As New WeddingList.dal_WeddingList()
  Try
    obj_daa_WeddingList.AddParty(strXML)
    ContextUtil.SetComplete()
  Catch
    ContextUtil.SetAbort()
    Exit Try
  Finally
    ContextUtil.DeactivateOnReturn = True
  End Try
  ' Check for a null resource.
  If Not (obj_daa_WeddingList Is Nothing) Then
    obj_daa_WeddingList.Dispose()
  End If
End Sub

<AutoComplete()> _
Public Sub UpdateParty(ByVal strXML As String)
  Dim obj_daa_WeddingList As New WeddingList.dal_WeddingList()
  Try
    obj_daa_WeddingList.UpdateParty(strXML)
    ContextUtil.SetComplete()
  Catch
    ContextUtil.SetAbort()
    Exit Try
  Finally
    ContextUtil.DeactivateOnReturn = True
  End Try
  ' Check for a null resource.
```

```
      If Not (obj_daa_WeddingList Is Nothing) Then
        obj_daa_WeddingList.Dispose()
      End If
    End Sub

    <AutoComplete()> _
    Public Sub DeleteParty(ByVal strXML As String)
      Dim obj_daa_WeddingList As New WeddingList.dal_WeddingList()
      Try
        obj_daa_WeddingList.DeleteParty(strXML)
        ContextUtil.SetComplete()
      Catch
        ContextUtil.SetAbort()
        Exit Try
      Finally
        ContextUtil.DeactivateOnReturn = True
      End Try
      ' Check for a null resource.
      If Not (obj_daa_WeddingList Is Nothing) Then
        obj_daa_WeddingList.Dispose()
      End If
```

Enterprise Services Checklist

Here is a quick and dirty checklist for building the WeddingList assembly to leverage Enterprise Services. The checklist effectively summarizes what you have already done. Use this checklist for future reference when creating new Serviced Components:

1. Create a new class library project.

2. Add the appropriate classes and methods.

3. Organize your code using Regions:

```
#Region " Business Level Logic "
    Public Class MyClass
        Public Function MyFunction() As DataSet
            'Do work. . .
        End Function
    End Class
#End Region
```

4. Organize code in the middle tier to perform these specific functions:

- **Business Level Logic (BLL)** is a component layer whose sole purpose is to enforce business rules. This layer has no knowledge of the data source.
- **Data Access Layer (DAL)** is the only layer that has any real knowledge of the datasource. All database activity is performed by this layer affectively abstracting the data source from the rest of the application. This promotes code reuse and database independence as this is the only layer that need to be modified to work with another database platform.

5. Add the appropriate Imports for your code:

```
Example: Imports System.Data.SqlClient
```

6. Apply all methods to classes.
7. Add assembly information to the `AssemblyInfo.vb` file (especially the version).
8. Add a Strong Name (SN) file to your project.
9. If using C#, move the new `KeyPair.snk` file to the `bin` directory. If using VB leave it in the project directory.
10. Add the Key File assembly attribute to the `AssemblyInfo.vb` file:

```
<Assembly: AssemblyKeyFile("Keypair.snk")>
```

11. Compile your project to create the strongly named assembly.
12. Add the new assembly to the Global Assembly Cache (GAC):

```
gacutil /I WeddingList.dll
```

13. Add a reference from the client application to the `WeddingList.dll`.
14. Configure connection pooling in your connection string:

```
    "Data Source=localhost;Initial Catalog=WeddingList" & _
                     ";User Id=sa;Pwd=;" & _
    "Pooling=true;Min Pool Size=1;Max Pool Size=3"
```

15. Add a reference to the System.EnterrpiseServices.dll.
16. Add the appropriate Enterprise Services import statements:

```
'COM+/Enterprise Services Imports
Imports System.EnterpriseServices
Imports System.Runtime.CompilerServices
Imports System.Reflection
```

17. Inherit the `ServicedComponent` class into each class:

```
Public Class MyClass
        Inherits ServicedComponents
```

18. Add new Assembly attributes to the `AssemblyInfo.vb` file supporting Serviced Components:

```
' COM+ Application Name
<Assembly: ApplicationName("WeddingList")>
' COM+ Activation Type (In this case Server which is out-of-process)
<Assembly: ApplicationActivation(ActivationOption.Server)>
```

19. Create the COM+ application and register the assemblies as Serviced Components:

```
regsvcs /c WeddingList
```

20. Modify the client to enable use of Serviced Components by adding a reference to the `System.EnterpriseServices` assembly and adding the following import statement:

```
Imports System.EnterpriseServices
```

21. Add the appropriate Serviced Components attributes to each class, then re-compile and deploy the assembly:

```
<JustInTimeActivation(True)>
<Transaction(TransactionOption.Required)>
<ObjectPooling(MinPoolsize:=2, MaxPoolsize:=5)>
<EventTrackingEnabled(True)>
```

Creating a Façade Layer with Web Services

While this lengthy example has demonstrated the implementation of many technologies, it hasn't demonstrated the flexibility built into your layered model. Currently your `Visual Basic .NET` application accesses your `bll_WeddingList` layer directly, which is fine for applications that reside on the same network or intranet. But what if your application does not?

As discussed in Chapter 9, "Retrieving Data," you have web services in your arsenal. The next example will show you how you can simply add a Façade layer with web services to WeddingList. Good design early in the application makes it easy to extend your Weddinglist application.

You'll create a Façade layer with web services, as shown in Figure 12-17. This layer will contain absolutely no business logic, but will provide extensibility so that your application will continue to function beyond your local network and across the internet, while functioning through any firewall on port 80.

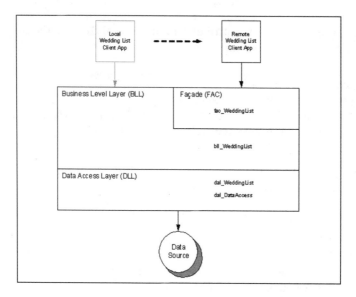

Figure 12-17: The logical view of the model with web services.

The physical view of this the WeddingList application with web services is shown in Figure 12-18. Most firewalls secure their networks by closing TCP/IP ports that are not used for web browsing. This includes many ports used by RPC protocols such as DCOM and CORBA, which are used to allow remote clients access to distributed applications. Your application, using web services, communicates across port 80 that is used for web access, allowing client applications easier access to web applications. Figure 12-18 shows a remote client application gaining access to your Serviced Components, hosted in COM+, through a firewall.

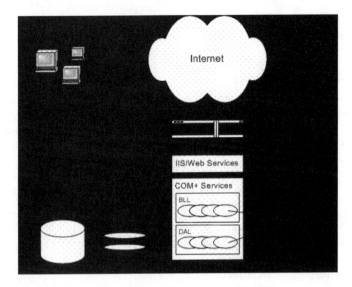

Figure 12-18: The physical view of the model with web services.

The first step in extending the WeddingList application beyond the local network is to create a web services project. Your web services are responsible for accepting the same parameters the bll_WeddingList assembly is expecting, then returning the same. In this scenario, the web service participates as a Façade layer component level, effectively passing all requests through to lower layers.

NOTE *Web services can participate in applications to a much larger degree than the Façade layer. This is simply how you are implementing web services in the WeddingList application.*

Creating the Web Service Façade

To create the web service Façade layer, follow these steps:

1. Create a new Visual Basic .NET Project using the ASP.NET Web Service template.

2. Change the project Location to http://localhost/ws_WeddingList.

3. Rename the Service1.asmx file to fac_WeddingList.asmx.

4. Open the code window for WeddingList.asmx:

Rename the Service1 class to fac_WeddingList.

---

5. Add a reference to the EnterpriseServices.dll.

6. Add the System.EnterpriseServices imports statement:

Imports System.EnterpriseServices

---

7. Add a reference to the WeddingList assembly. You will need to select browse and navigate to the WeddingList.dll and press OK.

Adding Web Methods

At this point, the web service is correctly configured and ready for you to add your pass-through web methods. Start by adding the GetPartyList method and then test it. If all goes well, you can continue to add a web method for each method in the bll_WeddingList class:

1. Open the fac_WeddingList code window and replace the commended web method that demonstrates the HelloWorld method with the following code:

```
<WebMethod()> Public Function GetPartyList() As DataSet
    Dim objbll_WeddingList As New WeddingList.bll_WeddingList()
    Dim objDataSet As DataSet
    objDataSet = objbll_WeddingList.GetPartyList
    ' Check for a null resource.
    If Not (objbll_WeddingList Is Nothing) Then
      objbll_WeddingList.Dispose()
    End If
    Return objDataSet
End Function
```

2. Let's go ahead and test our new web method. Press F5 and a browser pointing to the fac_WeddingList.asmx file loads (Figure 12-19).

3. Select the GetPartyList bulleted list item.

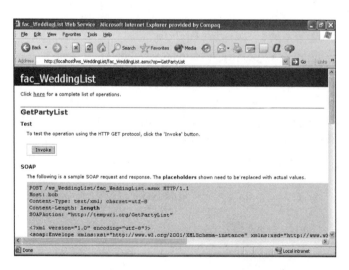

Figure 12-19: Generated test screen for the GetPartyList *web method.*

4. Since there are no required parameters simply press the Invoke button.

NOTE *If everything is working correctly, another browser will open, displaying the XML that represents the returned dataset (Figure 12-20).*

Figure 12-20: Results of the GetPartyList web method test.

5. Go ahead and add the necessary code for the rest of this class:

```
<WebMethod()> Public Function GetPartyListDetail( _
ByVal strXML As String) As DataSet
    Dim objbll_WeddingList As New WeddingList.bll_WeddingList()
    Dim objDataSet As DataSet
    objDataSet = objbll_WeddingList.GetPartyListDetail(strXML)
    If Not (objbll_WeddingList Is Nothing) Then
      objbll_WeddingList.Dispose()
    End If
    Return objDataSet
    'Use for testing
    '<Parties>
    ' <Party>
    ' <ID>1</ID>
    ' </Party>
    '</Parties>
  End Function

  <WebMethod()> Public Sub AddParty(ByVal strXML As String)
    Dim objbll_WeddingList As New WeddingList.bll_WeddingList()
```

(continued on next page)

```
      objbll_WeddingList.AddParty(strXML)
      If Not (objbll_WeddingList Is Nothing) Then
        objbll_WeddingList.Dispose()
      End If
      '<Parties>
      ' <Party>
      ' <PartyName></PartyName>
      ' <Guests></Guests>
      ' <GuestOf></GuestOf>
      ' <Status></Status>
      ' </Party>
      '</Parties>
    End Sub

    <WebMethod()> Public Sub DeleteParty(ByVal strXML As String)
      Dim objbll_WeddingList As New WeddingList.bll_WeddingList()
      objbll_WeddingList.DeleteParty(strXML)
      If Not (objbll_WeddingList Is Nothing) Then
        objbll_WeddingList.Dispose()
      End If
      '<Parties>
      ' <Party>
      ' <ID></ID>
      ' </Party>
      '</Parties>
    End Sub

    <WebMethod()> Public Sub UpdateParty(ByVal strXML As String)
      Dim objbll_WeddingList As New WeddingList.bll_WeddingList()
      objbll_WeddingList.UpdateParty(strXML)
      If Not (objbll_WeddingList Is Nothing) Then
        objbll_WeddingList.Dispose()
      End If
      '<Parties>
      ' <Party>
      ' <ID></ID>
      ' <PartyName></PartyName>
      ' <Guests></Guests>
      ' <GuestOf></GuestOf>
      ' <Status></Status>
      ' </Party>
      '</Parties>
    End Sub
```

6. Press F5 and a new browser listing all the available methods will open. Feel
    free to select each method and test them.

NOTE *Where parameters are required, you will need to provide the appropriate XML string that the clients pass or the method will fail.*

Reconfiguring the Client for Web Services

As you have architected this solution for extensibility, all you need to do in the client is change its references and make a few minor adjustments:

1. Open the WindowsFormWeddingList project.
2. Expand the References folder in the Solutions Explorer.
3. Right-click on WeddingList and select Remove.
4. Right-click on References and select Add Web Reference.
5. Place the following Address in the Address list box and press Enter:

```
http://localhost/ws_WeddingList/fac_WeddingList.asmx
```

6. Press the Add Reference button.
7. Expand the Web References folder. Right click on localhost and rename it WeddingList.

NOTE *If you named the* `fac_WeddingList` *class of the Web Service* `bll_WeddingList`, *no other changes to the client will be required.*

8. Review the `WindowsFormWeddingList` project code and replace all references to `bll_WeddingList` with `fac_WeddingList`.
9. Rebuild the project by selecting Rebuild Solution from the Build menu.
10. Press F5 to run the application.

Typically, you could go ahead and deploy your application; however, you made a reference to your web services using localhost as your machine's name:

```
http://localhost/ws_WeddingList/fac_WeddingList.asmx
```

To distribute the client, you must reference the actual machine name or IP address of the web server, exposing your web service like this:

```
http://MyServer.com/ws_WeddingList/fac_WeddingList.asmx
```

or this:

```
http://192.168.1.1/ws_WeddingList/fac_WeddingList.asmx
```

Where Do You Go from Here?

If you've made it this far, you should have a good understanding of Visual Studio .NET and at least possess a basic understanding of a host of .NET Framework technologies. Your next step should be to focus on each of these technologies, either by investigating MSDN further, studying books that specialize in specific technologies such as ADO.NET or ASP.NET, or simply building your own applications.

Learning how to program using the .NET Framework is an enormous task. I hope this book has helped you understand the .NET Framework, Visual Studio .NET, and associated technologies. Best wishes!

INDEX

boxing, 123

Breakpoint Condition dialog
box, *94*

Breakpoint window, 93–94

btnAdd_Click event, 323

btnDelete_Click event, 324

btnModify_Click event, 321–22

BtnStringBuilder value, *124*

btnString value, *124*

Business Level Layer (BLL), 22,
119, 342

business problems, addressed by
.NET technology, 5–7

business processes, 24–25

business rules, 15, 17–18
data-specific, 24
downside in, 26
in three-tier applications, 20

Business Services tier, 18, 20, 21

button links, 168–69

byte data type, *76*

C

C# programming language, 11, 20,
57–58

Cab Project, 96

Call Stack window, 93

captions, *87*

Catch statement, 133

centralized computing, 6

centralized management, 14

central processing units (CPUs), 8

char data type, *76*

check constraints, 26, 114

Chrome data, 31

click events, 190–92

client-controlled model, 6

client/server model, 5–7
See also two-tier development
implementing business rules in,
17–18
and network performance, 16–17

clients, 6, 16
debugging Web services
from, 262
maintaining application
state in, 28

Clipboard Ring tab, 51

CLR (Common Language
Runtime), 11, 72, 133

cluster-management, 16

COBRA (Common Object Request
Broker Architecture), 10

code management
in .NET Framework, 72
in three-tier applications, 19
in two-tier applications, 16

code review, 325–30

COM+, 145–46, 283
adding functionality to clients in,
317–18
applications, 285–89
history of, 284–85
Just-In-Time Activation (JITA) in,
339–40
middle-tier components in, 307
object pooling in, 336
retrieving detailed information
in, 319–24
Serviced Components, 289–90
using XML (Extensible Markup
Language) in, 324

COM (Component Object Model),
265–66
building assemblies in, 266–68
building COM components in,
268–73

K

knowledge base, MSDN, 48

L

LAN (local area network), 17
late binding, 147
lblStringBuildingDisplay value, *124*
lblStringDisplay value, *124*
LEC (Local Event
    Concentrator), 117
level of expertise need for this
    book, 2
Linux operating system, 61
ListBoxWeddingList_DoubleClick
    method, 319–20
local area network (LAN), 17
Local Event Concentrator
    (LEC), 117
Locals window, 90
long data type, *76*

M

machine code, 73
Macro development environ-
    ment, *42*
Macro Explorer, 43
Macro Recorder, 42
macros, 41–43
Main Business classes, 22–23
mainframe model, 5
manifests, 73–74
memory, required, 36
Merge Module Project, 100
Message property, 139
metadata, 72
methods, 143–44

Microsoft Application Center
    Server 2000, *9*, 14
Microsoft Application Server
    2000, *9*
Microsoft BizTalk Server 2000, *9*
Microsoft Commerce Server
    2000, *9*
Microsoft Exchange 2000, *9*
Microsoft Host Integration 2000, *9*
Microsoft Intermediate Language
    (MSIL), 11–12, 72–73
Microsoft Internet Security and
    Acceleration Server 2000, *9*
Microsoft Message Queue Server
    (MSMQ), 31
Microsoft Solution Developer
    Network (MSDN), 40–41
Microsoft SQL Server 2000, *9*
Microsoft Transaction Services
    (MTS), 285
Microsoft.VisualBasic namespace,
    130
Microsoft.VSA namespace, *130*
Microsoft.Win32 namespace, *130*
Middle-Tier Components, 307–14
    bll_WeddingList class, 311–14
    dal_DataAccess component,
        307–9
    dal_WeddingList class, 310–11
monitors
    settings for, 36
    support for, 39
MSDN knowledge base, 48
MSDN (Microsoft Solution
    Developer Network), 40–41
MSIL (Microsoft Intermediate
    Language), 11–12, 72–73
MSMQ (Microsoft Message Queue
    Server), 31

System.Data.InvalidConstraint-
Exception class, *134*
System.Data.NoNullAllowed-
Exception class, *135*
System.Data.odbc namespace, 195
System.Data.Ole.Db namespace,
195
System.Data.SqlClient namespace,
195
System.Diagnostics namespace, *131*
System.DirectoryServices
namespace, *131*
System.DivideByZeroException
class, *134*
System.DllNotFoundException
class, *134*
System.EnterpriseService
namespace, *131*
System.Globalization namespace,
131
System.IndexOutofRangeException
class, *134*
System.Int 32 data type, 75
System.InvalidCaseException
class, *134*
System.IO.DirectoryNotFound-
Exception class, *135*
System.IO.FileLoadException
class, *135*
System.IO.IOException class, *135*
System.IO namespace, *131*
System.IO.PathToLongException
class, *135*
System.Management namespace,
131
System.Messaging namespace, *132*
System.Net namespace, *132*

System.NullReferenceException
class, *134*
System.Object class, 147
System.OutOfMemoryException
class, *134*
System.OverflowException
class, *134*
System.RankException class, *134*
System.Reflection namespace, *132*
System.Runtime.Remoting
namespace, *132*
System.Runtime.Remoting.Remot-
ingException class, *135*
System.Runtime.Remoting.Remot-
ingServerException class, *135*
System.Runtime.Remoting.Remot-
ingTimeOutException
class, *135*
System.Runtime.Serialization
namespace, *132*
System.Runtime.Serialization.Serial-
izationException class, *135*
System.Security namespace, *132*
System.ServiceProcess namespace,
132
System.SystemException class, *134*
System.Text namespace, *132*
System.Timer namespace, *132*
System.Tread namespace, *132*
System.Web namespace, *132*
System.Web.httpException
class, *135*
System.Windows.Forms
namespace, *132*
System.XML namespace, *132*
System.XML.XmlException
class, *135*

T

U

UDDI (Universal Description, Discovery, and Integration), 253–54
uint data type, *76*
UI (User Interface), 117
ulong data type, *76*
Uniform Resource Locators (URLs), 32, 60
unique constraints, 25, 114
Universal Description, Discovery, and Integration (UDDI), 253–54
UNIX operating system, 61
UpdateRecord function, 240
URLs (Uniform Resource Locators), 32, 60
User Control Designer, 106–7
user controls, creating, 106
user experience, 15, 32
user ID, 196
User Interface (UI), 117
User Services tier, 18
ushort data type, *76*

V

Validate_Party event, 320–21
Validation Summary control, 169–70
variables, 123–26
.vb files, 128
.vbproj files, 128
Visual Basic .NET
  adding "Hello World" code, 56–57
  building project, 57
  code window, *102*
  creating application, 55–56
  new features in, 122
  regions, 126
  running "Hello World" application, 57
  structures, 126
  variable scope, 126
  variables, 123–25
  Windows Forms, 127–28
Visual C++ programming language, 11, 20
visual database tools, 107–13
Visual Interdev, *9*, 48
Visual J++ programming language, 48–49
Visual Source Safe, 54
Visual Studio Analyzer (VSA), 115–17
Visual Studio .NET
  See also tools
  Command Window, 49–51
  customizing IDE (Integrated Development Environment) of, 39–47
  designers, 10–11
  development environment, 47–49
  development features and enhancements, 10–11
  hardware requirements, 36
  installing, 36–39
  Project Solution in, 128
  system requirements, 164
  Tool Box Window, 51–53
Visual Web Page Editor, 11
VSA Client, 116–17
VSA Server, 115–17
VSA (Visual Studio Analyzer), 115–17

W

Windows 2000 operating system,
61, 81
Windows Component Update, 37
windows, dockable, 41
Windows Forms, 127–28
Designer, 10, 101–2
template, 291–94
Windows NT 3.1 operating system,
81
Windows Registry, 145–46
Window XP operating system, 81
wizards, 95
Add-in Wizard, 44–47
Deployment Wizard, 96–100,
96–100
wl_AddParty_isp stored procedure,
303–5
wl_DeleteParty_dsp stored
procedure, 306
wl_GetInvited_ssp stored
procedure, 307
wl_GetPartyListDetail_ssp stored
procedure, 302–3
wl_GetPartyList_ssp stored
procedure, 300–1
wl_UpdateParty_usp stored
procedure, 305–6
WriteOnly keyword, 142
WSDL (Web Service Definition
Language), 253

X

XCopy command, 95
XML Data Designer, 10
XML Designer, 104–6
XML (Extensible Markup
Language), 8, 61
advantages of, 324
batch insert example, 247–50
in COM+, 324
.NET server support to, 9
and stored procedures, 241–45
in Web Services, 10, 252–53
XML Schema, *129*, 253
XML Web Services page, 40
XML_GetDataSet connection pools,
332
XSLT (eXtensible Stylesheet
Language Transformation),
253

More No-Nonsense Books from **no starch press**

THE BOOK OF VB .NET
.NET Insight for VB Developers

by MATTHEW MACDONALD

This complete introduction to development with Visual Basic .NET teaches experienced Visual Basic programmers with real-world examples that cover web development, XML, databases, web services, and user interface design.

"The stuff Visual Studio Basic 6 programmers desperately need to know about VB .NET is exactly the stuff [author] Matthew MacDonald has put into this book."
–BarnesandNoble.com

2002, 468 PP., $39.95 ($59.95 CDN)
ISBN 1-886411-82-4

THE BOOK OF SAX
The Simple API for XML

by W. SCOTT MEANS AND MICHAEL A. BODIE

Everything Java and XML developers need to know to write SAX applications, with tutorials on developing a fully functioning SAX application as well as picoSAX, a complete, non-validating XML 1.0 parser that implements the SAX 2.0 API. Learn to use SAX to solve XML parsing problems that are difficult to address with tree-based technologies.

". . . an all-in-one manual for the SAX programmer and offers great value for money." –Linux Format

2002, 312 PP., $29.95 ($44.95 CDN)
ISBN 1-886411-77-8

HOW NOT TO PROGRAM IN C++
111 Broken Programs and 3 Working Ones, or Why 2+2=5986

by STEVE OUALLINE

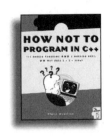

Find the bugs in these broken programs and become a better programmer. Based on real-world errors, the puzzles range from easy (one wrong character) to mind twisting (errors with multiple threads). Match your wits against the author's and polish your language skills as you try to fix broken programs. Clues help along the way, and answers are provided at the back of the book.

2002, 304 PP., $24.95 ($37.95 CDN)
ISBN 1-886411-95-6

STEAL THIS COMPUTER BOOK 2
What They Won't Tell You About the Internet

by WALLACE WANG

This bestseller will open your eyes to the Internet underground, with coverage of everything from viruses and password theft to Trojan Horse programs and encryption. The CD-ROM includes over 200 anti-hacker and security tools.

"An engaging look at the darker side of the information superhighway."
–Amazon.com

2000, 462 PP. W/ CD-ROM, $24.95 ($38.95 CDN)
ISBN 1-886411-42-5

Phone:

1 (800) 420-7240 OR
(415) 863-9900
MONDAY THROUGH FRIDAY,
9 A.M. TO 5 P.M. (PST)

Fax:

(415) 863-9950
24 HOURS A DAY,
7 DAYS A WEEK

Email:

SALES@NOSTARCH.COM

Web:

HTTP://WWW.NOSTARCH.COM

Mail:

NO STARCH PRESS
555 DE HARO STREET, SUITE 250
SAN FRANCISCO, CA 94107
USA

Distributed in the U.S. by Publishers Group West

SOURCE CODE AND SUPPORTING FILES

Source code and supporting files can be downloaded from the No Starch Press website at **http:www.nostarch.com/vsdotnet.htm**. After you have downloaded the source code file from the website, you can extract the files using WinZip. The directory structure will then be created and all the sample project files will be distributed.

UPDATES AND ERRATA

Visit **http://www.nostarch.com/vsdotnet_updates.htm** for updates, errata, and other information.